A STREETCAR N

AND OTHER PLAYS

Tennessee Williams was born in 1911 in Columbus, Mississippi, where his grandfather was the episcopal clergyman. When his father, a travelling salesman, moved with his family to St Louis some years later, both he and his sister found it impossible to settle down to city life. He entered college during the Depression and left after a couple of years to take a clerical job in a shoe company. He stayed there for two years, spending the evenings writing. He entered the University of Iowa in 1938 and completed his course, at the same time holding a large number of part-time jobs of great diversity. He received a Rockefeller Fellowship in 1940 for his play *Battle of Angels*, and he won the Pulitzer Prize in 1948 and 1955. Among his many other plays Penguin have published *Summer and Smoke* (1948), *The Rose Tattoo* (1951), *Camino Real* (1953), *Cat on a Hot Tin Roof* (1955), *Baby Doll* (1957), *Orpheus Descending* (1957), *Something Unspoken* (1958), *Suddenly Last Summer* (1958), *Period of Adjustment* (1960), *The Night of the Iguana* (1961), *The Milk Train Doesn't Stop Here Anymore* (1963), and *Small Craft Warnings* (1972). Tennessee Williams died in 1983.

Peter Shaffer has written of Tennessee Williams: 'He was a born dramatist as few are ever born. Whatever he put on paper, superb or superfluous, glorious or gaudy, could not fail to be electrifyingly actable. He could not write a dull scene . . . Tennessee Williams will live as long as drama itself.'

TENNESSEE WILLIAMS

A Streetcar Named Desire and Other Plays

SWEET BIRD OF YOUTH
A STREETCAR NAMED DESIRE
THE GLASS MENAGERIE

EDITED BY
E. MARTIN BROWNE

PENGUIN BOOKS
in association with Martin Secker & Warburg Ltd

PENGUIN BOOKS

Published by the Penguin Group
Penguin Books Ltd, 27 Wrights Lane, London W8 5TZ, England
Penguin Putnam Inc., 375 Hudson Street, New York, New York 10014, USA
Penguin Books Australia Ltd, Ringwood, Victoria, Australia
Penguin Books Canada Ltd, 10 Alcorn Avenue, Toronto, Ontario, Canada M4V 3B2
Penguin Books (NZ) Ltd, 182–190 Wairau Road, Auckland 10, New Zealand

Penguin Books Ltd, Registered Offices: Harmondsworth, Middlesex, England

A Streetcar Named Desire and *The Glass Menagerie*
published together in Penguin Books 1959
Reprinted with *Sweet Bird of Youth* 1962
49 50 48

ACKNOWLEDGEMENTS
The lines from Hart Crane are reprinted from *Collected Poems of Hart Crane*,
by permission of Liveright Publishing Corp., N. Y. *It's Only a Paper Moon*,
copyright 1933 by Harms, Inc. Used by permission
All rights reserved including the right of reproduction in whole or in part in any form

Printed in England by Clays Ltd, St Ives plc
Set in Monotype Baskerville

CONTENTS

SWEET BIRD OF YOUTH

Relentless caper for all those who step
The legend of their youth into the noon

HART CRANE

TO CHERYL CRAWFORD

FOREWORD*

WHEN I came to my writing desk on a recent morning, I found lying on my desk top an unmailed letter that I had written. I began reading it and found this sentence: 'We are all civilized people, which means that we are all savages at heart but observing a few amenities of civilized behaviour.' Then I went on to say: 'I am afraid that I observe fewer of these amenities than you do. Reason? My back is to the wall and has been to the wall for so long that the pressure of my back on the wall has started to crumble the plaster that covers the bricks and mortar.'

Isn't it odd that I said the wall was giving way, not my back? I think so. Pursuing this course of free association, I suddenly remembered a dinner date I once had with a distinguished colleague. During the course of this dinner, rather close to the end of it, he broke a long, mournful silence by lifting to me his sympathetic gaze and saying to me, sweetly, 'Tennessee, don't you feel that you are blocked as a writer?'

I didn't stop to think of an answer; it came immediately off my tongue without any pause for planning. I said, 'Oh, yes, I've always been blocked as a writer but my desire to write has been so strong that it has always broken down the block and gone past it.'

Nothing untrue comes off the tongue that quickly. It is planned speeches that contain lies or dissimulations, not what you blurt out so spontaneously in one instant.

It was literally true. At the age of fourteen I discovered writing as an escape from a world of reality in which I felt acutely uncomfortable. It immediately became my place of retreat, my cave, my refuge. From what? From being called

* Written prior to the Broadway opening of *Sweet Bird of Youth* and published in the *New York Times* on Sunday, 8 March 1959.

a sissy by the neighbourhood kids, and Miss Nancy by my father, because I would rather read books in my grand-father's large and classical library than play marbles and baseball and other normal kid games, a result of a severe childhood illness and of excessive attachment to the female members of my family, who had coaxed me back into life.

I think no more than a week after I started writing I ran into the first block. It's hard to describe it in a way that will be understandable to anyone who is not a neurotic. I will try. All my life I have been haunted by the obsession that to desire a thing or to love a thing intensely is to place yourself in a vulnerable position, to be a possible, if not a probable, loser of what you most want. Let's leave it like that. That block has always been there and always will be, and my chance of getting, or achieving, anything that I long for will always be gravely reduced by the interminable existence of that block.

I described it once in a poem called 'The Marvellous Children'.

'He, the demon, set up barricades of gold and purple tin-foil, labelled Fear (and other august titles), which they, the children, would leap lightly over, always tossing backwards their wild laughter.'

But having, always, to contend with this adversary of fear, which was sometimes terror, gave me a certain tendency towards an atmosphere of hysteria and violence in my writing, an atmosphere that has existed in it since the beginning.

In my first published work, for which I received the big sum of thirty-five dollars, a story published in the July or August issue of *Weird Tales* in the year 1928, I drew upon a paragraph in the ancient histories of Herodotus to create a story of how the Egyptian queen, Nitocris, invited all of her enemies to a lavish banquet in a subterranean hall on the shores of the Nile, and how, at the height of this banquet, she excused herself from the table and opened sluice gates admitting the waters of the Nile into the locked banquet hall, drowning her unloved guests like so many rats.

I was sixteen when I wrote this story, but already a confirmed writer, having entered upon this vocation at the age of fourteen, and, if you're well acquainted with my writings since then, I don't have to tell you that it set the keynote for most of the work that has followed.

My first four plays, two of them performed in St Louis, were correspondingly violent or more so. My first play professionally produced and aimed at Broadway was *Battle of Angels* and it was about as violent as you can get on the stage.

During the nineteen years since then I have only produced five plays that are *not* violent: *The Glass Menagerie*, *You Touched Me*, *Summer and Smoke*, *The Rose Tattoo*, and, recently in Florida, a serious comedy called *Period of Adjustment*, which is still being worked on.

What surprises me is the degree to which both critics and audience have accepted this barrage of violence. I think I was surprised, most of all, by the acceptance and praise of *Suddenly Last Summer*. When it was done off Broadway, I thought I would be critically tarred and feathered and ridden on a fence rail out of the New York theatre, with no future haven except in translation for theatres abroad, who might mistakenly construe my work as a castigation of American morals, not understanding that I write about violence in American life only because I am not so well acquainted with the society of other countries.

Last year I thought it might help me as a writer to undertake psychoanalysis and so I did. The analyst, being acquainted with my work and recognizing the psychic wounds expressed in it, asked me, soon after we started, 'Why are you so full of hate, anger, and envy?'

Hate was the word I contested. After much discussion and argument, we decided that 'hate' was just a provisional term and that we would only use it till we had discovered the more precise term. But unfortunately I got restless and started hopping back and forth between the analyst's couch and some Caribbean beaches. I think before we called it quits I had persuaded the doctor that hate was not the right word, that there was some other thing, some other word for it, which we had not yet uncovered, and we left it like that.

Anger, oh yes! And envy, yes! But not hate. I think that hate is a thing, a feeling, that can only exist where there is no understanding. Significantly, good physicians never have it. They never hate their patients, no matter how hateful their patients may seem to be, with their relentless, maniacal concentration on their own tortured egos.

Since I am a member of the human race, when I attack its behaviour towards fellow members I am obviously including myself in the attack, unless I regard myself as not human but superior to humanity. I don't. In fact, I can't expose a human weakness on the stage unless I know it through having it myself. I have exposed a good many human weaknesses and brutalities and consequently I have them.

I don't even think that I am more conscious of mine than any of you are of yours. Guilt is universal. I mean a strong sense of guilt. If there exists any area in which a man can rise above his moral condition, imposed upon him at birth, and long before birth, by the nature of his breed, then I think it is only a willingness to know it, to face its existence in him, and I think that, at least below the conscious level, we all face it. Hence guilty feelings, and hence defiant aggressions, and hence the deep dark of despair that haunts our dreams, our creative work, and makes us distrust each other.

Enough of these philosophical abstractions, for now. To get back to writing for the theatre, if there is any truth in the Aristotelian idea that violence is purged by its poetic representation on a stage, then it may be that my cycle of violent plays have had a moral justification after all. I know that I have felt it. I have always felt a release from the sense of meaninglessness and death when a work of tragic intention has seemed to me to have achieved that intention, even if only approximately, nearly.

I would say that there is something much bigger in life and death than we have become aware of (or adequately recorded) in our living and dying. And, further, to compound this shameless romanticism, I would say that our serious theatre is a search for that something that is not yet successful but is still going on.

THE CHARACTERS

Sweet Bird of Youth was presented at the Martin Beck Theatre in New York on 10 March 1959 by Cheryl Crawford. It was directed by Elia Kazan; the stage settings and lighting were by Jo Mielziner, the costumes by Anna Hill Johnstone, and the music by Paul Bowles; production stage manager, David Pardoll. The cast was as follows:

CHANCE WAYNE	*Paul Newman*
THE PRINCESS KOSMONOPOLIS	*Geraldine Page*
FLY	*Milton J. Williams*
MAID	*Patricia Ripley*
GEORGE SCUDDER	*Logan Ramsey*
HATCHER	*John Napier*
BOSS FINLEY	*Sidney Blackmer*
TOM JUNIOR	*Rip Torn*
AUNT NONNIE	*Martine Bartlett*
HEAVENLY FINLEY	*Diana Hyland*
CHARLES	*Earl Sydnor*
STUFF	*Bruce Dern*
MISS LUCY	*Madeleine Sherwood*
THE HECKLER	*Charles Tyner*
VIOLET	*Monica May*
EDNA	*Hilda Brawner*
SCOTTY	*Charles McDaniel*
BUD	*Jim Jeter*
MEN IN BAR	*Duke Farley*
	Ron Harper
	Kenneth Blake
PAGE	*Glenn Stensel*

SYNOPSIS OF SCENES

TIME: Modern, an Easter Sunday, from late morning till late night.

SETTING and 'SPECIAL EFFECTS': The stage is backed by a cyclorama that should give a poetic unity of mood to the several specific settings. There are non-realistic projections on this 'cyc', the most important and constant being a grove of royal palm trees. There is nearly always a wind among these very tall palm trees, sometimes loud, sometimes just a whisper, and sometimes it blends into a thematic music which will be identified, when it occurs, as the 'Lament'.

During the daytime scenes the cyclorama projection is a poetic abstraction of semi-tropical sea and sky in fair spring weather. At night it is the palm garden with its branches among the stars.

The specific settings should be treated as freely and sparingly as the sets for *Cat on a Hot Tin Roof* or *Summer and Smoke*. They'll be described as you come to them in the script.

Act One

SCENE ONE

A bedroom of an old-fashioned but still fashionable hotel somewhere along the Gulf Coast in a town called St Cloud. I think of it as resembling one of those 'Grand Hotels' around Sorrento or Monte Carlo, set in a palm garden. The style is vaguely 'Moorish'. The principal set-piece is a great double bed which should be raked towards the audience. In a sort of Moorish corner, backed by shuttered windows, is a wicker tabouret and two wicker stools, over which is suspended a Moorish lamp on a brass chain. The windows are floor length and they open out upon a gallery. There is also a practical door frame, opening on to a corridor: the walls are only suggested.

On the great bed are two figures, a sleeping woman, and a young man awake, sitting up, in the trousers of white silk pyjamas. The sleeping woman's face is partly covered by an eyeless black satin domino to protect her from morning glare. She breathes and tosses on the bed as if in the grip of a nightmare. The young man is lighting his first cigarette of the day.

> [*Outside the windows there are heard the soft, urgent cries of birds, the sound of their wings. Then a coloured waiter,* FLY, *appears at the door on the corridor, bearing coffee-service for two. He knocks.* CHANCE *rises, pauses a moment at a mirror in the fourth wall to run a comb through his slightly thinning blond hair before he crosses to open the door.*]

CHANCE: Aw, good, put it in there.

FLY: Yes, suh.

CHANCE: Give me the Bromo first. You better mix it for me,
   I'm –

FLY: Hands kind of shaky this mawnin'?

CHANCE [*shuddering after the Bromo*]: Open the shutters a little. Hey, I said a little, not much, not that much!

[*As the shutters are opened we see him clearly for the first time: he's in his late twenties and his face looks slightly older than that; you might describe it as a 'ravaged young face' and yet it is still exceptionally good-looking. His body shows no decline, yet it's the kind of a body that white silk pyjamas are, or ought to be, made for. A church bell tolls, and from another church, nearer, a choir starts singing the 'Hallelujah Chorus'. It draws him to the window, and as he crosses he speaks.*]

I didn't know it was – Sunday.

FLY: Yes, suh, it's *Easter* Sunday.

CHANCE [*leaning out a moment, hands gripping the shutters*]: Uh-huh . . .

FLY: That's the Episcopal Church they're singin' in. The bell's from the Catholic Church.

CHANCE: I'll put your tip on the check.

FLY: Thank you, Mr Wayne.

CHANCE [*as FLY starts for the door*]: Hey. How did you know my name?

FLY: I waited tables in the Grand Ballroom when you used to come to the dances on Saturday nights, with that real pretty girl you used to dance so good with, Mr Boss Finley's daughter.

CHANCE: I'm increasing your tip to five dollars in return for a favour which is not to remember that you have recognized me or anything else at all. Your name is Fly – Shoo, Fly. Close the door with no noise.

VOICE OUTSIDE: Just a minute.

CHANCE: Who's that?

VOICE OUTSIDE: George Scudder.

[*Slight pause. FLY exits.*]

CHANCE: How did you know I was here?

[GEORGE SCUDDER *enters: a coolly nice-looking, business-like young man who might be the head of the Junior Chamber of Commerce but is actually a young doctor, about thirty-six or -seven.*]

SCUDDER: The assistant manager that checked you in here last night phoned me this morning that you'd come back to St Cloud.

CHANCE: So you came right over to welcome me home?

SCUDDER: Your lady friend sounds like she's coming out of ether.

CHANCE: The Princess had a rough night.

SCUDDER: You've latched on to a Princess? [*mockingly*] Gee.

CHANCE: She's travelling incognito.

SCUDDER: Golly, I should think she would, if she's checking in hotels with *you*.

CHANCE: George, you're the only man I know that still says 'gee', 'golly', and 'gosh'.

SCUDDER: Well, I'm not the sophisticated type, Chance.

CHANCE: That's for sure. Want some coffee?

SCUDDER: Nope. Just came for a talk. A quick one.

CHANCE: O.K. Start talking, man.

SCUDDER: Why've you come back to St Cloud?

CHANCE: I've still got a mother and a girl in St Cloud. How's Heavenly, George?

SCUDDER: We'll get around to that later. [*He glances at his watch.*] I've got to be in surgery at the hospital in twenty-five minutes.

CHANCE: You operate now, do you?

SCUDDER [*opening doctor's bag*]: I'm chief of staff there now.

CHANCE: Man, you've got it made.

SCUDDER: Why have you come back?

CHANCE: I heard that my mother was sick.

SCUDDER: But you said 'How's Heavenly?' not 'How's my mother?' Chance. [CHANCE *sips coffee.*] Your mother died a couple of weeks ago ...

[CHANCE *slowly turns his back on the man and crosses to the window. Shadows of birds sweep the blind. He lowers it a little before he turns back to* SCUDDER.]

CHANCE: Why wasn't I notified?

SCUDDER: You were. A wire was sent you three days before she died, at the last address she had for you which was General Delivery, Los Angeles. We got no answer from that and another wire was sent you after she died, the same day of her death and we got no response from that either. Here's the Church Record. The church took up a collection for her hospital and funeral expenses. She was buried nicely in your family plot and the church has also given her a very nice headstone. I'm giving you these details in spite of the fact that I know and everyone here in town knows that you had no interest in her, less than people who knew her only slightly, such as myself.

CHANCE: How did she go?

SCUDDER: She had a long illness, Chance. You know about that.

CHANCE: Yes. She was sick when I left here the last time.

SCUDDER: She was sick at heart as well as sick in her body at that time, Chance. But people were very good to her, especially people who knew her in church, and the Reverend Walker was with her at the end.

[CHANCE *sits down on the bed. He puts out his unfinished cigarette and immediately lights another. His voice becomes thin and strained.*]

CHANCE: She never had any luck.

SCUDDER: Luck? Well, that's all over with now. If you want to know anything more about that, you can get in touch with Reverend Walker about it, although I'm afraid he won't be likely to show much cordiality to you.

CHANCE: She's gone. Why talk about it?

SCUDDER: I hope you haven't forgotten the letter I wrote you soon after you last left town.

CHANCE: No. I got no letter.

SCUDDER: I wrote you in care of an address your mother gave me, about a very important private matter.

CHANCE: I've been moving a lot.

SCUDDER: I didn't even mention names in the letter.

CHANCE: What was the letter about?

SCUDDER: Sit over here so I don't have to talk loud about this. Come over here. I can't talk loud about this. [SCUDDER *indicates the chair by the tabouret.* CHANCE *crosses and rests a foot on the chair*.] In this letter I just told you that a certain girl we know had to go through an awful experience, a tragic ordeal, because of past contact with you. I told you that I was only giving you this information so that you would know better than to come back to St Cloud, but you didn't know better.

CHANCE: I told you I got no letter. Don't tell me about a letter, I didn't get any letter.

SCUDDER: I'm telling you what I told you in this letter.

CHANCE: All right. Tell me what you told me, don't – don't talk to me like a club, a chamber of something. What did you tell me? What ordeal? What girl? Heavenly? Heavenly? George?

SCUDDER: I see it's not going to be possible to talk about this quietly and so I . . .

CHANCE [*rising to block* SCUDDER's *way*]: Heavenly? What ordeal?

SCUDDER: We will not mention names. Chance, I rushed over here this morning as soon as I heard you were back in St Cloud, before the girl's father and brother could hear that you were back in St Cloud, to stop you from trying to get in touch with the girl and to get you out of here. That is absolutely all I have to say to you in this room at this moment . . . But I hope I have said it in a way to impress you with the vital urgency of it, so you will leave. . . .

CHANCE: Jesus! If something's happened to Heavenly, will you please tell me – what?

SCUDDER: I said no names. We are not alone in this room. Now when I go downstairs now, I'll speak to Dan Hatcher, assistant manager here ... he told me you'd checked in here ... and tell him you want to check out, so you'd better get Sleeping Beauty and yourself ready to travel, and I suggest that you keep on travelling till you've crossed the State line. ...

CHANCE: You're not going to leave this room till you've explained to me what you've been hinting at about my girl in St Cloud.

SCUDDER: There's a lot more to this which we feel ought not to be talked about to anyone, least of all to you, since you have turned into a criminal degenerate, the only right term for you, but, Chance, I think I ought to remind you that once long ago the father of this girl wrote out a prescription for you, a sort of medical prescription, which is castration. You'd better think about that, that would deprive you of all you've got to get by on. [*He moves towards the steps.*]

CHANCE: I'm used to that threat. I'm not going to leave St Cloud without my girl.

SCUDDER [*on the steps*]: You don't have a girl in St Cloud. Heavenly and I are going to be married next month. [*He leaves abruptly.*]

[CHANCE, *shaken by what he has heard, turns and picks up phone, and kneels on the floor.*]

CHANCE: Hello? St Cloud 525. Hello, Aunt Nonnie? This is Chance, yes Chance. I'm staying at the Royal Palms and I ... what's the matter, has something happened to Heavenly? Why can't you talk now? George Scudder was here and ... Aunt Nonnie? Aunt Nonnie?

[*The other end hangs up. The sleeping woman suddenly cries out in her sleep.* CHANCE *drops the phone on its cradle and runs to the bed.*]

CHANCE [*bending over her as she struggles out of a nightmare*]: Princess! Princess! Hey, *Princess Kos*! [*He removes her eyemask; she sits up gasping and staring wild-eyed about her.*]

PRINCESS: Who are you? Help!

CHANCE [*on the bed*]: Hush now. ...

PRINCESS: Oh ... I ... had ... a *terrible* dream.

CHANCE: It's all right. Chance's with you.

PRINCESS: Who?

CHANCE: Me.

PRINCESS: I don't know who you are!

CHANCE: You'll remember soon, Princess.

PRINCESS: I don't know, I don't know. ...

CHANCE: It'll come back to you soon. What are you reachin' for, honey?

PRINCESS: Oxygen! Mask!

CHANCE: Why? Do you feel short-winded?

PRINCESS: Yes! I have ... air ... shortage!

CHANCE [*looking for the correct piece of luggage*]: Which bag is your oxygen in? I can't remember which bag we packed it in. Aw, yeah, the crocodile case, the one with the combination lock. Wasn't the first number zero ...? [*He comes back to the bed and reaches for a bag under its far side.*]

PRINCESS [*as if with her dying breath*]: Zero, zero. Two zeros to the right and then back around to ...

CHANCE: Zero, three zeros, two of them to the right and the last one to the left. ...

PRINCESS: Hurry! I can't breathe, I'm dying!

CHANCE: I'm getting it, Princess.

PRINCESS: *HURRY!*

CHANCE: Here we are, I've got it. ...

[*He has extracted from case a small oxygen cylinder and mask. He fits the inhalator over her nose and mouth. She falls back on the pillow. He places the other pillow under her head. After a moment, her panicky breath subsiding, she growls at him.*]

PRINCESS: Why in hell did you lock it up in that case?

CHANCE [*standing at the head of the bed*]: You said to put all your valuables in that case.

PRINCESS: I meant my jewellery, and you know it, you bastard!

CHANCE: Princess, I didn't think you'd have these attacks any more. I thought that having me with you to protect you would stop these attacks of panic, I . . .

PRINCESS: Give me a pill.

CHANCE: Which pill?

PRINCESS: A pink one, a pinkie, and vodka. . . .

> [*He puts the tank on the floor, and goes over to the trunk. The phone rings.* CHANCE *gives the* PRINCESS *a pill, picks up the vodka bottle, and goes to the phone. He sits down with the bottle between his knees.*]

CHANCE [*pouring a drink, phone held between shoulder and ear*]: Hello? Oh, hello, Mr Hatcher – Oh? But Mr Hatcher, when we checked in here last night we weren't told that, and Miss Alexandra Del Lago . . .

PRINCESS [*shouting*]: *Don't use my name!*

CHANCE: . . . is suffering from exhaustion, she's not at all well, Mr Hatcher, and certainly not in any condition to travel. . . . I'm sure you don't want to take the responsibility for what might happen to Miss Del Lago. . . .

PRINCESS [*shouting again*]: *Don't use my name!*

CHANCE: . . . if she attempted to leave here today in the condition she's in . . . do you?

PRINCESS: *Hang up!* [*He does. He comes over with his drink and the bottle to the* PRINCESS.] I want to forget everything, I want to forget who I am. . . .

CHANCE [*handing her the drink*]: He said that . . .

PRINCESS [*drinking*]: Please shut up, I'm *forgetting*!

CHANCE [*taking the glass from her*]: Okay, go on, forget.

There's nothing better than that, I wish I could do it. . . .

PRINCESS: I can, I will. I'm forgetting . . . I'm forgetting. . . .

[*She lies down.* CHANCE *moves to the foot of the bed, where he seems to be struck with an idea. He puts the bottle down on the floor, runs to the chaise, and picks up a tape recorder. Taking it back to the bed, he places the recorder on the floor. As he plugs it in, he coughs.*]

What's going on?

CHANCE: Looking for my toothbrush.

PRINCESS [*throwing the oxygen mask on the bed*]: Will you please take that away.

CHANCE: Sure you've had enough of it?

PRINCESS [*laughing breathlessly*]: Yes, for God's sake, take it away. I must look hideous in it.

CHANCE [*taking the mask*]: No, no, you just look exotic, like a Princess from Mars or a big magnified insect.

PRINCESS: Thank you, check the cylinder please.

CHANCE: For what?

PRINCESS: Check the air left in it; there's a gauge on the cylinder that gives the pressure. . . .

CHANCE: You're still breathing like a quarter horse that's been run a full mile. Are you sure you don't want a doctor?

PRINCESS: No, for God's sake . . . no!

CHANCE: Why are you so scared of doctors?

PRINCESS [*hoarsely, quickly*]: I don't need them. What happened is nothing at all. It happens frequently to me. Something disturbs me . . . adrenalin's pumped in my blood and I get short-winded, that's all, that's all there is to it. . . . I woke up, I didn't know where I was or who I was with, I got panicky . . . adrenalin was released and I got short-winded. . . .

CHANCE: Are you okay now, Princess? Huh? [*He kneels on the bed, and helps straighten up the pillows.*]

PRINCESS: Not quite yet, but I will be. I will be.

CHANCE: You're full of complexes, plump lady.

PRINCESS: What did you call me?

CHANCE: Plump lady.

PRINCESS: Why do you call me that? Have I let go of my figure?

CHANCE: You put on a good deal of weight after that disappointment you had last month.

PRINCESS [*hitting him with a small pillow*]: What disappointment? I don't remember any.

CHANCE: Can you control your memory like that?

PRINCESS: Yes. I've had to learn to. What is this place, a hospital? And you, what are you, a male nurse?

CHANCE: I take care of you but I'm not your nurse.

PRINCESS: But you're employed by me, aren't you? For some purpose or other?

CHANCE: I'm not on salary with you.

PRINCESS: What are you on? Just expenses?

CHANCE: Yep. You're footing the bills.

PRINCESS: I see. Yes, I see.

CHANCE: Why're you rubbing your eyes?

PRINCESS: My vision's so cloudy! Don't I wear glasses, don't I have any glasses?

CHANCE: You had a little accident with your glasses.

PRINCESS: What was that?

CHANCE: You fell on your face with them on.

PRINCESS: Were they completely demolished?

CHANCE: One lens cracked.

PRINCESS: Well, please give me the remnants. I don't mind waking up in an intimate situation with someone, but I like to see who it's with, so I can make whatever adjustment seems called for. ...

CHANCE [*rising and going to the trunk, where he lights cigarette*]: You know what I look like.

PRINCESS: No, I don't.

CHANCE: You did.

PRINCESS: I tell you I don't remember, it's all gone away!

CHANCE: I don't believe in amnesia.

PRINCESS: Neither do I. But you have to believe a thing that happens to you.

CHANCE: Where did I put your glasses?

PRINCESS: Don't ask me. You say I fell on them. If I was in that condition I wouldn't be likely to know where anything is I had with me. What happened last night?

[*He has picked them up but not given them to her.*]

CHANCE: You knocked yourself out.

PRINCESS: Did we sleep here together?

CHANCE: Yes, but I didn't molest you.

PRINCESS: Should I thank you for that, or accuse you of cheating? [*She laughs sadly.*]

CHANCE: I like you, you're a nice monster.

PRINCESS: Your voice sounds young. Are you young?

CHANCE: My age is twenty-nine years.

PRINCESS: That's young for anyone but an Arab. Are you very good-looking?

CHANCE: I used to be the best-looking boy in this town.

PRINCESS: How large is the town?

CHANCE: Fair-sized.

PRINCESS: Well, I like a good mystery novel, I read them to put me to sleep and if they don't put me to sleep, they're good; but this one's a little too good for comfort. I wish you would find me my glasses. . . .

[*He reaches over headboard to hand the glasses to her. She puts them on and looks him over. Then she motions him to come nearer and touches his bare chest with her finger tips.*]

Well, I may have done better, but God knows I've done worse.

CHANCE: What are you doing now, Princess?

PRINCESS: The tactile approach.

CHANCE: You do that like you were feeling a piece of goods to see if it was genuine silk or phony. . . .

PRINCESS: It feels like silk. Genuine! This much I do remember, that I like bodies to be hairless, silky-smooth
gold!

CHANCE: Do I meet these requirements?

PRINCESS: You seem to meet those requirements. But I still
have a feeling that something is not satisfied in the rela-
tion between us.

CHANCE [*moving away from her*]: You've had your experiences, I've had mine. You can't expect everything to be
settled at once. ... Two different experiences of two
different people. Naturally there's some things that have
to be settled between them before there's any absolute
agreement.

PRINCESS [*throwing the glasses on the bed*]: Take that
splintered lens out before it gets in my eye.

CHANCE [*obeying this instruction by knocking the glasses sharply
on the bed table*]: You like to give orders, don't you?

PRINCESS: It's something I seem to be used to.

CHANCE: How would you like to *take* them? To be a slave?

PRINCESS: What time is it?

CHANCE: My watch is in hock somewhere. Why don't you
look at yours?

PRINCESS: Where's mine?

[*He reaches lazily over to the table, and hands it to her.*]

CHANCE: It's stopped, at five past seven.

PRINCESS: Surely it's later than that, or earlier, that's no
hour when I'm ...

CHANCE: Platinum, is it?

PRINCESS: No, it's only white gold. I never travel with
anything very expensive.

CHANCE: Why? Do you get robbed much? Huh? Do you
get 'rolled' often?

PRINCESS: Get what?

CHANCE: 'Rolled'. Isn't that expression in your vocabulary?

PRINCESS: Give me the phone.

CHANCE: For what?

PRINCESS: I said give me the phone.

CHANCE: I know. And I said for what?

PRINCESS: I want to inquire where I am and who is with me?

CHANCE: Take it easy.

PRINCESS: Will you give me the phone?

CHANCE: Relax. You're getting short-winded again. ...

[*He takes hold of her shoulders.*]

PRINCESS: Please let go of me.

CHANCE: Don't you feel secure with me? Lean back. Lean back against me.

PRINCESS: Lean back?

CHANCE: This way, this way. There ...

[*He pulls her into his arms. She rests in them, panting a little like a trapped rabbit.*]

PRINCESS: It gives you an awful trapped feeling this, this memory block. ... I feel as if someone I loved had died lately, and I don't want to remember who it could be.

CHANCE: Do you remember your name?

PRINCESS: Yes, I do.

CHANCE: What's your name?

PRINCESS: I think there's some reason why I prefer not to tell you.

CHANCE: Well, I happen to know it. You registered under a phony name in Palm Beach but I discovered your real one. And you admitted it to me.

PRINCESS: I'm the Princess Kosmonopolis.

CHANCE: Yes, and you used to be known as ...

PRINCESS [*sitting up sharply*]: No, stop ... will you let me do it? Quietly, in my own way? The last place I remember ...

CHANCE: What's the last place you remember?

PRINCESS: A town with the crazy name of Tallahassee.

CHANCE: Yeah. We drove through there. That's where I reminded you that today would be Sunday and we ought to lay in a supply of liquor to get us through it without us being dehydrated too severely, and so we stopped there but it was a college town and we had some trouble locating a package store, open. ....

PRINCESS: But we did, did we?

CHANCE [*getting up for the bottle and pouring her a drink*]: Oh, sure, we bought three bottles of vodka. You curled up in the back seat with one of those bottles and when I looked back you were blotto. I intended to stay on the old Spanish Trail straight through to Texas, where you had some oil wells to look at. I didn't stop here ... I was stopped.

PRINCESS: What by, a cop? Or ...

CHANCE: No. No cop, but I was arrested by something.

PRINCESS: My car. Where is my car?

CHANCE [*handing her the drink*]: In the hotel parking lot, Princess.

PRINCESS: Oh, then, this is a hotel?

CHANCE: It's the elegant old Royal Palms Hotel in the town of St Cloud.

[*Gulls fly past window, shadows sweeping the blind: they cry out with soft urgency.*]

PRINCESS: Those pigeons out there sound hoarse. They sound like gulls to me. Of course, they could be pigeons with laryngitis.

[CHANCE *glances at her with his flickering smile and laughs softly.*]

Will you help me please? I'm about to get up.

CHANCE: What do you want? I'll get it.

PRINCESS: I want to go to the window.

CHANCE: What for?

PRINCESS: To look out of it.

CHANCE: I can describe the view to you.

PRINCESS: I'm not sure I'd trust your description. *WELL?*

CHANCE: Okay, *oopsa-daisy.*

PRINCESS: My God! I said help me up, not ... toss me on to the carpet! [*Sways dizzily a moment, clutching bed. Then draws a breath and crosses to the window.*]

[*The* PRINCESS *pauses as she gazes out, squinting into noon's brilliance.*]

CHANCE: Well, what do you see? Give me your description of the view, Princess?

PRINCESS [*facing the audience*]: I see a palm garden.

CHANCE: And a four-lane highway just past it.

PRINCESS [*squinting and shielding her eyes*]: Yes, I see that and a strip of beach with some bathers and then, an infinite stretch of nothing but water and ... [*She cries softly and turns away from the window.*]

CHANCE: What? ...

PRINCESS: Oh God, I remember the thing I wanted not to. The goddam end of my life! [*She draws a deep shuddering breath.*]

CHANCE: [*running to her aid*]: What's the matter?

PRINCESS: Help me back to bed. Oh God, no wonder I didn't want to remember, I was no fool!

[*He assists her to the bed. There is an unmistakable sympathy in his manner, however shallow.*]

CHANCE: Oxygen?

PRINCESS [*drawing another deep shuddering breath*]: No! Where's the stuff? Did you leave it in the car?

CHANCE: Oh, the stuff? Under the mattress. [*Moving to the other side of the bed, he pulls out a small pouch.*]

PRINCESS: A stupid place to put it.

CHANCE [*sitting at the foot of the bed*]: What's wrong with under the mattress?

PRINCESS [*sitting up on the edge of the bed*]: There's such a thing as chambermaids in the world, they make up beds, they come across lumps in a mattress.

CHANCE: This isn't pot. What is it?

PRINCESS: Wouldn't that be pretty? A year in jail in one of those model prisons for distinguished addicts. What is it? Don't you know what it is, you beautiful, stupid young man? It's hashish, Moroccan, the finest.

CHANCE: Oh, hash! How'd you get it through customs when you came back for your come-back?

PRINCESS: I didn't get it through customs. The ship's doctor gave me injections while this stuff was winging over the ocean to a shifty young gentleman who thought he could blackmail me for it. [*She puts on her slippers with a vigorous gesture.*]

CHANCE: Couldn't he?

PRINCESS: Of course not. I called his bluff.

CHANCE: You took injections coming over?

PRINCESS: With my neuritis? I had to. Come on, give it to me.

CHANCE: Don't you want it packed right?

PRINCESS: You talk too much. You ask too many questions. I need something quick. [*She rises.*]

CHANCE: I'm a new hand at this.

PRINCESS: I'm sure, or you wouldn't discuss it in a hotel room. . . .

[*She turns to the audience, and intermittently changes the focus of her attention.*]

For years they all told me that it was ridiculous of me to feel that I couldn't go back to the screen or the stage as a middle-aged woman. They told me I was an artist, not just a star whose career depended on youth. But I knew in my heart that the legend of Alexandra del Lago couldn't be separated from an appearance of youth. . . .

There's no more valuable knowledge than knowing the right time to go. I knew it. I went at the right time to go.

RETIRED! Where to? To what? To that dead planet the moon. ...

There's nowhere else to retire to when you retire from an art because, believe it or not, I really was once an artist. So I retired to the moon, but the atmosphere of the moon doesn't have any oxygen in it. I began to feel breathless, in that withered, withering country, of time coming after time not meant to come after, and so I discovered ... Haven't you fixed it yet?

[CHANCE *rises and goes to her with a cigarette he has been preparing.*]

Discovered this!

And other practices like it, to put to sleep the tiger that raged in my nerves. ... Why the unsatisfied tiger? In the nerves' jungle? Why is anything, anywhere, unsatisfied, and raging? ...

Ask somebody's good doctor. But don't believe his answer because it isn't ... the answer ... if I had just been old but you see, I wasn't old. ...

I just wasn't young, not young, young. I just wasn't young any more. ...

CHANCE: Nobody's young any more. ...

PRINCESS: But you see, I couldn't get old with that tiger still in me raging.

CHANCE: Nobody can get old. ...

PRINCESS: Stars in retirement sometimes give acting lessons. Or take up painting, paint flowers on pots, or landscapes. I could have painted the landscapes of the endless, withering country in which I wandered like a lost nomad. If I could paint deserts and nomads, if I could paint ... hahaha. ...

CHANCE: Sh-Sh-sh-

PRINCESS: Sorry!

CHANCE: Smoke.

PRINCESS: Yes, smoke! And then the young lovers. ...

CHANCE: Me?

PRINCESS: You? Yes, finally you. But you come after the come-back. Ha ... Ha ... The glorious come-back, when I turned fool and came back. ... The screen's a very clear mirror. There's a thing called a close-up. The camera advances and you stand still and your head, your face, is caught in the frame of the picture with a light blazing on it and all your terrible history screams while you smile. ...

CHANCE: How do you know? Maybe it wasn't a failure, maybe you were just scared, just chicken, Princess ... ha-ha-ha. ...

PRINCESS: Not a failure ... after that close-up they gasped. ... People gasped. ... I heard them whisper, their shocked whispers. Is that her? Is that her? Her? ... I made the mistake of wearing a very elaborate gown to the *première*, a gown with a train that had to be gathered up as I rose from my seat and began the interminable retreat from the city of flames, up, up, up the unbearably long theatre aisle, gasping for breath and still clutching up the regal white train of my gown, all the way up the forever ... length of the aisle, and behind me some small unknown man grabbing at me, saying, stay, stay! At last the top of the aisle, I turned and struck him, then let the train fall, forgot it, and tried to run down the marble stairs, tripped of course, fell and rolled, rolled, like a sailor's drunk whore to the bottom ... hands, merciful hands without faces, assisted me to get up. After that? Flight, just flight, not interrupted until I woke up this morning. ... Oh God it's gone out. ...

CHANCE: Let me fix you another. Huh? Shall I fix you another?

PRINCESS: Let me finish yours. You can't retire with the out-crying heart of an artist still crying out, in your body, in your nerves, in your what? Heart? Oh, no, that's gone, that's ...

CHANCE [*He goes to her, takes the cigarette out of her hand and*

gives her a fresh one.]: Here, I've fixed you another one ...
Princess, I've fixed you another. .... [*He sits on the floor,
leaning against the foot of the bed.*]

PRINCESS: Well, sooner or later, at some point in your life,
the thing that you lived for is lost or abandoned, and then
... you die, or find something else. This is my something
else. .... [*She approaches the bed.*] And ordinarily I take the
most fantastic precautions against ... detection. .... [*She
sits on the bed, then lies down on her back, her head over the foot,
near his.*] I cannot imagine what possessed me to let you
know. Knowing so little about you as I seem to know.

CHANCE: I must've inspired a good deal of confidence in
you.

PRINCESS: If that's the case, I've gone crazy. Now tell me
something. What is that body of water, that sea, out past
the palm garden and four-lane highway? I ask you
because I remember now that we turned west from the
sea when we went on to that highway called the Old
Spanish Trail.

CHANCE: We've come back to the sea.

PRINCESS: What sea?

CHANCE: The Gulf.

PRINCESS: The Gulf?

CHANCE: The Gulf of misunderstanding between me and
you. ....

PRINCESS: We don't understand each other? And lie here
smoking this stuff?

CHANCE: Princess, don't forget that this stuff is yours, that
you provided me with it.

PRINCESS: What are you trying to prove? [*Church bells toll.*]
Sundays go on a long time.

CHANCE: You don't deny it was yours.

PRINCESS: What's mine?

CHANCE: You brought it into the country, you smuggled it
through customs into the U.S.A., and you had a fair
supply of it at that hotel in Palm Beach and were asked to

check out before you were ready to do so, because its aroma drifted into the corridor one breezy night.

PRINCESS: What are you trying to prove?

CHANCE: You don't deny that you introduced me to it?

PRINCESS: Boy, I doubt very much that I have any vice that I'd need to introduce to you. . . .

CHANCE: Don't call me 'boy'.

PRINCESS: Why not?

CHANCE: It sounds condescending. And all my vices were caught from other people.

PRINCESS: What are you trying to prove? My memory's come back now. Excessively clearly. It was this mutual practice that brought us together. When you came in my cabaña to give me one of those papaya cream rubs, you sniffed, you grinned, and said you'd like a stick too.

CHANCE: That's right. I knew the smell of it.

PRINCESS: What are you trying to prove?

CHANCE: You asked me four or five times what I'm trying to prove, the answer is nothing. I'm just making sure that your memory's cleared up now. You do remember me coming in your cabaña to give you those papaya cream rubs?

PRINCESS: Of course I do, Carl!

CHANCE: My name is not Carl. It's Chance.

PRINCESS: You called yourself Carl.

CHANCE: I always carry an extra name in my pocket.

PRINCESS: You're not a criminal, are you?

CHANCE: No ma'am, not me. You're the one that's committed a federal offence.

[*She stares at him a moment, and then goes to the door leading to the hall, looks out and listens.*]

What did you do that for?

PRINCESS [*closing the door*]: To see if someone was planted outside the door.

CHANCE: You still don't trust me?

PRINCESS: Someone that gives me a false name?

CHANCE: You registered under a phony one in Palm Beach.

PRINCESS: Yes, to avoid getting any reports or condolences on the disaster I ran from. [*She crosses to the window. There is a pause followed by the 'Lament'.*] And so we've not arrived at any agreement?

CHANCE: No ma'am, not a complete one.

[*She turns her back to the window and gazes at him from there.*]

PRINCESS: What's the gimmick? The hitch?

CHANCE: The usual one.

PRINCESS: What's that?

CHANCE: Doesn't somebody always hold out for something?

PRINCESS: Are you holding out for something?

CHANCE: Uh-huh ...

PRINCESS: What?

CHANCE: You said that you had a large block of stock, more than half-ownership in a sort of a second-rate Hollywood studio, and could put me under contract. I doubted your word about that. You're not like any phony I've met before, but phonies come in all types and sizes. So I held out, even after we locked your cabaña door for the papaya cream rubs. .... You wired for some contract papers we signed. It was notarized and witnessed by three strangers found in a bar.

PRINCESS: Then why did you hold out, still?

CHANCE: I didn't have much faith in it. You know, you can buy those things for six bits in novelty stores. I've been conned and tricked too often to put much faith in anything that could still be phony.

PRINCESS: You're wise. However, I have the impression that there's been a certain amount of intimacy between us.

CHANCE: A certain amount. No more. I wanted to hold your interest.

PRINCESS: Well, you miscalculated. My interest always increases with satisfaction.

CHANCE: Then you're unusual in that respect, too.

PRINCESS: In all respects I'm not common.

CHANCE: But I guess the contract we signed is full of loopholes?

PRINCESS: Truthfully, yes, it is. I can get out of it if I wanted to. And so can the studio. Do you have any talent?

CHANCE: For what?

PRINCESS: Acting, baby, *ACTING* !

CHANCE: I'm not as positive of it as I once was. I've had more chances than I could count on my fingers, and made the grade almost, but not quite, every time. Something always blocks me. . . .

PRINCESS: What? What? Do you *know*? [*He rises. The lamentation is heard very faintly.*] Fear?

CHANCE: No not fear, but terror . . . otherwise would I be your goddam caretaker, hauling you across the country? Picking you up when you fall? Well would I? Except for that block, be anything less than a star?

PRINCESS: *CARL!*

CHANCE: Chance . . . Chance Wayne. You're stoned.

PRINCESS: Chance, come back to your youth. Put off this false, ugly hardness and . . .

CHANCE: And be took in by every con-merchant I meet?

PRINCESS: I'm not a phony, believe me.

CHANCE: Well, then, what is it you want? Come on, say it, Princess.

PRINCESS: Chance, come here. [*He smiles but doesn't move.*] Come here and let's comfort each other a little. [*He crouches by the bed; she encircles him with her bare arms.*]

CHANCE: Princess! Do you know something? All this conversation has been recorded on tape?

PRINCESS: What are you talking about?

CHANCE: Listen. I'll play it back to you. [*He uncovers the tape recorder; approaches her with the earpiece.*]

PRINCESS: How did you get that thing?

CHANCE: You bought it for me in Palm Beach. I said that I wanted it to improve my diction. . . .

[*He presses the 'play' button on the recorder. The following in the left column can either be on a public address system, or can be cut.*]

(PLAYBACK)

PRINCESS: What is it? Don't you know what it is, you beautiful, stupid, young man? It's hashish, Moroccan, the finest.

CHANCE: Oh, hash! How'd you get it through customs when you came back for your come-back?

PRINCESS: I didn't get it through customs. The ship's doctor. . . .

PRINCESS: What a smart cookie you are.

CHANCE: How does it feel to be over a great big barrel?

[*He snaps off the recorder and picks up the reels.*]

PRINCESS: This is blackmail is it? Where's my mink stole?

CHANCE: Not stolen.

[*He tosses it to her contemptuously from a chair.*]

PRINCESS: Where is my jewel case?

CHANCE [*picking it up off the floor and throwing it on the bed*]: Here.

PRINCESS [*opening it up and starting to put on some jewellery*]: Every piece is insured and described in detail. Lloyd's in London.

CHANCE: *Who's* a smart cookie, Princess? You want your purse now so you can count your money?

PRINCESS: I don't carry currency with me, just travellers' cheques.

CHANCE: I noted that fact already. But I got a fountain pen you can sign them with.

PRINCESS: Ho, Ho!

CHANCE: 'Ho, ho!' What an insincere laugh; if that's how you fake a laugh, no wonder you didn't make good in your come-back picture. . . .

PRINCESS: Are you serious about this attempt to blackmail me?

CHANCE: You'd better believe it. Your trade's turned dirt on you, Princess. You understand that language.

PRINCESS: The language of the gutter is understood anywhere that anyone ever fell in it.

CHANCE: Aw, then you *do* understand.

PRINCESS: And if I shouldn't comply with this order of yours?

CHANCE: You still got a name, you're still a personage, Princess. You wouldn't want *Confidential* or *Whisper* or *Hush-Hush* or the narcotics department of the F.B.I. to get hold of one of these tape-records, would you? And I'm going to make lots of copies. Huh? Princess?

PRINCESS: You are trembling and sweating . . . you see this part doesn't suit you, you just don't play it well, Chance. . . . [CHANCE *puts the reels in a suitcase.*] I hate to think of what kind of desperation has made you try to intimidate me, *ME? ALEXANDRA DEL LAGO?* with that ridiculous threat. Why it's so silly, it's touching, downright endearing, it makes me feel close to you, Chance. You were well born, weren't you? Born of good Southern stock, in a genteel tradition, with just one disadvantage, a laurel wreath on your forehead, given too early, without enough effort to earn it . . . where's your scrapbook, Chance? [*He crosses to the bed, takes a travellers' chequebook out*

of her purse, and extends it to her.] Where's your book full of
little theatre notices and stills that show you in the background of . . .

CHANCE: Here! Here! Start signing . . . or . . .

PRINCESS [*pointing to the bathroom*]: Or *WHAT*? Go take a
shower under cold water. I don't like hot sweaty bodies in
a tropical climate. Oh, you, I do want and will accept, still
. . . under certain conditions which I will make very clear
to you.

CHANCE: Here. [*Throws the chequebook towards the bed.*]

PRINCESS: Put this away. And your leaky fountain pen. . . .
When monster meets monster, one monster has to give
way, *AND IT WILL NEVER BE ME*. I'm an older
hand at it . . . with much more natural aptitude at it than
you have. . . . Now then, you put the cart a little in front of
the horse. Signed cheques are payment, delivery comes
first. Certainly I can afford it, I could deduct you, as my
caretaker, Chance, remember that I was a star before big
taxes . . . and had a husband who was a great merchant
prince. He taught me to deal with money. . . . Now,
Chance, please pay close attention while I tell you the
very special conditions under which I will keep you in my
employment . . . after this miscalculation. . . .

Forget the legend that I was and the ruin of that legend.
Whether or not I do have a disease of the heart that places
an early terminal date on my life, no mention of that, no
reference to it ever. No mention of death, never, never a
word on that odious subject. I've been accused of having
a death wish but I think it's life that I wish for, terribly,
shamelessly, on any terms whatsoever.

When I say now, the answer must not be later. I have
only one way to forget these things I don't want to
remember and that's through the act of love-making.
That's the only dependable distraction so when I say now,
because I need that distraction, it has to be now, not
later.

[*She crosses to the bed. He rises from the opposite side of the bed and goes to the window. She gazes at his back as he looks out of the window. Pause: 'Lament'.*]

PRINCESS [*finally, softly*]: Chance, I need that distraction. It's time for me to find out if you're able to give it to me. You mustn't hang on to your silly little idea that you can increase your value by turning away and looking out of a window when somebody wants you. ... I want you. ... I say now and I mean now, then and not until then will I call downstairs and tell the hotel cashier that I'm sending a young man down with some travellers' cheques to cash for me. ...

CHANCE: [*turning slowly from the window*]: Aren't you ashamed, a little?

PRINCESS: Of course I am. Aren't you?

CHANCE: More than a little. ...

PRINCESS: Close the shutters, draw the curtain across them.

[*He obeys these commands.*]

Now get a little sweet music on the radio and come here to me and make me almost believe that we're a pair of young lovers without any shame.

SCENE TWO

[*As the curtain rises, the* PRINCESS *has a fountain pen in hand and is signing cheques.* CHANCE, *now wearing dark slacks, socks, and shoes of the fashionable loafer type, is putting on his shirt and speaks as the curtain opens.*]

CHANCE: Keep on writing, has the pen gone dry?

PRINCESS: I started at the back of the book where the big ones are.

CHANCE: Yes, but you stopped too soon.

PRINCESS: All right, one more from the front of the book as a token of some satisfaction. I said some, not complete.

CHANCE [*picking up the phone*]: Operator – Give me the cashier please.

PRINCESS: What are you doing that for?

CHANCE: You have to tell the cashier you're sending me down with some travellers' cheques to cash for you.

PRINCESS: Have to? Did you say have to?

CHANCE: Cashier? Just a moment. The Princess Kosmonopolis. [*He thrusts the phone at her.*]

PRINCESS [*into the phone*]: Who is this? But I don't want the cashier. My watch has stopped and I want to know the right time ... five after three? Thank you ... he says it's five after three. [*She hangs up and smiles at* CHANCE.] I'm not ready to be left alone in this room. Now let's not fight any more over little points like that, let's save our strength for the big ones. I'll have the cheques cashed for you as soon as I've put on my face. I just don't want to be left alone in this place till I've put on the face that I face the world with, baby. Maybe after we get to know each other, we won't fight over little points any more, the struggle will stop, maybe we won't even fight over big points, baby. Will you open the shutters a little bit, please? [*He doesn't seem to hear her. The 'Lament' is heard.*] I won't be able to see my face in the mirror. . . . Open the shutters, I won't be able to see my face in the mirror.

CHANCE: Do you want to?

PRINCESS [*pointing*]: Unfortunately I have to! Open the shutters!

[*He does. He remains by the open shutters, looking out as the Lament in the air continues.*]

CHANCE: — I was born in this town. I was born in St Cloud.

PRINCESS: That's a good way to begin to tell your life story. Tell me your life story. I'm interested in it, I really would like to know it. Let's make it your audition, a sort of screen test for you. I can watch you in the mirror while I put my face on. And tell me your life story, and if you hold my attention with your life story, I'll know you have talent, I'll wire my studio on the Coast that I'm still alive and I'm on my way to the Coast with a young man named Chance Wayne that I think is cut out to be a great young star.

CHANCE [*moving out on the forestage*]: Here is the town I was born in, and lived in till ten years ago, in St Cloud. I was a twelve-pound baby, normal and healthy, but with some kind of quantity 'X' in my blood, a wish or a need to be different. . . . The kids that I grew up with are mostly still here and what they call 'settled down', gone into business, married, and bringing up children; the little crowd I was in with, that I used to be the star of, was the snobset, the ones with the big names and money. I didn't have either. . . . [*The* PRINCESS *utters a soft laugh in her dimmed-out area.*] What I had was . . . [*The* PRINCESS *half-turns, brush poised in a faint, dusty beam of light.*]

PRINCESS: *BEAUTY!* Say it! Say it! What you had was beauty! I had it! I say it with pride, no matter how sad, being gone, now.

CHANCE: Yes, well . . . the others . . . [*The* PRINCESS

resumes brushing hair and the sudden cold beam of light on her goes out again] ... are all now members of the young social set here. The girls are young matrons, bridge-players, and the boys belong to the Junior Chamber of Commerce and some of them, clubs in New Orleans such as Rex and Comus and ride on the Mardi Gras floats. Wonderful? No, boring ... I wanted, expected, intended to get, something better. ... Yes, and I did, I got it. I did things that fat-headed gang never dreamed of. Hell, when they were still freshmen at Tulane or L.S.U. or Ole Miss, I sang in the chorus of the biggest show in New York, in *Oklahoma*, and had pictures in *Life* in a cowboy outfit, tossin' a ten-gallon hat in the air! *YIP* ... *EEEEEE!* Ha-ha. ... And at the same time pursued my other vocation. ...

Maybe the one one I was truly meant for, love-making ... slept in the social register of New York! Millionaires' widows and wives and débutante daughters of such famous names as Vanderbrook and Masters and Halloway and Connaught, names mentioned daily in columns, whose credit cards are their faces. ... And ...

PRINCESS: What did they pay you?

CHANCE: I gave people more than I took. Middle-aged people I gave back a feeling of youth. Lonely girls? Understanding, appreciation! An absolutely convincing show of affection. Sad people, lost people? Something light and uplifting! Eccentrics? Tolerance, even odd things they long for. ...

But always just at the point when I might get something back that would solve my own need, which was great, to rise to their level, the memory of my girl would pull me back home to her ... and when I came home for those visits, man oh man how that town buzzed with excitement. I'm telling you, it would blaze with it, and then that thing in Korea came along. I was about to be sucked into the Army so I went into the Navy, because a sailor's uniform suited me better, the uniform was all that suited me, though. . . .

PRINCESS: Ah-ha!

CHANCE [*mocking her*]: Ah-ha. I wasn't able to stand the goddam routine, discipline. . . .

I kept thinking, this stops everything. I was twenty-three, that was the peak of my youth, and I knew my youth wouldn't last long. By the time I got out, Christ knows, I might be nearly thirty! Who would remember Chance Wayne? In a life like mine, you just can't stop, you know, can't take time out between steps, you've got to keep going right on up from one thing to the other; once you drop out, it leaves you and goes on without you and you're washed up.

PRINCESS: I don't think I know what you're talking about.

CHANCE: I'm talking about the parade. *THE* parade! The parade! the boys that go places, that's the parade I'm talking about, not a parade of swabbies on a wet deck. And so I ran my comb through my hair one morning and noticed that eight or ten hairs had come out, a warning signal of a future baldness. My hair was still thick. But would it be, five years from now, or even three? When the war would be over, that scared me, that speculation. I started to have bad dreams. Nightmares and cold sweats at night, and I had palpitations, and on my leaves I got drunk and woke up in strange places with faces on the next pillow I had never seen before. My eyes had a wild look in them in the mirror. . . . I got the idea I wouldn't live through the war, that I wouldn't come back, that all the excitement and glory of being Chance Wayne would go up in smoke at the moment of contact between my brain and a bit of hot steel that happened to be in the air at the same time and place that my head was . . . that thought didn't comfort me any. Imagine a

whole lifetime of dreams and ambitions and hopes
dissolving away in one instant, being blacked out like
some arithmetic problem washed off a blackboard by a
wet sponge, just by some little accident like a bullet, not
even aimed at you but just shot off in space, and so I
cracked up, my nerves did. I got a medical discharge out
of the service and I came home in civvies, then it was
when I noticed how different it was, the town and the
people in it. Polite? Yes, but not cordial. No headlines
in the papers, just an item that measured one inch at
the bottom of page five saying that Chance Wayne, the
son of Mrs Emily Wayne of North Front Street had
received an honorable discharge from the Navy as the
result of illness and was home to recover ... that was
when Heavenly became more important to me than
anything else. ...

PRINCESS: Is Heavenly a girl's name?

CHANCE: Heavenly is the name of my girl in St Cloud.

PRINCESS: Is Heavenly why we stopped here?

CHANCE: What other reason for stopping here can you
think of?

PRINCESS: So ... I'm being used. Why not? Even a dead
race horse is used to make glue. Is she pretty?

CHANCE [*handing* PRINCESS *a snapshot*]: This is a flashlight photo I took of her, nude, one night on Diamond
Key, which is a little sandbar about half a mile off-shore
which is under water at high tide. This was taken with
the tide coming in. The water is just beginning to lap
over her body like it desired her like I did and still do
and will always, always. [CHANCE *takes back the snapshot*.]
Heavenly was her name. You can see that it fits her. This
was her at fifteen.

PRINCESS: Did you have her that early?

CHANCE: I was just two years older, we had each other
that early.

PRINCESS: Sheer luck!

CHANCE: Princess, the great difference between people in
this world is not between the rich and the poor or the
good and the evil, the biggest of all differences in this
world is between the ones that had or have pleasure in
love and those that haven't and hadn't any pleasure in
love, but just watched it with envy, sick envy. The
spectators and the performers. I don't mean just ordinary
pleasure or the kind you can buy, I mean great pleasure,
and nothing that's happened to me or to Heavenly since
can cancel out the many long nights without sleep when
we gave each other such pleasure in love as very few
people can look back on in their lives. . . .

PRINCESS: No question, go on with your story.

CHANCE: Each time I came back to St Cloud I had her
love to come back to. . . .

PRINCESS: Something permanent in a world of change?

CHANCE: Yes, after each disappointment, each failure
at something, I'd come back to her like going to a
hospital.

PRINCESS: She put cool bandages on your wounds? Why
didn't you marry this Heavenly little physician?

CHANCE: Didn't I tell you that Heavenly is the daughter of
Boss Finley, the biggest political wheel in this part of the
country? Well, if I didn't I made a serious omission.

PRINCESS: He disapproved?

CHANCE: He figured his daughter rated someone a hundred, a thousand per cent better than me, Chance
Wayne. . . . The last time I came back here, she phoned
me from the drugstore and told me to swim out to
Diamond Key, that she would meet me there. I waited a
long time, till almost sunset, and the tide started coming
in before I heard the put-put of an outboard motor-boat
coming out to the sandbar. The sun was behind her, I
squinted. She had on a silky wet tank suit and fans of
water and mist made rainbows about her . . . she stood

up in the boat as if she was water-skiing, shouting things at me an' circling around the sandbar, around and around it!

PRINCESS: She didn't come to the sandbar?

CHANCE: No, just circled around it, shouting things at me. I'd swim toward the boat, I would just about reach it and she'd race it away, throwing up misty rainbows, disappearing in rainbows and then circling back and shouting things at me again. . . .

PRINCESS: What things?

CHANCE: Things like, 'Chance go away.' 'Don't come back to St Cloud.' 'Chance, you're a liar.' 'Chance, I'm sick of your lies!' 'My father's right about you!' 'Chance, you're no good any more.' 'Chance, stay away from St Cloud.' The last time around the sandbar she shouted nothing, just waved good-bye and turned the boat back to shore.

PRINCESS: Is that the end of the story?

CHANCE: Princess, the end of the story is up to you. You want to help me?

PRINCESS: I want to help you. Believe me, not everybody wants to hurt everybody. I don't want to hurt you, can you believe me?

CHANCE: I can if you prove it to me.

PRINCESS: How can I prove it to you?

CHANCE: I have something in mind.

PRINCESS: Yes, what?

CHANCE: O.K., I'll give you a quick outline of this project I have in mind. Soon as I've talked to my girl and shown her my contract, we go on, you and me. Not far, just to New Orleans, Princess. But no more hiding away, we check in at the Hotel Roosevelt there as Alexandra Del Lago and Chance Wayne. Right away the newspaper call you and you give a Press conference. . . .

PRINCESS: Oh?

CHANCE: Yes! The idea briefly, a local contest of talent to find a pair of young people to star as unknowns in a picture you're planning to make to show your faith in *YOUTH*, Princess. You stage this contest, you invite other judges, but your decision decides it!

PRINCESS: And you and ...?

CHANCE: Yes, Heavenly and I win it. We get her out of St Cloud, we go to the West Coast together.

PRINCESS: And me?

CHANCE: You?

PRINCESS: Have you forgotten, for instance, that any public attention is what I least want in the world?

CHANCE: What better way can you think of to show the public that you're a person with bigger than personal interest?

PRINCESS: Oh, yes, yes, but not true.

CHANCE: You could pretend it was true.

PRINCESS: If I didn't despise pretending!

CHANCE: I understand. Time does it. Hardens people. Time and the world that you've lived in.

PRINCESS: Which you want for yourself. Isn't that what you want? [*She looks at him, goes to the phone, then speaks into phone*] Cashier?
Hello Cashier? This is the Princess Kosmonopolis speaking. I'm sending down a young man to cash some travellers' cheques for me. [*She hangs up.*]

CHANCE: And I want to borrow your Cadillac for a while. ...

PRINCESS: What for, Chance?

CHANCE [*posturing*]: I'm pretentious. I want to be seen in your car on the streets of St Cloud. Drive all around town in it, blowing those long silver trumpets and dressed in the fine clothes you bought me. ... Can I?

PRINCESS: Chance, you're a lost little boy that I really would like to help find himself.

CHANCE: I passed the screen test!

PRINCESS: Come here, kiss me, I love you. [*She faces the audience.*] Did I say that? Did I mean it? [*Then to* CHANCE *with arms outstretched.*] What a child you are. . . . Come here. . . . [*He ducks under her arms, and escapes to the chair.*]

CHANCE: I want this big display. Big phony display in your Cadillac around town. And a wad of dough to flash in their faces and the fine clothes you've bought me, on me.

PRINCESS: Did I buy you fine clothes?

CHANCE [*picking up his jacket from the chair*]: The finest. When you stopped being lonely because of my company at that Palm Beach Hotel, you bought me the finest. That's the deal for tonight, to toot those silver horns and drive slowly around in the Cadillac convertible so everybody that thought I was washed up will see me. And I have taken my false or true contract to flash in the faces of various people that called me washed up. All right, that's the deal. Tomorrow you'll get the car back and what's left of your money. Tonight's all that counts.

PRINCESS: How do you know that as soon as you walk out of this room I won't call the police?

CHANCE: You wouldn't do that, Princess. [*He puts on his jacket.*] You'll find the car in back of the hotel parking lot, and the left-over dough will be in the glove compartment of the car.

PRINCESS: Where will you be?

CHANCE: With my girl, or nowhere.

PRINCESS: Chance Wayne! This was not necessary, all this. I'm not a phony and I wanted to be your friend.

CHANCE: Go back to sleep. As far as I know you're not a bad person, but you just got into bad company on this occasion.

PRINCESS: I am your friend and I'm not a phony. [CHANCE *turns and goes to the steps.*] When will I see you?

CHANCE [*at the top of the steps*]: I don't know — maybe never.

Act Two

SCENE ONE

The terrace of Boss Finley's house, which is a frame house of Victorian Gothic design, suggested by a door frame at the right and a single white column. As in the other scenes, there are no walls, the action occurring against the sky and sea cyclorama.

The Gulf is suggested by the brightness and the gulls crying as in Act One. There is only essential porch furniture, Victorian wicker but painted bone white. The men should also be wearing white or off-white suits: the tableau is all blue and white, as strict as a canvas of Georgie O'Keefe's.

[*At the rise of the curtain,* BOSS FINLEY *is standing in the centre and* GEORGE SCUDDER *nearby.*]

BOSS FINLEY: Chance Wayne had my daughter when she was fifteen.

SCUDDER: That young.

BOSS: When she was fifteen he had her. Know how I know? Some flashlight photos were made of her, naked, on Diamond Key.

SCUDDER: By Chance Wayne?

BOSS: My little girl was fifteen, barely out of her childhood when – [*calling offstage*] Charles –

[CHARLES *enters*]

BOSS: Call Miss Heavenly –

CHARLES [*concurrently*]: Miss Heavenly. Miss Heavenly. Your daddy wants to see you.

[CHARLES *leaves.*]

BOSS [*to* SCUDDER]: By Chance Wayne? Who the hell else do you reckon? I seen them. He had them developed by some studio in Pass Christian that made more copies of them than Chance Wayne ordered and these photos were circulated. I seen them. That was when I first warned the son-of-a-bitch to git out of St Cloud. But he's back in St Cloud right now. I tell you –

SCUDDER: Boss, let me make a suggestion. Call off this rally, I mean your appearance at it, and take it easy tonight. Go out on your boat, you and Heavenly take a short cruise on *THE STARFISH*. . . .

BOSS: I'm not about to start sparing myself. Oh, I know, I'll have me a coronary and go like that. But not because Chance Wayne had the unbelievable gall to come back to St Cloud. [*Calling offstage*] Tom Junior!

TOM JUNIOR [*offstage*]: Yes, sir!

BOSS: Has he checked out yet?

TOM JUNIOR [*entering*]: Hatcher says he called their room at the Royal Palms, and Chance Wayne answered the phone, and Hatcher says . . .

BOSS: Hatcher says – who's Hatcher?

TOM JUNIOR: Dan Hatcher.

BOSS: I hate to expose my ignorance like this but the name Dan Hatcher has no more meaning to me than the name of Hatcher, which is none whatsoever.

SCUDDER [*quietly, deferentially*]: Hatcher, Dan Hatcher, is the assistant manager of the Royal Palms Hotel, and the man that informed me this morning that Chance Wayne was back in St Cloud.

BOSS: Is this Hatcher a talker, or can he keep his mouth shut?

SCUDDER: I think I impressed him how important it is to handle this thing discreetly.

BOSS: Discreetly, like you handled that operation you done on my daughter, so discreetly that a hillbilly heckler is shouting me questions about it wherever I speak?

SCUDDER: I went to fantastic lengths to preserve the secrecy of that operation.

TOM JUNIOR: When Papa's upset he hits out at anyone near him.

BOSS: I just want to know – Has Wayne left?

TOM JUNIOR: Hatcher says that Chance Wayne told him that this old movie star that he's latched on to ...

SCUDDER: Alexandra Del Lago.

TOM JUNIOR: She's not well enough to travel.

BOSS: Okay, your'e a doctor, remove her to a hospital. Call an ambulance and haul her out of the Royal Palms Hotel.

SCUDDER: Without her consent?

BOSS: Say she's got something contagious, typhoid, bubonic plague. Haul her out and slap a quarantine on her hospital door. That way you can separate them. We can remove Chance Wayne from St Cloud as soon as this Miss Del Lago is removed from Chance Wayne.

SCUDDER: I'm not so sure that's the right way to go about it.

BOSS: Okay, you think of a way. My daughter's no whore, but she had a whore's operation after the last time he had her. I don't want him passin' another night in St Cloud. Tom Junior.

TOM JUNIOR: Yes, sir.

BOSS: I want him gone by tomorrow – tomorrow commences at midnight.

TOM JUNIOR: I know what to do, Papa. Can I use the boat?

BOSS: Don't ask me, don't tell me nothin' –

TOM JUNIOR: Can I have *The Starfish* tonight?

BOSS: I don't want to know how, just go about it. Where's your sister?

[CHARLES *appears on the gallery, points out* HEAVENLY *lying on the beach to Boss and exits.*]

TOM JUNIOR: She's lyin' out on the beach like a dead body washed up on it.

BOSS [*calling*]: Heavenly!

TOM JUNIOR: Gawge, I want you with me on this boat trip tonight, Gawge.

BOSS [*calling*]: Heavenly!

SCUDDER: I know what you mean, Tom Junior, but I couldn't be involved in it. I can't even know about it.

BOSS [*calling again*]: Heavenly!

TOM JUNIOR: Okay, don't be involved in it. There's a pretty fair doctor that lost his licence for helping a girl out of trouble, and he won't be so goddam finicky about doing this absolutely just thing.

SCUDDER: I don't question the moral justification, which is complete without question. . . .

TOM JUNIOR: Yeah, complete without question.

SCUDDER: But I am a reputable doctor, I haven't lost my licence. I'm chief of staff at the great hospital put up by your father. . . .

TOM JUNIOR: I said, don't know about it.

SCUDDER: No, sir, I won't know about it . . . [BOSS *starts to cough.*] I can't afford to, and neither can your father. . . .

[SCUDDER *goes to gallery writing prescription.*]

BOSS: Heavenly! Come up here, sugar. [*To* SCUDDER] What's that you're writing?

SCUDDER: Prescription for that cough.

BOSS: Tear it up, throw it away. I've hawked and spit all my life, and I'll be hawking and spitting in the hereafter. You all can count on that.

[*Auto horn is heard.*]

TOM JUNIOR [*leaps up on the gallery and starts to leave*]: Papa, he's drivin' back by.

BOSS: Tom Junior.

[TOM JUNIOR *stops.*]

TOM JUNIOR: Is Chance Wayne insane?

SCUDDER: Is a criminal degenerate sane or insane is a

question that lots of law courts haven't been able to
settle.

BOSS: Take it to the Supreme Court, they'll hand you down
a decision on that question. They'll tell you a handsome
young criminal degenerate like Chance Wayne is the
mental and moral equal of any white man in the country.

TOM JUNIOR: He's stopped at the foot of the drive.

BOSS: Don't move, don't move, Tom Junior.

TOM JUNIOR: I'm not movin', Papa.

CHANCE [offstage]: Aunt Nonnie! Hey, Aunt Nonnie!

BOSS: What's he shouting?

TOM JUNIOR: He's shouting at Aunt Nonnie.

BOSS: Where is she?

TOM JUNIOR: Runnin' up the drive like a dog-track rabbit.

BOSS: He ain't followin', is he?

TOM JUNIOR: Nope. He's drove away.

[AUNT NONNIE *appears before the veranda, terribly flustered,
rooting in her purse for something, apparently blind to the
men on the veranda.*]

BOSS: Whatcha lookin' for, Nonnie?

NONNIE [*stopping short*]: Oh – I didn't notice you, Tom. I
was looking for my *door*-key.

BOSS: Door's open, Nonnie, it's wide open, like a church
door.

NONNIE [*laughing*]: Oh, ha, ha ...

BOSS: Why didn't you answer that good-lookin' boy in the
Cadillac car that shouted at you, Nonnie?

NONNIE: Oh. I hoped you hadn't seen him. [*Draws a deep
breath and comes on to the terrace, closing her white purse.*]
That was Chance Wayne. He's back in St Cloud, he's at
the Royal Palms, he's –

BOSS: Why did you snub him like that? After all these
years of devotion?

NONNIE: I went to the Royal Palms to warn him not to
stay here but –

BOSS: He was out showing off in that big white Cadillac with the trumpet horns on it.

NONNIE: I left a message for him, I –

TOM JUNIOR: What was the message, Aunt Nonnie? Love and kisses?

NONNIE: Just get out of St Cloud right away, Chance.

TOM JUNIOR: He's gonna git out, but not in that fish-tail Caddy.

NONNIE [*to* TOM JUNIOR]: I hope you don't mean violence – [*turning to* BOSS] does he, Tom? Violence don't solve problems. It never solves young people's problems. If you will leave it to me, I'll get him out of St Cloud. I can, I will, I promise. I don't think Heavenly knows he's back in St Cloud. Tom, you know, Heavenly says it wasn't Chance that – She says it wasn't Chance.

BOSS: You're like your dead sister, Nonnie, gullible as my wife was. You don't know a lie if you bump into it on a street in the daytime. Now go out there and tell Heavenly I want to see her.

NONNIE: Tom, she's not well enough to –

BOSS: Nonnie, you got a whole lot to answer for.

NONNIE: Have I?

BOSS: Yes, you sure have, Nonnie. You favoured Chance Wayne, encouraged, aided, and abetted him in his corruption of Heavenly over a long, long time. You go get her. You sure do have a lot to answer for. You got a helluva lot to answer for.

NONNIE: I remember when Chance was the finest, nicest, sweetest boy in St Cloud, and he stayed that way till you, till you –

BOSS: Go get her, go get her!

[*She leaves by the far side of the terrace. After a moment her voice is heard calling,* 'Heavenly? Heavenly?']

It's a curious thing, a mighty peculiar thing, how often a man that rises to high public office is drug back down by every soul he harbours under his roof. He harbours them under his roof, and they pull the roof down on him. Every last living one of them.

TOM JUNIOR: Does that include me, Papa?

BOSS: If the shoe fits, put it on you.

TOM JUNIOR: How does that shoe fit me?

BOSS: If it pinches your foot, just slit it down the sides a little – it'll feel comfortable on you.

TOM JUNIOR: Papa, you are *UNJUST*.

BOSS: What do you want credit for?

TOM JUNIOR: I have devoted the past year to organizin' the 'Youth for Tom Finley' clubs.

BOSS: I'm carryin' Tom Finley Junior on my ticket.

TOM JUNIOR: You're lucky to have me on it.

BOSS: How do you figure I'm lucky to have you on it?

TOM JUNIOR: I got more newspaper coverage in the last six months than ...

BOSS: Once for drunk drivin', once for a stag party you thrown in Capitol City that cost me five thousand dollars to hush it up!

TOM JUNIOR: You are so unjust, it ...

BOSS: And everyone knows you had to be drove through school like a blazeface mule pullin' a plough uphill: flunked out of college with grades that only a moron would have an excuse for.

TOM JUNIOR: I got re-admitted to college.

BOSS: At my insistence. By fake examinations, answers provided beforehand, stuck in your fancy pockets. And your promiscuity. Why, these 'Youth for Tom Finley' clubs are practically nothin' but gangs of juvenile delinquents, wearin' badges with my name and my photograph on them.

TOM JUNIOR: How about your well-known promiscuity, Papa? How about your Miss Lucy?

BOSS: Who is Miss Lucy?

TOM JUNIOR [*laughing so hard he staggers*]: Who is Miss

Lucy? You don't even know who she is, this woman you keep in a fifty-dollar-a-day hotel suite at the Royal Palms, Papa?

BOSS: What're you talkin' about?

TOM JUNIOR: That rides down the Gulf Stream Highway with a motor-cycle escort blowin' their sirens like the Queen of Sheba was going into New Orleans for the day. To use her charge accounts there. And you ask who's Miss Lucy? She don't even talk good of you. She says you're too old for a lover.

BOSS: That is a goddam lie. Who says Miss Lucy says that?

TOM JUNIOR: She wrote it with lipstick on the ladies' room mirror at the Royal Palms.

BOSS: Wrote what?

TOM JUNIOR: I'll quote it to you exactly. 'Boss Finley,' she wrote, 'is too old to cut the mustard.'

[*Pause: the two stags, the old and the young one, face each other, panting.* SCUDDER *has discreetly withdrawn to a far end of porch.*]

BOSS: I don't believe this story!

TOM JUNIOR: Don't believe it.

BOSS: I will check on it, however.

TOM JUNIOR: I already checked on it. Papa, why don't you get rid of her, huh, Papa?

[BOSS FINLEY *turns away, wounded, baffled: stares out at the audience with his old, bloodshot eyes as if he thought that someone out there had shouted a question at him which he didn't quite hear.*]

BOSS: Mind your own goddam business. A man with a mission, which he holds sacred, and on the strength of which he rises to high public office – crucified in this way, publicly, by his own offspring. [HEAVENLY *has entered on the gallery.*] Ah, here she is, here's my little girl. [*Stopping* HEAVENLY] You stay here, honey. I think

you all had better leave me alone with Heavenly now,
huh – yeah. ... [TOM JUNIOR *and* SCUDDER *exit.*]
Now, honey, you stay here. I want to have a talk with you.
HEAVENLY: Papa, I can't talk now.
BOSS: It's necessary.
HEAVENLY: I can't, I can't talk now.
BOSS: All right, don't talk, just listen.

[*But she doesn't want to listen, starts away. He would have
restrained her forcibly if an old coloured manservant,
CHARLES, had not, at that moment, come out on the porch,
He carries a stick, a hat, a package, wrapped as a present.
Puts them on a table.*]

CHARLES: It's five o'clock, Mister Finley.
BOSS: Huh? Oh – thanks ...

[CHARLES *turns on a coach lamp by the door. This marks
a formal division in the scene. The light change is not
realistic; the light doesn't seem to come from the coach lamp
but from a spectral radiance in the sky, flooding the terrace.*

The sea wind sings. HEAVENLY *lifts her face to it. Later
that night may be stormy, but now there is just a quickness and
freshness coming in from the Gulf.* HEAVENLY *is always
looking that way, towards the Gulf, so that the light from
Point Lookout catches her face with its repeated soft stroke of
clarity.*

*In her father, a sudden dignity is revived. Looking at his
very beautiful daughter, he becomes almost stately. He
approaches her, as soon as the coloured man returns inside, like an
aged courtier comes deferentially up to a Crown Princess or
Infanta. It's important not to think of his attitude towards her
in the terms of crudely conscious incestuous feeling, but just
in the natural terms of almost any ageing father's feeling for a
beautiful young daughter who reminds him of a dead wife that
he desired intensely when she was the age of his daughter.*

At this point there might be a phrase of stately, Mozartian]

[*music, suggesting a court dance. The flagged terrace may suggest the parquet floor of a ballroom and the two players' movements may suggest the stately, formal movements of a court dance of that time; but if this effect is used, it should be just a suggestion. The change towards 'stylization' ought to be held in check.*]

BOSS: You're still a beautiful girl.

HEAVENLY: Am I, Papa?

BOSS: Of course you are. Lookin' at you nobody could guess that –

HEAVENLY [*laughs*]: The embalmers must have done a good job on me, Papa. ...

BOSS: You got to quit talkin' like that. [*Then, seeing* CHARLES] Will you get back in the house! [*Phone rings.*]

CHARLES: Yes, sir, I was just –

BOSS: Go on in! If that phone-call is for me, I'm in only to the governor of the state and the president of the Tidewater Oil Corporation.

CHARLES [*offstage*]: It's for Miss Heavenly again.

BOSS: Say she ain't in.

CHARLES: Sorry, she ain't in.

[HEAVENLY *has moved upstage to the low parapet or sea wall that separates the courtyard and lawn from the beach. It is early dusk. The coach lamp has cast a strange light on the setting which is neo-romantic;* HEAVENLY *stops by an ornamental urn containing a tall fern that the salty Gulf wind has stripped nearly bare. The* BOSS *follows her, baffled.*]

BOSS: Honey, you say and do things in the presence of people as if you had no regard of the fact that people have ears to hear you and tongues to repeat what they hear. And so you become a issue.

HEAVENLY: Become what, Papa?

BOSS: A issue, a issue, subject of talk, of scandal – which can defeat the mission that –

HEAVENLY: Don't give me your 'Voice of God' speech. Papa, there was a time when you could have saved me, by letting me marry a boy that was still young and clean, but instead you drove him away, drove him out of St Cloud. And when he came back, you took me out of St Cloud, and tried to force me to marry a fifty-year-old money bag that you wanted something out of –

BOSS: Now, honey –

HEAVENLY: – and then another, another, all of them ones that you wanted something out of. I'd gone, so Chance went away. Tried to compete, make himself big as these big-shots you wanted to use me for a bond with. He went. He tried. The right doors wouldn't open, and so he went in the wrong ones, and – Papa, you married for love, why wouldn't you let me do it, while I was alive, inside, and the boy still clean, still decent?

BOSS: Are you reproaching me for –?

HEAVENLY [*shouting*]: Yes, I am, Papa, I am. You married for love, but you wouldn't let me do it, and even though you'd done it, you broke Mama's heart, Miss Lucy had been your mistress –

BOSS: Who is Miss Lucy?

HEAVENLY: Oh, Papa, she was your mistress long before Mama died. And Mama was just a front for you. Can I go in now, Papa? Can I go in now?

BOSS: No, no, not till I'm through with you. What a terrible, terrible thing for my baby to say … [*He takes her in his arms.*] Tomorrow, tomorrow morning, when the big after-Easter sales commence in the stores – I'm gonna send you in town with a motor-cycle escort, straight to the Maison Blanche. When you arrive at the store, I want you to go directly up to the office of Mr Harvey C. Petrie and tell him to give you unlimited credit there. Then go down and outfit yourself as if you was – buyin' a trousseau to marry the Prince of Monaco. … Purchase a full wardrobe, includin' furs. Keep 'em in storage until winter. Gown? Three, four, five, the most lavish. Slippers? Hell, pairs and pairs of 'em. Not one hat – but a dozen. I made a pile of dough on a deal involvin' the sale of rights to oil under water here lately, and, baby, I want you to buy a piece of jewellery. Now about that, you better tell Harvey to call me. Or better still, maybe Miss Lucy had better help you select it. She's wise as a backhouse rat when it comes to a stone – that's for sure. ... Now where'd I buy that clip that I give your mama? D'you remember the clip I bought your mama? Last thing I give your mama before she died. ... I knowed she was dyin' when I bought her that clip, and I bought that clip for fifteen thousand dollars mainly to make her think she was going to get well. ... When I pinned it on her on the nightgown she was wearing, that poor thing started crying. She said, for God's sake, Boss, what does a dying woman want with such a big diamond? I said to her, honey, look at the price tag on it. What does the price tag say? See them five figures, that one and that five and them three oughts on there? Now, honey, make sense, I told her. If you was dying, if there was any chance of it, would I invest fifteen grand in a diamond clip to pin on the neck of a shroud? Ha, haha. That made the old lady laugh. And she sat up as bright as a little bird in that bed with the diamond clip on, receiving callers all day, and laughing and chatting with them, with that diamond clip on inside and she died before midnight, with that diamond clip on her. And not till the very last minute did she believe that the diamonds wasn't a proof that she wasn't dying. [*He moves to terrace, takes off robe, and starts to put on tuxedo coat.*]

HEAVENLY: Did you bury her with it?

BOSS: Bury her with it? Hell, no. I took it back to the jewellery store in the morning.

HEAVENLY: Then it didn't cost you fifteen grand after all.

BOSS: Hell, did I care what it cost me? I'm not a small man. I wouldn't have cared one hoot if it cost me a million ... if at that time I had that kind of loot in my pockets. It would have been worth that money to see that one little smile your mama bird give me at noon of the day she was dying.

HEAVENLY: I guess that shows, demonstrates very clearly, that you have got a pretty big heart after all.

BOSS: Who doubts it then? Who? Who ever? [*He laughs.*]

[HEAVENLY *starts to laugh and then screams hysterically. She starts going towards the house.*

BOSS *throws down his cane and grabs her.*]

Just a minute, Missy. Stop it. Stop it. Listen to me, I'm gonna tell you something. Last week in New Bethesda, when I was speaking on the threat of desegregation to white women's chastity in the South, some heckler in the crowd shouted out, 'Hey, Boss Finley, how about your daughter? How about that operation you had done on your daughter at the Thomas J. Finley hospital in St Cloud? Did she put on black in mourning for her appendix?' Same heckler, same question when I spoke in the Coliseum at the state capitol.

HEAVENLY: What was your answer to him?

BOSS: He was removed from the hall at both places and roughed up a little outside it.

HEAVENLY: Papa, you have got an illusion of power.

BOSS: I have power, which is not an illusion.

HEAVENLY: Papa, I'm sorry my operation has brought this embarrassment on you, but can you imagine it, Papa? I felt worse than embarrassed when I found out that Dr George Scudder's knife had cut the youth out of my body, made me an old childless woman. Dry, cold, empty, like an old woman. I feel as if I ought to rattle like a dead dried-up vine when the Gulf Wind blows, but, Papa – I won't embarrass you any more. I've made up my mind about something. If they'll let me, accept me, I'm going into a convent.

BOSS [*shouting*]: You ain't going into no convent. This state is a Protestant region and a daughter in a convent would politically ruin me. Oh, I know, you took your mama's religion because in your heart you always wished to defy me. Now, tonight, I'm addressing the 'Youth for Tom Finley' clubs in the ballroom of the Royal Palms Hotel. My speech is going out over a national TV network, and Missy, you're going to march in the ballroom on my arm. You're going to be wearing the stainless white of a virgin, with a 'Youth for Tom Finley' button on one shoulder and a corsage of lilies on the other. You're going to be on the speaker's platform with me, you on one side of me and Tom Junior on the other, to scotch these rumours about your corruption. And you're gonna wear a proud happy smile on your face, you're gonna stare straight out at the crowd in the ballroom with pride and joy in your eyes. Lookin' at you, all in white like a virgin, nobody would dare to speak or believe the ugly stories about you. I'm relying a great deal on this campaign to bring in young voters for the crusade I'm leading. I'm all that stands between the South and the black days of Reconstruction. And you and Tom Junior are going to stand there beside me in the grand crystal ballroom, as shining examples of white Southern youth – in danger.

HEAVENLY [*defiant*]: Papa, I'm not going to do it.

BOSS: I didn't say would you, I said you would, and you will.

HEAVENLY: Suppose I still say I won't.

BOSS: Then you won't, that's all. If you won't, you won't. But there would be consequences you might not like. [*Phone rings.*] Chance Wayne is back in St Cloud.

CHARLES [*offstage*]: Mr Finley's residence. Miss Heavenly? Sorry, she's not in.

BOSS: I'm going to remove him, he's going to be removed

from St Cloud. How do you want him to leave, in that white Cadillac he's riding around in, or in the scow that totes the garbage out to the dumping place in the Gulf?

HEAVENLY: You wouldn't dare.

BOSS: You want to take a chance on it!

CHARLES [*enters*]: That call was for you again, Miss Heavenly.

BOSS: A lot of people approve of taking violent action against corrupters. And on all of them that want to adulterate the pure white blood of the South. Hell, when I was fifteen, I come down barefoot out of the red clay hills as if the Voice of God called me. Which it did, I believe. I firmly believe He called me. And nothing, nobody, nowhere is gonna stop me, never. . . . [*He motions to* CHARLES *for gift.* CHARLES *hands it to him.*] Thank you, Charles. I'm gonna pay me an early call on Miss Lucy.

[*A sad, uncertain note has come into his voice on this final line. He turns and plods wearily, doggedly off at left.*

THE CURTAIN FALLS
House remains dark for short intermission.]

A corner of cocktail lounge and of outside gallery of the Royal Palms Hotel. This corresponds in style to the bedroom set: Victorian with Moorish influence. Royal palms are projected on the cyclorama which is deep violet with dusk. There are Moorish arches between gallery and interior: over the single table, inside, is suspended the same lamp, stained glass, and ornately wrought metal, that hung in the bedroom. Perhaps on the gallery there is a low stone balustrade that supports, where steps descend into the garden, an electric-light standard with five branches and pear-shaped globes of a dim pearly lustre. Somewhere out of the sight-lines an entertainer plays a piano or novachord.

> [*The interior table is occupied by two couples that represent society in St Cloud. They are contemporaries of* CHANCE'S. *Behind the bar is* STUFF *who feels the dignity of his recent advancement from drugstore soda-fountain to the Royal Palms cocktail lounge: he has on a white mess-jacket, a scarlet cummerbund, and light-blue trousers, flatteringly close-fitted.* CHANCE WAYNE *was once barman here;* STUFF *moves with an indolent male grace that he may have unconsciously remembered admiring in* CHANCE.
>
> *Boss Finley's mistress,* MISS LUCY, *enters the cocktail lounge dressed in a ball gown elaborately ruffled and very bouffant like an antebellum Southern belle's. A single blonde curl is arranged to switch girlishly at one side of her sharp little terrier face. She is outraged over something and her glare is concentrated on* STUFF *who 'plays it cool' behind the bar.*]

STUFF: Ev'nin', Miss Lucy.

MISS LUCY: I wasn't allowed to sit at the banquet table. No. I was put at a little side-table, with a couple of state legislators an' wives. [*She sweeps behind the bar in a*

proprietary fashion.] Where's your Grant's twelve-year-old?
Hey! Do you have a big mouth? I used to remember a
kid that jerked sodas at Walgreen's that had a big
mouth. ... Put some ice in this. ... Is yours big, huh?
I want to tell you something.

STUFF: What's the matter with your finger?

[*She catches him by his scarlet cummerbund.*]

MISS LUCY: I'm going to tell you just now. The boss came
over to me with a big candy Easter egg for me. The top of
the egg unscrewed. He told me to unscrew it. So I unscrewed it. Inside was a little blue velvet jewel box, no
not little, a big one, as big as somebody's mouth, too.

STUFF: Whose mouth?

MISS LUCY: The mouth of somebody who's not a hundred
miles from here.

STUFF [*going off at the left*]: I got to set my chairs. [STUFF
re-enters at once carrying two chairs. Sets them at tables while
MISS LUCY *talks.*]

MISS LUCY: I open the jewel box an' start to remove the
great big diamond clip in it. I just got my fingers on it,
and start to remove it and the old son of a bitch slams the
lid of the box on my fingers. One fingernail is still blue.
And the boss says to me, 'Now go downstairs to the cocktail lounge and go in the ladies' room and describe this
diamond clip with lipstick on the ladies'-room mirror
down there. Hanh?' – and he put the jewel box in his
pocket and slammed the door so hard goin' out of my
suite that a picture fell off the wall.

STUFF [*setting the chairs at the table*]: Miss Lucy, you are the
one that said, 'I wish you would see what's written with
lipstick on the ladies'-room mirror' las' Saturday night.

MISS LUCY: To you! Because I thought I could trust you.

STUFF: Other people were here an' all of them heard it.

MISS LUCY: Nobody but you at the bar belonged to the
'Youth for Boss Finley' Club.

[*Both stop short. They've noticed a tall man who has entered the cocktail lounge. He has the length and leanness and luminous pallor of face that El Greco gave to his saints. He has a small bandage near the hairline. His clothes are country.*]

Hey, you.

HECKLER: Evenin', ma'am.

MISS LUCY: You with the Hillbilly Ramblers? You with the band?

HECKLER: I'm a hillbilly, but I'm not with no band.

[*He notices* MISS LUCY'S *steady, interested stare.* STUFF *leaves with a tray of drinks.*]

MISS LUCY: What do you want here?

HECKLER: I come to hear Boss Finley talk. [*His voice is clear but strained. He rubs his large Adam's apple as he speaks.*]

MISS LUCY: You can't get in the ballroom without a jacket and a tie on. .... I know who you are. You're the heckler, aren't you?

HECKLER: I don't heckle. I just ask questions, one question or two or three questions, depending on how much time it takes them to grab me and throw me out of the hall.

MISS LUCY: Those questions are loaded questions. You gonna repeat them tonight?

HECKLER: Yes, ma'am, if I can get in the ballroom, and make myself heard.

MISS LUCY: What's wrong with your voice?

HECKLER: When I shouted my questions in New Bethesda last week I got hit in the Adam's apple with the butt of a pistol, and that affected my voice. It still ain't good, but it's better. [*Starts to go.*]

MISS LUCY [*goes to back of bar, where she gets jacket, the kind kept in places with dress regulations, and throws it to* HECKLER]: Wait. Here, put this on. The Boss's talking on a national TV hookup tonight. There's a tie in the pocket. You sit perfectly still at the bar till the Boss starts speaking. Keep your face back of this *Evening Banner*. Okay?

HECKLER [*opening the paper in front of his face*]: I thank you.

MISS LUCY: I thank you, too, and I wish you more luck than you're likely to have.

[STUFF *re-enters and goes to back of the bar.*]

FLY [*entering on the gallery*]: Paging Chance Wayne. [*Auto horn offstage*] Mr Chance Wayne, please. Paging Chance Wayne. [*He leaves.*]

MISS LUCY [*to* STUFF, *who has re-entered*]: Is Chance Wayne back in St Cloud?

STUFF: You remember Alexandra Del Lago?

MISS LUCY: I guess I do. I was president of her local fan club. Why?

CHANCE [*offstage*]: Hey, Boy, park that car up front and don't wrinkle them fenders.

STUFF: She and Chance Wayne checked in here last night.

MISS LUCY: Well I'll be a dawg's mother. I'm going to look into that. [LUCY *exits.*]

CHANCE [*entering and crossing to the bar*]: Hey, Stuff! [*He takes a cocktail off the bar and sips it.*]

STUFF: Put that down. This ain't no cocktail party.

CHANCE: Man, don't you know ... phew ... nobody drinks gin martinis with olives. Everybody drinks vodka martinis with lemon twist nowadays, except the squares in St Cloud. When I had your job, when I was the barman here at the Royal Palms, I created that uniform you've got on. ... I copied it from an outfit Vic Mature wore in a Foreign Legion picture, and I looked better in it than he did, and almost as good in it as you do, ha, ha. ...

AUNT NONNIE [*who has entered at the right*]: Chance. Chance. ...

CHANCE: Aunt Nonnie! [*to* STUFF] Hey, I want a

tablecloth on that table, and a bucket of champagne. . . .
Mumm's Cordon Rouge. . . .

AUNT NONNIE: You come out here.

CHANCE: But, I just ordered champagne in here. [*Suddenly
his effusive manner collapses, as she stares at him gravely.*]

AUNT NONNIE: I can't be seen talking to you. . . .

> [*She leads him to one side of the stage. A light change has
> occurred which has made it a royal palm grove with a bench.
> They cross to it solemnly,* STUFF *busies himself at the bar,
> which is barely lit. After a moment he exits with a few drinks to
> main body of the cocktail lounge off left. Bar music: 'Quiereme
> Mucho'.*]

CHANCE [*following her*]: Why?

AUNT NONNIE: I've got just one thing to tell you, Chance,
get out of St Cloud.

CHANCE: Why does everybody treat me like a low criminal
in the town I was born in?

AUNT NONNIE: Ask yourself that question, ask your conscience that question.

CHANCE: What question?

AUNT NONNIE: You know, and I know you know. . . .

CHANCE: Know what?

AUNT NONNIE: I'm not going to talk about it. I just can't
talk about it. Your head and your tongue run wild. You
can't be trusted. We have to live in St Cloud. . . . Oh,
Chance, why have you changed like you've changed?
Why do you live on nothing but wild dreams now, and
have no address where anybody can reach you in time
to – reach you?

CHANCE: Wild dreams! Yes. Isn't life a wild dream? I
never heard a better description of it. . . . [*He takes a pill
and a swallow from a flask.*]

AUNT NONNIE: What did you just take, Chance? You took
something out of your pocket and washed it down with
liquor.

CHANCE: Yes, I took a wild dream and – washed it down with another wild dream, Aunt Nonnie, that's my life now. ...

AUNT NONNIE: Why, son?

CHANCE: Oh, Aunt Nonnie, for God's sake, have you forgotten what was expected of me?

AUNT NONNIE: People that loved you expected just one thing of you – sweetness and honesty and ...

[STUFF *leaves with tray*.]

CHANCE [*kneeling at her side*]: No, not after the brilliant beginning I made. Why, at seventeen, I put on, directed, and played the leading role in *The Valiant*, that one-act play that won the state drama contest. Heavenly played in it with me, and have you forgotten? You went with us as the girls' chaperon to the national contest held in. ...

AUNT NONNIE: Son, of course I remember.

CHANCE: In the parlour car? How we sang together?

AUNT NONNIE: You were in love even then.

CHANCE: God, yes, we were in love!

[*He sings softly*]

  'If you like-a me, like I like-a you,
  And we like-a both the same'

TOGETHER:
  'I'd like-a say, this very day,
  I'd like-a change your name.'

[CHANCE *laughs softly, wildly, in the cool light of the palm grove.* AUNT NONNIE *rises abruptly.* CHANCE *catches her hands*.]

AUNT NONNIE: You – *Do* – Take unfair advantage. ...

CHANCE: Aunt Nonnie, we didn't win that lousy national contest, we just placed second.

AUNT NONNIE: Chance, you didn't place second. You got

honourable mention. Fourth place, except it was just called honourable mention.

CHANCE: Just honourable mention. But in a national contest, honourable mention means something. ... We would have won it, but I blew my lines. Yes, I that put on and produced the damn thing, couldn't even hear the damn lines being hissed at me by that fat girl with the book in the wings. [*He buries his face in his hands.*]

AUNT NONNIE: I loved you for that, son, and so did Heavenly, too.

CHANCE: It was on the way home in the train that she and I –

AUNT NONNIE [*with a flurry of feeling*]: I know, I – I –

CHANCE [*rising*]: I bribed the Pullman Conductor to let us use for an hour a vacant compartment on that sad, home-going train –

AUNT NONNIE: I know, I – I –

CHANCE: Gave him five dollars, but that wasn't enough, and so I gave him my wrist-watch, and my collar pin and tie clip and signet ring and my suit, that I'd bought on credit to go to the contest. First suit I'd ever put on that cost more than thirty dollars.

AUNT NONNIE: Don't go back over that.

CHANCE: – To buy the first hour of love that we had together. When she undressed, I saw that her body was just then, barely, beginning to be a woman's and ...

AUNT NONNIE: Stop, Chance.

CHANCE: I said, oh, Heavenly, no, but she said yes, and I cried in her arms that night, and didn't know that what I was crying for was – youth, that would go.

AUNT NONNIE: It was from that time on, you've changed.

CHANCE: I swore in my heart that I'd never again come in second in any contest, especially not now that Heavenly was my – Aunt Nonnie, look at this contract.

[*He snatches out papers and lights lighter.*]

AUNT NONNIE: I don't want to see false papers.

CHANCE: These are genuine papers. Look at the notary's seal and the signatures of the three witnesses on them. Aunt Nonnie, do you know who I'm with? I'm with Alexandra Del Lago, the Princess Kosmonopolis is my –

AUNT NONNIE: Is your what?

CHANCE: Patroness! Agent! Producer! She hasn't been seen much lately, but still has influence, power, and money – money that can open all doors. That I've knocked at all these years till my knuckles are bloody.

AUNT NONNIE: Chance, even now, if you came back here simply saying, 'I couldn't remember the lines, I lost the contest, I – failed,' but you've come back here again with –

CHANCE: Will you just listen one minute more? Aunt Nonnie, here is the plan. A local-contest-of-Beauty.

AUNT NONNIE: Oh, Chance.

CHANCE: A local contest of talent that she will win.

AUNT NONNIE: Who?

CHANCE: Heavenly.

AUNT NONNIE: No, Chance. She's not young now, she's faded, she's ...

CHANCE: Nothing goes that quick, not even youth.

AUNT NONNIE: Yes, it does.

CHANCE: It will come back like magic. Soon as I ...

AUNT NONNIE: For what? For a fake contest?

CHANCE: For love. The moment I hold her.

AUNT NONNIE: Chance.

CHANCE: It's not going to be a local thing, Aunt Nonnie. It's going to get national coverage. The Princess Kosmonopolis's best friend is that sob sister, Sally Powers. Even you know Sally Powers. Most powerful movie columnist in the world. Whose name is law in the motion ...

AUNT NONNIE: Chance, lower your voice.

CHANCE: I want people to hear me.

AUNT NONNIE: No, you don't, no you don't. Because if your voice gets to Boss Finley, you'll be in great danger, Chance.

CHANCE: I go back to Heavenly, or I don't. I live or die. There's nothing in between for me.

AUNT NONNIE: What you want to go back to is your clean, unashamed youth. And you can't.

CHANCE: You still don't believe me, Aunt Nonnie?

AUNT NONNIE: No, I don't. Please go. Go away from here, Chance.

CHANCE: Please.

AUNT NONNIE: No, no, go away!

CHANCE: Where to? Where can I go? This is the home of my heart. Don't make me homeless.

AUNT NONNIE: Oh, Chance.

CHANCE: Aunt Nonnie. Please.

AUNT NONNIE [rises and starts to go]: I'll write to you. Send me an address. I'll write to you.

[She exits through bar. STUFF enters and moves to bar.]

CHANCE: Aunt Nonnie ...

[She's gone.

CHANCE removes a pint bottle of vodka from his pocket and something else which he washes down with the vodka. He stands back as two couples come up the steps and cross the gallery into the bar: they sit at a table. CHANCE takes a deep breath. FLY enters lighted area inside, singing out 'Paging Mr Chance Wayne, Mr Chance Wayne, pagin' Mr Chance Wayne.' — Turns about smartly and goes back out through lobby. The name has stirred a commotion at the bar and table visible inside.]

EDNA: Did you hear that? Is Chance Wayne back in St Cloud?

[CHANCE *draws a deep breath. Then, he stalks back into the main part of the cocktail lounge like a matador entering a bull ring.*]

VIOLET: My God, yes – there he is.

[CHANCE *reads Fly's message.*]

CHANCE [*to* FLY]: Not now, later, later.

[*The entertainer off left begins to play a piano. . . . The 'evening' in the cocktail lounge is just beginning.*
FLY *leaves through the gallery.*]

Well! Same old place, same old gang. Time doesn't pass in St Cloud. [*To* BUD *and* SCOTTY] Hi!

BUD: How are you . . .?

CHANCE [*shouting offstage as* FLY *enters and stands on terrace*]: Hey, Jackie . . . [*Piano stops.* CHANCE *crosses over to the table that holds the foursome.*] . . . remember my song? Do you – remember my song? . . . You see, he remembers my song. [*The entertainer swings into 'It's a Big Wide Wonderful World'.*] Now I feel at home. In my home town . . . Come on, everybody – sing!

[*This token of apparent acceptance reassures him. The foursome at the table on stage studiously ignore him. He sings.*]

'When you're in love you're a master
Of all you survey, you're a gay Santa Claus.
There's a great big star-spangled sky up above you,
When you're in love you're a hero. . . .'

Come on! Sing, ev'rybody!

[*In the old days they did; now they don't. He goes on, singing a bit; then his voice dies out on a note of embarrassment. Somebody at the bar whispers something and another laughs.* CHANCE *chuckles uneasily and speaks.*]

What's wrong here? The place is dead.

STUFF: You been away too long, Chance.

CHANCE: Is that the trouble?

STUFF: That's all. . . .

[JACKIE, *off, finishes with an arpeggio. The piano lid slams. There is a curious hush in the bar.* CHANCE *looks at the table.* VIOLET *whispers something to* BUD. *Both girls rise abruptly and cross out of the bar.*]

BUD [*yelling at* STUFF]: Check, Stuff.

CHANCE [*with exaggerated surprise*]: Well, *Bud and Scotty.* I didn't see you at all. Wasn't that Violet and Edna at your table? [*He sits at the table between* BUD *and* SCOTTY.]

SCOTTY: I guess they didn't recognize you, Chance.

BUD: Violet did.

SCOTTY: Did Violet?

BUD: She said, 'My God, Chance Wayne.'

SCOTTY: That's recognition and profanity, too.

CHANCE: I don't mind. I've been snubbed by experts, and I've done some snubbing myself. . . . Hey! [MISS LUCY *has entered at left.* CHANCE *sees her and goes towards her.*] — Is that Miss Lucy or is that Scarlett O'Hara?

MISS LUCY: Hello there, Chance Wayne. Somebody said that you were back in St Cloud, but I didn't believe them. I said I'd have to see it with my own eyes before . . . Usually there's an item in the paper, in Gwen Phillips's column saying 'St Cloud youth home on visit is slated to play featured role in important new picture,' and me being a movie fan I'm always thrilled by it. . . . [*She ruffles his hair.*]

CHANCE: Never do that to a man with thinning hair.

[CHANCE'S *smile is unflinching; it gets harder and brighter.*]

MISS LUCY: Is your hair thinning, baby? Maybe that's the difference I noticed in your appearance. Don't go 'way till I get back with my drink. . . .

[*She goes to back of bar to mix herself a drink. Meanwhile* CHANCE *combs his hair.*]

SCOTTY [*to* CHANCE]: Don't throw away those golden hairs you combed out, Chance. Save 'em and send 'em each in letters to your fan clubs.

BUD: Does Chance Wayne have a fan club?

SCOTTY: The most patient one in the world. They've been waiting years for him to show up on the screen for more than five seconds in a crowd scene.

MISS LUCY [*returning to the table*]: Y'know, this boy Chance Wayne used to be so attractive I couldn't stand it. But now I can, almost stand it. Every Sunday in summer I used to drive out to the municipal beach and watch him dive off the high tower. I'd take binoculars with me when he put on those free divin' exhibitions. You still dive, Chance? Or have you given that up?

CHANCE [*uneasily*]: I did some diving last Sunday.

MISS LUCY: Good, as ever?

CHANCE: I was a little off form, but the crowd didn't notice. I can still get away with a double back somersault and a –

MISS LUCY: Where was this, in Palm Beach, Florida, Chance?

[HATCHER *enters.*]

CHANCE [*stiffening*]: Why Palm Beach? Why there?

MISS LUCY: Who was it said they seen you last month in Palm Beach? Oh yes, Hatcher – that you had a job as a beach-boy at some big hotel there?

HATCHER [*stopping at steps of the terrace, then leaving across the gallery*]: Yeah, that's what I heard.

CHANCE: Had a job – as a beach-boy?

STUFF: Rubbing oil into big fat millionaires.

CHANCE: What joker thought up that one? [*His laugh is a little too loud.*]

SCOTTY: You ought to get their names and sue them for slander.

CHANCE: I long ago gave up tracking down sources of

rumours about me. Of course, it's flattering, it's gratifying to know that you're still being talked about in your old home town, even if what they say is completely fantastic. Hahaha.

[*Entertainer returns, sweeps into 'Quiereme Mucho'.*]

MISS LUCY: Baby, you've changed in some way, but I can't put my finger on it. You all see a change in him, or has he just gotten older? [*She sits down next to* CHANCE.]

CHANCE [*quickly*]: To change is to live, Miss Lucy, to live is to change, and not to change is to die. You know that, don't you? It used to scare me sometimes. I'm not scared of it now. Are you scared of it, Miss Lucy? Does it scare you?

[*Behind* CHANCE'S *back one of the girls has appeared and signalled the boys to join them outside.* SCOTTY *nods and holds up two fingers to mean they'll come in a couple of minutes. The girl goes back out with an angry head-toss.*]

SCOTTY: Chance, did you know Boss Finley was holding a 'Youth for Tom Finley' rally upstairs tonight?

CHANCE: I saw the announcements of it all over town.

BUD: He's going to state his position on that emasculation business that's stirred up such a mess in the state. Had you heard about that?

CHANCE: No.

SCOTTY: He must have been up in some earth satellite if he hasn't heard about that.

CHANCE: No, just out of St Cloud.

SCOTTY: Well, they picked out a nigger at random and castrated the bastard to show they mean business about white women's protection in this state.

BUD: Some people think they went too far about it. There's been a whole lot of Northern agitation all over the country.

SCOTTY: The Boss is going to state his own position about

that thing before the 'Youth for Boss Finley' rally upstairs in the Crystal Ballroom.

CHANCE: Aw. Tonight?

STUFF: Yeah, t'night.

BUD: They say that Heavenly Finley and Tom Junior are going to be standing on the platform with him.

PAGEBOY [*entering*]: Paging Chance Wayne. Paging. ...

> [*He is stopped short by* EDNA.]

CHANCE: I *doubt* that story, somehow I *doubt* that story.

SCOTTY: You doubt they cut that nigger?

CHANCE: Oh, no, that I don't doubt. You know what that is, don't you? Sex-envy is what that is, and the revenge for sex-envy which is a widespread disease that I have run into personally too often for me to doubt its existence or any manifestation. [*The group push back their chairs, snubbing him.* CHANCE *takes the message from the* PAGEBOY, *reads it, and throws it on the floor.*] Hey, Stuff – What d'ya have to do, stand on your head to get a drink around here? – Later, tell her. – Miss Lucy, can you get that Walgreen's soda jerk to give me a shot of vodka on the rocks? [*She snaps her fingers at* STUFF. *He shrugs and sloshes some vodka on to ice.*]

MISS LUCY: Chance? You're too loud, baby.

CHANCE: Not loud enough, Miss Lucy. No. What I meant that I doubt is that Heavenly Finley, that only I know in St Cloud, would stoop to stand on a platform next to her father while he explains and excuses on TV this random emasculation of a young Nigra caught on a street after midnight. [CHANCE *is speaking with an almost incoherent excitement, one knee resting on the seat of his chair, swaying the chair back and forth. The* HECKLER *lowers his newspaper from his face; a slow fierce smile spreads over his face as he leans forward with tensed throat muscles to catch* CHANCE'S *burst of oratory.*] No! That's what I do not believe. If I believed it, oh, I'd give you a diving exhibition. I'd dive off municipal pier and swim straight out to Diamond Key and past it, and keep on swimming till sharks and barracuda took me for live bait, brother. [*His chair topples over backward, and he sprawls to the floor. The* HECKLER *springs up to catch him.* MISS LUCY *springs up too, and sweeps between* CHANCE *and the* HECKLER, *pushing the* HECKLER *back with a quick, warning look or gesture. Nobody notices the* HECKLER. CHANCE *scrambles back to his feet, flushed, laughing.* BUD *and* SCOTTY *outlaugh him.* CHANCE *picks up his chair and continues. The laughter stops.*] Because I have come back to St Cloud to take her out of St Cloud. Where I'll take her is not to a place anywhere except to her place in my heart. [*He has removed a pink capsule from his pocket, quickly and furtively, and drunk it down with his vodka.*]

BUD: Chance, what did you swallow just now?

CHANCE: Some hundred-proof vodka.

BUD: You washed something down with it that you took out of your pocket.

SCOTTY: It looked like a little pink pill.

CHANCE: Oh, ha, ha. Yes, I washed down a goof-ball. You want one? I got a bunch of them. I always carry them with me. When you're not having fun, it makes you have it. When you're having fun, it makes you have more of it. Have one and see.

SCOTTY: Don't that damage the brain?

CHANCE: No, the contrary. It stimulates the brain cells.

SCOTTY: Don't it make your eyes look different, Chance?

MISS LUCY: Maybe that's what I noticed. [*As if wishing to change the subject*] Chance, I wish you'd settle an argument for me.

CHANCE: What argument, Miss Lucy?

MISS LUCY: About who you're travelling with. I heard you checked in here with a famous old movie star.

[*They all stare at him. . . . In a way he now has what he*

wants. He's the centre of attraction; everybody is looking at him,
even though with hostility, suspicion, and a cruel sense of sport.]

CHANCE: Miss Lucy, I'm travelling with the vice-president
and major-stockholder of the film studio which just
signed me.

MISS LUCY: Wasn't she once in the movies and very well
known?

CHANCE: She was and still is and never will cease to be an
important, a legendary figure in the picture industry,
here and all over the world, and I am now under personal
contract to her.

MISS LUCY: What's her name, Chance?

CHANCE: She doesn't want her name known. Like all great
figures, world-known, she doesn't want or need and
refuses to have the wrong type of attention. Privacy is a
luxury to great stars. Don't ask me her name. I respect
her too much to speak her name at this table. I'm
obligated to her because she has shown faith in me. It
took a long hard time to find that sort of faith in my
talent that this woman has shown me. And I refuse to
betray it at this table. [*His voice rises; he is already 'high'.*]

MISS LUCY: Baby, why are you sweating and your hands
shaking so? You're not sick, are you?

CHANCE: Sick? Who's sick? I'm the least sick one you know.

MISS LUCY: Well, baby, you know you oughtn't to stay in
St Cloud. Y'know that, don't you? I couldn't believe my
ears when I heard you were back here. [*To the two boys*]
Could you all believe he was back here?

SCOTTY: What did you come back for?

CHANCE: I wish you would give me one reason why I
shouldn't come back to visit the grave of my mother and
pick out a monument for her, and share my happiness
with a girl that I've loved many years. It's her, Heavenly
Finley, that I've fought my way up for, and now that
I've made it, the glory will be hers, too. And I've just

about persuaded the powers to be to let her appear with me in a picture I'm signed for. Because I . . .

BUD: What is the name of this picture?

CHANCE: . . . Name of it? *Youth*!

BUD: Just *Youth*?

CHANCE: Isn't that a great title for a picture introducing young talent? You all look doubtful. If you don't believe me, well, look. Look at this contract. [*Removes it from his pocket.*]

SCOTTY: You carry the contract with you?

CHANCE: I happen to have it in this jacket pocket.

MISS LUCY: Leaving, Scotty? [SCOTTY *has risen from the table.*]

SCOTTY: It's getting too deep at this table.

BUD: The girls are waiting.

CHANCE [*quickly*]: Gee, Bud, that's a clean set of rags you're wearing, but let me give you a tip for your tailor. A guy of medium stature looks better with natural shoulders, the padding cuts down your height, it broadens your figure, and gives you a sort of squat look.

BUD: Thanks, Chance.

SCOTTY: You got any helpful hints for my tailor, Chance?

CHANCE: Scotty, there's no tailor on earth than can disguise a sedentary occupation.

MISS LUCY: Chance, Baby . . .

CHANCE: You still work down at the bank? You sit on your can all day countin' century notes and once every week they let you slip one in your pockets? That's a fine set-up, Scotty, if you're satisfied with it but it's starting to give you a little pot and a can.

VIOLET [*appearing in the door, angry*]: Bud! Scotty! Come on.

SCOTTY: I don't get by on my looks, but I drive my own car. It isn't a Caddy, but it's my own car. And if my own mother died, I'd bury her myself; I wouldn't let a church take up a collection to do it.

VIOLET [*impatiently*]: Scotty, if you all don't come now I'm going home in a taxi.

[*The two boys follow her into the Palm Garden. There they can be seen giving their wives cab money, and indicating they are staying.*]

CHANCE: The squares have left us, Miss Lucy.

MISS LUCY: Yeah.

CHANCE: Well ... I didn't come back here to fight with old friends of mine. ... Well, it's quarter past seven.

MISS LUCY: Is it?

[*There are a number of men, now, sitting around in the darker corners of the bar, looking at him. They are not ominous in their attitudes. They are simply waiting for something, for the meeting to start upstairs, for something. . ... MISS LUCY stares at CHANCE and the men, then again at CHANCE, nearsightedly, her head cocked like a puzzled terrier's. CHANCE is discomfited.*]

CHANCE: Yep ... How is that Hickory Hollow for steaks? Is it still the best place in town for a steak?

STUFF [*answering the phone at the bar*]: Yeah, it's him. He's here. [*Looks at CHANCE ever so briefly, hangs up.*]

MISS LUCY: Baby, I'll go to the checkroom and pick up my wrap and call for my car and I'll drive you out to the airport. They've got an air-taxi out there, a whirly-bird taxi, a helicopter, you know, that'll hop you to New Orleans in fifteen minutes.

CHANCE: I'm not leaving St Cloud. What did I say to make you think I was?

MISS LUCY: I thought you had sense enough to know that you'd better.

CHANCE: Miss Lucy, you've been drinking, it's gone to your sweet little head.

MISS LUCY: Think it over while I'm getting my wrap. You still got a friend in St Cloud.

CHANCE: I still have a girl in St Cloud, and I'm not leaving without her.

PAGEBOY [*offstage*]: Paging Chance Wayne, Mr Chance Wayne, please.

PRINCESS [*entering with* PAGEBOY]: Louder, young man, louder. .... Oh, never mind, here he is!

[*But* CHANCE *has already rushed out on to the gallery. The* PRINCESS *looks as if she had thrown on her clothes to escape a building on fire. Her blue-sequined gown is unzipped, or partially zipped, her hair is dishevelled, her eyes have a dazed, drugged brightness; she is holding up the eyeglasses with the broken lens, shakily, hanging on to her mink stole with the other hand; her movements are unsteady.*]

MISS LUCY: I know who you are. Alexandra Del Lago.

[*Loud whispering. A pause.*]

PRINCESS [*on the step to the gallery*]: What? Chance!

MISS LUCY: Honey, let me fix that zipper for you. Hold still just a second. Honey, let me take you upstairs. You mustn't be seen down here in this condition. ....

[CHANCE *suddenly rushes in from the gallery: he conducts the* PRINCESS *outside: she is on the verge of panic. The* PRINCESS *rushes half-down the steps to the palm garden: leans panting on the stone balustrade under the ornamental light standard with its five great pearls of light. The interior is dimmed as* CHANCE *comes out behind her.*]

PRINCESS: Chance! Chance! Chance! Chance!

CHANCE [*softly*]: If you'd stayed upstairs that wouldn't have happened to you.

PRINCESS: I did, I stayed.

CHANCE: I told you to wait.

PRINCESS: I waited.

CHANCE: Didn't I tell you to wait till I got back?

PRINCESS: I did, I waited forever, I waited forever for you.

Then finally I heard those long sad silver trumpets blowing through the palm garden and then − Chance, the most wonderful thing has happened to me. Will you listen to me? Will you let me tell you?

MISS LUCY [*to the group at the bar*]: Shhh!

PRINCESS: Chance, when I saw you driving under the window with your head held high, with that terrible stiff-necked pride of the defeated which I know so well; I knew that your come-back had been a failure like mine. And I felt something in my heart for you. That's a miracle, Chance. That's the wonderful thing that happened to me. I felt something for someone besides myself. That means my heart's still alive, at least some part of it is, not all of my heart is dead yet. Part's alive still. . . . Chance, please listen to me. I'm ashamed of this morning. I'll never degrade you again, I'll never degrade myself, you and me, again by − I wasn't always this monster. Once I wasn't this monster. And what I felt in my heart when I saw you returning, defeated, to this palm garden, Chance, gave me hope that I could stop being a monster. Chance, you've got to help me stop being the monster that I was this morning, and you can do it, can help me. I won't be ungrateful for it. I almost died this morning, suffocated in a panic. But even through my panic, I saw your kindness. I saw a true kindness in you that you have almost destroyed, but that's still there, a little. . . .

CHANCE: What kind thing did I do?

PRINCESS: You gave my oxygen to me.

CHANCE: Anyone would do that.

PRINCESS: It could have taken you longer to give it to me.

CHANCE: I'm not that kind of monster.

PRINCESS: You're no kind of monster. You're just −

CHANCE: What?

PRINCESS: Lost in the beanstalk country, the ogre's country

at the top of the beanstalk, the country of the flesh-hungry, blood-thirsty ogre –

[*Suddenly a voice is heard from off.*]

VOICE: Wayne?

[*The call is distinct but not loud.* CHANCE *hears it, but doesn't turn towards it; he freezes momentarily, like a stag scenting hunters. Among the people gathered inside in the cocktail lounge we see the speaker,* DAN HATCHER. *In appearance, dress, and manner he is the apotheosis of the assistant hotel manager, about Chance's age, thin, blond-haired, trim blond moustache, suave, boyish, betraying an instinct for murder only by the ruby-glass studs in his matching cuff-links and tie-clip.*]

HATCHER: Wayne!

[*He steps forward a little and at the same instant* TOM JUNIOR *and* SCOTTY *appear behind him, just in view.* SCOTTY *strikes a match for* TOM JUNIOR'S *cigarette as they wait there.* CHANCE *suddenly gives the* PRINCESS *his complete and tender attention, putting an arm around her and turning her towards the Moorish arch to the bar entrance.*]

CHANCE [*loudly*]: I'll get you a drink, and then I'll take you upstairs. You're not well enough to stay down here.

HATCHER [*crossing quickly to the foot of the stairs*]: Wayne!

[*The call is too loud to ignore:* CHANCE *half-turns and calls back.*]

CHANCE: Who's that?

HATCHER: Step down here a minute!

CHANCE: Oh, *Hatcher*! I'll be right with you.

PRINCESS: Chance, don't leave me alone.

[*At this moment the arrival of* BOSS FINLEY *is heralded by the sirens of several squad cars. The forestage is suddenly brightened from off left, presumably the floodlights of the cars arriving at the entrance to the hotel. This is the signal the*

*men at the bar have been waiting for. Everybody rushes off
left. In the hot light all alone on stage is* CHANCE; *behind
him is the* PRINCESS. *And the* HECKLER *is at the bar. The
entertainer plays a feverish tango. Now, off left,* BOSS
FINLEY *can be heard, his public personality very much ' on'.
Amid the flash of flash bulbs we hear off:*]

BOSS [*off*]: Hahaha! Little Bit, smile! Go on, smile for the
birdie! Ain't she Heavenly, ain't that the right name for
her!

HEAVENLY [*off*]: Papa, I want to go in!

[*At this instant she runs in – to face* CHANCE. . . . *The*
HECKLER *rises. For a long instant,* CHANCE *and*
HEAVENLY *stand there: he on the steps leading to the Palm
Garden and gallery; she in the cocktail lounge. They simply
look at each other . . . the* HECKLER *between them. Then the*
BOSS *comes in and seizes her by the arm. . . . And there he is
facing the* HECKLER *and* CHANCE *both. . . . For a split
second he faces them, half-lifts his cane to strike at them, but
doesn't strike . . . then pulls* HEAVENLY *back off left stage
. . . where the photographing and interviews proceed during
what follows.* CHANCE *has seen that* HEAVENLY *is going
to go on the platform with her father. . . . He stands there
stunned. . . .*]

PRINCESS: Chance! Chance? [*He turns to her blindly.*] Call
the car and let's go. Everything's packed, even the . . .
tape recorder with my shameless voice on it. . . .

[*The* HECKLER *has returned to his position at the bar. Now*
HATCHER *and* SCOTTY *and a couple of other of the boys
have come out. . . . The* PRINCESS *sees them and is silent . . . .
She's never been in anything like this before. . . .*]

HATCHER: Wayne, step down here, will you.
CHANCE: What for, what do you want?
HATCHER: Come down here, I'll tell you.
CHANCE: You come up here and tell me.

TOM JUNIOR: Come on, you chicken-gut bastard.

CHANCE: Why, hello, Tom Junior. Why are you hiding down there?

TOM JUNIOR: You're hiding, not me, chicken-gut.

CHANCE: You're in the dark, not me.

HATCHER: Tom Junior wants to talk to you privately down here.

CHANCE: He can talk to me privately up here.

TOM JUNIOR: Hatcher, tell him I'll talk to him in the washroom on the mezzanine floor.

CHANCE: I don't hold conversations with people in washrooms. . . .

[TOM JUNIOR, *infuriated, starts to rush forward. Men restrain him.*]

What is all this anyhow? It's fantastic. You all having a little conference there? I used to leave places when I was told to. Not now. That time's over. Now I leave when I'm ready. Hear that, Tom Junior? Give your father that message. This is my town. I was born in St Cloud, not him. He was just called here. He was just called down from the hills to preach hate. I was born here to make love. Tell him about that difference between him and me, and ask him which he thinks has more right to stay here. . . . [*He gets no answer from the huddled little group which is restraining* TOM JUNIOR *from perpetrating murder right there in the cocktail lounge. After all, that would be a bad incident to precede the* BOSS'S *all-South-wide* TV *appearance . . . and they all know it.* CHANCE, *at the same time, continues to taunt them.*] Tom, Tom Junior! What do you want me for? To pay me back for the ball game and picture-show money I gave you when you were cutting your father's yard grass for a dollar on Saturday? Thank me for the times I gave you my motor-cycle and got you a girl to ride the buddy seat with you? Come here! I'll give you the keys to my Caddy. I'll give you the price of any whore in St Cloud.

You still got credit with me because you're Heavenly's
brother.

TOM JUNIOR [*almost bursting free*]: Don't say the name of
my sister !

CHANCE: I said the name of my girl !

TOM JUNIOR [*breaking away from the group*]: I'm all right,
I'm all right. Leave us alone, will you. I don't want
Chance to feel that he's outnumbered. [*He herds them out.*]
Okay? Come on down here.

PRINCESS [*trying to restrain* CHANCE]: No, Chance, don't.

TOM JUNIOR: Excuse yourself from the lady and come on
down here. Don't be scared to. I just want to talk to you
quietly. Just talk. Quiet talk.

CHANCE: Tom Junior, I know that since the last time I was
here something has happened to Heavenly and I –

TOM JUNIOR: Don't – speak the name of my sister. Just
leave her name off your tongue –

CHANCE: Just tell me what happened to her.

TOM JUNIOR: Just keep your ruttin' voice down.

CHANCE: I know I've done many wrong things in my life,
many more than I can name or number, but I swear I
never hurt Heavenly in my life.

TOM JUNIOR: You mean to say my sister was had by somebody else – diseased by somebody else the last time you
were in St Cloud? ... I know, it's possible, it's barely
possible that you didn't know what you done to my little
sister the last time you come to St Cloud. You remember
that time when you came home broke? My sister had to
pick up your tabs in restaurants and bars, and had to
cover bad cheques you wrote on banks where you had no
accounts. Until you met this rich bitch, Minnie, the
Texas one with the yacht, and started spending week-
ends on her yacht, and coming back Mondays with
money from Minnie to go on with my sister. I mean,
you'd sleep with Minnie, that slept with any goddam
gigolo bastard she could pick up on Bourbon Street or

the docks, and then you would go on sleeping again with my sister. And sometime, during that time, you got something besides your gigolo fee from Minnie and passed it on to my sister, my little sister that had hardly even heard of a thing like that, and didn't know what it was till it had gone on too long and –

CHANCE: I left town before I found out I –

[*The lamentation music is heard.*]

TOM JUNIOR: You found out! Did you tell my little sister?

CHANCE: I thought if something was wrong she'd write me or call me –

TOM JUNIOR: How could she write you or call you, there're no addresses, no phone numbers in gutters. I'm itching to kill you – here, on this spot! ... My little sister, Heavenly, didn't know about the diseases and operations of whores, till she had to be cleaned and cured – I mean spayed like a dawg by Dr George Scudder's knife. That's right – by the knife! ... And tonight – if you stay here tonight, if you're here after this rally, you're gonna get the knife, too. You know? The knife? That's all. Now go on back to the lady, I'm going back to my father. [TOM JUNIOR *exits.*]

PRINCESS [*as* CHANCE *returns to her*]: Chance, for God's sake, let's go now. ...

[*The 'Lament' is in the air. It blends with the wind-blown sound of the palms.*]

All day I've kept hearing a sort of lament that drifts through the air of this place. It says, 'Lost, lost, never to be found again.' Palm gardens by the sea and olive groves on Mediterranean islands all have that lament drifting through them. 'Lost, lost'. ... The isle of Cyprus, Monte Carlo, San Remo, Torremolenas, Tangiers. They're all places of exile from whatever we loved. Dark glasses, wide-brimmed hats, and whispers,

'Is that her?' Shocked whispers. . . . Oh, Chance, believe
me, after failure comes flight. Nothing ever comes after
failure but flight. Face it. Call the car, have them bring
down the luggage, and let's go on along the Old Spanish
Trail. [*She tries to hold him.*]

CHANCE: Keep your grabbing hands off me.

[*Marchers offstage start to sing 'Bonnie Blue Flag'.*]

PRINCESS: There's no one but me to hold you back from
destruction in this place.

CHANCE: I don't want to be held.

PRINCESS: Don't leave me. If you do I'll turn into the
monster again. I'll be the first lady of the Beanstalk
Country.

CHANCE: Go back to the room.

PRINCESS: I'm going nowhere alone. I can't.

CHANCE [*in desperation*]: Wheel chair! [*Marchers enter from
the left,* TOM JUNIOR *and* BOSS *with them.*] Wheel chair!
Stuff, get the lady a wheel chair! She's having another
attack!

[STUFF *and a* BELLBOY *catch at her . . . but she pushes*
CHANCE *away and stares at him reproachfully. . . . The*
BELLBOY *takes her by the arm. She accepts this anonymous arm
and exits.* CHANCE *and the* HECKLER *are alone on stage.*]

CHANCE [*as if reassuring, comforting somebody besides himself*]:
It's all right, I'm alone now, nobody's hanging on to me.

[*He is panting. Loosens his tie and collar. Band in the
Crystal Ballroom, muted, strikes up a likely but lyrically
distorted variation of some such popular tune as the 'Lichten-
steiner Polka'.* CHANCE *turns towards the sound. Then,
from left stage, comes a drum majorette, bearing a gold and
purple silk banner inscribed, 'Youth for Tom Finley',
prancing and followed by* BOSS FINLEY, HEAVENLY, *and*
TOM JUNIOR, *with a tight grip on her arm, as if he were
conducting her to a death chamber.*]

TOM JUNIOR: Papa? Papa! Will you tell Sister to march?

BOSS: Little Bit, you hold you haid up *high* when we march into that ballroom. [*Music up high ... They march up the steps and on to the gallery in the rear ... then start across it. The* BOSS *calling out.*] Now march! [*And they disappear up the stairs.*]

VOICE [*offstage*]: Now let us pray. [*There is a prayer mumbled by many voices.*]

MISS LUCY [*who has remained behind*]: You still want to try it?

HECKLER: I'm going to take a shot at it. How's my voice?

MISS LUCY: Better.

HECKLER: I better wait here till he starts talkin', huh?

MISS LUCY: Wait till they turn down the chandeliers in the ballroom. ... Why don't you switch to a question that won't hurt his daughter?

HECKLER: I don't want to hurt his daughter. But he's going to hold her up as the fair white virgin exposed to black lust in the South, and that's his build-up, his lead into his Voice of God speech.

MISS LUCY: He honestly believes it.

HECKLER: I don't believe it. I believe that the silence of God, the absolute speechlessness of Him is a long, long and awful thing that the whole world is lost because of. I think it's yet to be broken to any man, living or any yet lived on earth — no exceptions, and least of all Boss Finley.

[STUFF *enters, goes to table, starts to wipe it. The chandelier lights go down.*]

MISS LUCY [*with admiration*]: It takes a hillbilly to cut down a hillbilly. ... [*to* STUFF] Turn on the television, baby.

VOICE [*offstage*]: I give you the beloved Thomas J. Finley.

[STUFF *makes a gesture as if to turn on the* TV, *which we play in the fourth wall. A wavering beam of light, flickering, narrow, intense, comes from the balcony rail.* STUFF *moves his head so that he's in it, looking into it. . . .* CHANCE *walks slowly downstage, his head also in the narrow flickering beam of light. As he walks downstage, there suddenly appears on the big* TV *screen, which is the whole back wall of the stage, the image of* BOSS FINLEY. *His arm is around* HEAVENLY *and he is speaking. . . . When* CHANCE *sees the Boss's arm around Heavenly, he makes a noise in his throat like a hard fist hit him low. . . . Now the sound, which always follows the picture by an instant, comes on . . . loud.*]

BOSS [*on* TV *screen*]: Thank you, my friends, neighbours, kinfolk, fellow Americans. . . . I have told you before, but I will tell you again. I got a mission that I hold sacred to perform in the Southland. . . . When I was fifteen I came down barefooted out of the red clay hills. . . . Why? Because the Voice of God called me to execute this mission.

MISS LUCY [*to* STUFF]: He's too loud.

HECKLER: Listen !

BOSS: And what is this mission? I have told you before but I will tell you again. To shield from pollution a blood that I think is not only sacred to me, but sacred to Him.

[*Upstage we see the* HECKLER *step up the last steps and makes a gesture as if he were throwing doors open. . . . He advances into the hall, out of our sight.*]

MISS LUCY: Turn it down, Stuff.

STUFF [*motioning to her*]: Shh !

BOSS: Who is the coloured man's best friend in the South? That's right . . .

MISS LUCY: Stuff, turn down the volume.

BOSS: It's me, Tom Finley. So recognized by both races.

STUFF [*shouting*]: He's speaking the word. Pour it on !

BOSS: However – I can't and will not accept, tolerate, condone this threat of a blood pollution.

[MISS LUCY *turns down the volume of the* TV *set.*]

BOSS: As you all know I had no part in a certain operation on a young black gentleman. I call that incident a deplorable thing. That is the one thing about which I am in total agreement with the Northern radical Press. It was a deplorable thing. However ... I understand the emotions that lay behind it. The passion to protect by this violent emotion something that we hold sacred: our purity of our own blood. But I had no part in, and I did not condone the operation performed on the unfortunate coloured gentleman caught prowling the midnight streets of our Capitol City. ...

CHANCE: Christ! What lies. What a liar!

MISS LUCY: Wait! ... Chance, you can still go. I can still help you, baby.

CHANCE [putting hands on MISS LUCY'S shoulders]: Thanks, but no thank you, Miss Lucy. Tonight, God help me, somehow, I don't know how, but somehow I'll take her out of St Cloud. I'll wake her up in my arms, and I'll give her life back to her. Yes, somehow, God help me, somehow!

[STUFF turns up volume of TV set.]

HECKLER [as voice on the TV]: Hey, Boss Finley! [The TV camera swings to show him at the back of the hall.] How about your daughter's operation? How about that operation your daughter had done on her at the Thomas J. Finley hospital here in St Cloud? Did she put on black in mourning for her appendix? ...

[We hear a gasp, as if the HECKLER had been hit.

Picture: HEAVENLY horrified. Sounds of a disturbance. Then the doors at the top of stairs up left burst open and the

HECKLER *tumbles down. ... The picture changes to* BOSS
FINLEY. *He is trying to dominate the disturbance in the*
hall.]

BOSS: Will you repeat that question? Have that man step
forward. I will answer his question. Where is he? Have
that man step forward, I will answer his question. ...
Last Friday ... Last Friday, Good Friday. I said last
Friday, Good Friday ... Quiet, may I have your attention
please. ... Last Friday, Good Friday, I seen a horrible
thing on the campus of our great State University, which
I built for the State. A hideous straw-stuffed effigy of myself, Tom Finley, was hung and set fire to in the main
quadrangle of the college. This outrage was inspired ...
inspired by the Northern radical Press. However, that
was Good Friday. Today is Easter. I say that was Good
Friday. Today is Easter Sunday and I am in St Cloud.

[*During this a gruesome, not-lighted, silent struggle has been*
going on. The HECKLER *defended himself, but finally has*
been overwhelmed and rather systematically beaten. ... The
tight intense follow-spot beam stayed on CHANCE. *If he*
had any impulse to go to the HECKLER'S *aid, he'd be dis-*
couraged by STUFF *and another man who stand behind him,*
watching him. ... At the height of the beating, there are
bursts of great applause. ... At a point during it, HEAVENLY
is suddenly escorted down the stairs, sobbing, and collapses.
...]

CURTAIN

Act Three

[*A while later that night: the hotel bedroom. The shutters in the Moorish Corner are thrown open on the Palm Garden: scattered sounds of disturbance are still heard: something burns in the Palm Garden: an effigy, an emblem? Flickering light from it falls on the* PRINCESS. *Over the interior scene, the constant serene projection of royal palms, branched among stars.*]

PRINCESS [*pacing with the phone*]: Operator! What's happened to my driver?

[CHANCE *enters on the gallery, sees someone approaching on other side – quickly pulls back and stands in shadows on the gallery.*]

You told me you'd get me a driver. ... Why can't you get me a driver when you said that you would? Somebody in this hotel can surely get me somebody to drive me at any price asked! – out of this infernal ...

[*She turns suddenly as* DAN HATCHER *knocks at the corridor door. Behind him appear* TOM JUNIOR, BUD, *and* SCOTTY, *sweaty, dishevelled from the riot in the Palm Garden.*]

Who's that?

SCOTTY: She ain't gonna open, break it in.

PRINCESS [*dropping phone*]: What do you want?

HATCHER: Miss Del Lago ...

BUD: Don't answer till she opens.

PRINCESS: Who's out there! What do you want?

SCOTTY [*to shaky* HATCHER]: Tell her you want her out of the goddam room.

HATCHER [*with forced note of authority*]: Shut up. Let me handle this ... Miss Del Lago, your check-out time was

three-thirty P.M., and it's now after midnight. ... I'm
sorry but you can't hold this room any longer.

PRINCESS [*throwing open the door*]: What did you say? Will
you repeat what you said! [*Her imperious voice, jewels, furs,
and commanding presence abash them for a moment.*]

HATCHER: Miss Del Lago ...

TOM JUNIOR [*recovering quickest*]: This is Mr Hatcher,
assistant manager here. You checked in last night with a
character not wanted here, and we been informed he's
stayin' in your room with you. We brought Mr Hatcher
up here to remind you that the check-out time is long
past and –

PRINCESS [*powerfully*]: My check-out time at any hotel in
the world is *when I want to check out*. ...

TOM JUNIOR: This ain't any hotel in the world.

PRINCESS [*making no room for entrance*]: Also, I don't talk to
assistant managers of hotels when I have complaints
to make about discourtesies to me, which I do most certainly have to make about my experiences here. I don't
even talk to managers of hotels, I talk to owners of them.
Directly to hotel owners about discourtesies to me. [*Picks
up satin sheets on bed.*] These sheets are mine, they go with
me. And I have never suffered such dreadful discourtesies
to me at any hotel at any time or place anywhere in the
world. Now I have found out the name of this hotel
owner. This is a chain hotel under the ownership of a
personal friend of mine whose guest I have been in
foreign capitals such as ... [TOM JUNIOR *has pushed past
her into the room.*] What in hell is he doing in my room?

TOM JUNIOR: Where is Chance Wayne?

PRINCESS: Is that what you've come here for? You can go
away then. He hasn't been in this room since he left this
morning.

TOM JUNIOR: Scotty, check the bathroom. ... [*He checks
a closet, stoops to peer under the bed.* SCOTTY *goes off at
right.*] Like I told you before, we know you're Alexandr.

Del Lago travelling with a degenerate that I'm sure you don't know. That's why you can't stay in St Cloud, especially after this ruckus that we – [SCOTTY *re-enters from the bathroom and indicates to* TOM JUNIOR *that Chance is not there.*] – Now if you need any help in getting out of St Cloud, I'll be –

PRINCESS [*cutting in*]: Yes. I want a driver. Someone to drive my car. I want to leave here. I'm desperate to leave here. I'm not able to drive. I have to be driven away!

TOM JUNIOR: Scotty, you and Hatcher wait outside while I explain something to her. . . . [*They go and wait outside the door, on the left end of the gallery.*] I'm gonna git you a driver, Miss Del Lago. I'll get you a state trooper, half a dozen state troopers if I can't get you no driver. Okay? Some time come back to our town 'n' see us, hear? We'll lay out a red carpet for you. Okay? G'night, Miss Del Lago.

> [*They disappear down the hall, which is then dimmed out.* CHANCE *now turns from where he's been waiting at the other end of the corridor and slowly, cautiously, approaches the entrance to the room. Wind sweeps the Palm Garden; it seems to dissolve the walls; the rest of the play is acted against the night sky. The shuttered doors on the veranda open and* CHANCE *enters the room. He has gone a good deal farther across the border of reason since we last saw him. The* PRINCESS *isn't aware of his entrance until he slams the shuttered doors. She turns, startled, to face him.*]

PRINCESS: Chance!

CHANCE: You had some company here.

PRINCESS: Some men were here looking for you. They told me I wasn't welcome in this hotel and this town because I had come here with 'a criminal degenerate'. I asked them to get me a driver so I can go.

CHANCE: I'm your driver. I'm still your driver, Princess.

PRINCESS: You couldn't drive through the palm garden.

CHANCE: I'll be all right in a minute.

PRINCESS: It takes more than a minute. Chance, will you
listen to me? Can you listen to me? I listened to you this
morning, with understanding and pity, I did, I listened
with pity to your story this morning. I felt something in
my heart for you which I thought I couldn't feel. I
remembered young men who were what you are or what
you're hoping to be. I saw them all clearly, all clearly,
eyes, voices, smiles, bodies clearly. But their names
wouldn't come back to me. I couldn't get their names
back without digging into old programmes of plays that
I starred in at twenty in which they said, 'Madam, the
Count's waiting for you,' or – Chance? They almost
made it. Oh, oh, Franz! Yes, Franz ... what? Albertzart.
Franz Albertzart, oh God, God, Franz Albertzart ... I
had to fire him. He held me too tight in the waltz scene,
his anxious fingers left bruises once so violent, they, they
dislocated a disc in my spine, and –

CHANCE: I'm waiting for you to shut up.

PRINCESS: I saw him in Monte Carlo not too long ago. He
was with a woman of seventy, and his eyes looked older
than hers. She held him, she led him by an invisible chain
through Grand Hotel ... lobbies and casinos and bars
like a blind, dying lap dog; he wasn't much older than
you are now. Not long after that he drove his Alfa-
Romeo or Ferrari off the Grand Corniche – acciden-
tally? – Broke his skull like an eggshell. I wonder what
they found in it? Old, despaired-of ambitions, little
treacheries, possibly even little attempts at blackmail
that didn't quite come off, and whatever traces are left of
really great charm and sweetness. Chance, Franz
Albertzart is Chance Wayne. Will you please try to face
it so we can go on together?

CHANCE [pulls away from her]: Are you through? Have you
finished?

PRINCESS: You didn't listen, did you?

CHANCE [*picking up the phone*]: I didn't have to. I told you that story this morning – I'm not going to drive off nothing and crack my head like an eggshell.

PRINCESS: No, because you can't drive.

CHANCE: Operator? Long distance.

PRINCESS: You would drive into a palm tree. Franz Albertzart . . .

CHANCE: Where's your address book, your book of telephone numbers?

PRINCESS: I don't know what you think that you are up to, but it's no good. The only hope for you now is to let me lead you by that invisible loving steel chain through Carltons and Ritzes and Grand Hotels and –

CHANCE: Don't you know, I'd die first? I would rather die first . . . [*into phone*] Operator? This is an urgent person-to-person call from Miss Alexandra Del Lago to Miss Sally Powers in Beverly Hills, California. . . .

PRINCESS: Oh, no ! . . . Chance !

CHANCE: Miss Sally Powers, the Hollywood columnist, yes, Sally Powers. Yes, well get information. I'll wait, I'll wait. . . .

PRINCESS: Her number is Coldwater five-nine thousand. . . . [*Her hand goes to her mouth – but too late.*]

CHANCE: In Beverly Hills, California, Coldwater five-nine thousand.

[*The* PRINCESS *moves out on to forestage; surrounding areas dim till nothing is clear behind her but the palm garden.*]

PRINCESS: Why did I give him the number? Well, why not, after all, I'd have to know sooner or later . . . I started to call several times, picked up the phone, put it down again. Well, let him do it for me. Something's happened. I'm breathing freely and deeply as if the panic was over. Maybe it's over. He's doing the dreadful thing for me, asking the answer for me. He doesn't exist for me now except as somebody making this awful call for me, asking the answer for me. The light's on me. He's almost invisible now. What does that mean? Does it mean that I still wasn't ready to be washed up, counted out?

CHANCE: All right, call Chasen's. Try to reach her at Chasen's.

PRINCESS: Well, one thing's sure. It's only this call I care for. I seem to be standing in light with everything else dimmed out. He's in the dimmed out background as if he'd never left the obscurity he was born in. I've taken the light again as a crown on my head to which I am suited by something in the cells of my blood and body from the time of my birth. It's mine, I was born to own it, as he was born to make this phone call for me to Sally Powers, dear faithful custodian of my outlived legend. [*Phone rings in distance.*] The legend that I've out-lived. . . . Monsters don't die early; they hang on long. Awfully long. Their vanity's infinite, almost as infinite as their disgust with themselves. . . . [*Phone rings louder: it brings the stage light back up on the hotel bedroom. She turns to* CHANCE *and the play returns to a more realistic level.*] The phone's still ringing.

CHANCE: They gave me another number. . . .

PRINCESS: If she isn't there, give my name and ask them where I can reach her.

CHANCE: Princess?

PRINCESS: What?

CHANCE: I have a personal reason for making this phone call.

PRINCESS: I'm quite certain of that.

CHANCE [*into phone*]: I'm calling for Alexandra Del Lago. She wants to speak to Miss Sally Powers – Oh, is there any number where the Princess could reach her?

PRINCESS: It will be a good sign if they give you a number.

CHANCE: Oh? – Good, I'll call that number . . . Operator? Try another number for Miss Sally Powers. It's Canyon seven-five thousand. ... Say it's urgent, it's Princess Kosmonopolis. ...

PRINCESS: Alexandra Del Lago.

CHANCE: Alexandra Del Lago is calling Miss Powers.

PRINCESS [*to herself*]: Oxygen, please, a little. ...

CHANCE: Is that you, Miss Powers? This is Chance Wayne talking. ... I'm calling for the Princess Kosmonopolis, she wants to speak to you. She'll come to the phone in a minute.

PRINCESS: I can't. ... Say I've ...

CHANCE [*stretching phone cord*]: This is as far as I can stretch the cord, Princess, you've got to meet it half-way.

[PRINCESS *hesitates; then advances to the extended phone.*]

PRINCESS [*in a low, strident whisper*]: Sally? Sally? Is it really you, Sally? Yes, it's me, Alexandra. It's what's left of me, Sally. Oh, yes, I was there, but I only stayed a few minutes. Soon as they started laughing in the wrong places, I fled up the aisle and into the street screaming 'Taxi' – and never stopped running till now. No, I've talked to nobody, heard nothing, read nothing ... just wanted – dark ... What? You're just being kind.

CHANCE [*as if to himself*]: Tell her that you've discovered a pair of new stars. Two of them.

PRINCESS: One moment, Sally, I'm – breathless!

CHANCE [*gripping her arm*]: And lay it on thick. Tell her to break it tomorrow in her column, in all of her columns, and in her radio talks ... that you've discovered a pair of young people who are the stars of tomorrow!

PRINCESS [*to* CHANCE]: Go into the bathroom. Stick your head under cold water. ... Sally ... Do you really think so? You're not just being nice, Sally, because of old times – Grown, did you say? My talent? In what way, Sally? More depth? More what, did you say? More power! well, Sally, God bless you, dear Sally.

CHANCE: Cut the chatter. Talk about me and *HEAVENLY*!

PRINCESS: No, of course I didn't read the reviews. I told you I flew, I flew. I flew as fast and fast as I could. Oh. Oh? Oh ... How very sweet of you, Sally. I don't even care if you're not altogether sincere in that statement, Sally. I think you know what the past fifteen years have been like, because I do have the – 'out-crying heart of an – artist'. Excuse me, Sally, I'm crying, and I don't have any Kleenex. Excuse me, Sally, I'm crying. ...

CHANCE [*hissing behind her*]: Hey. Talk about me! [*She kicks* CHANCE's *leg.*]

PRINCESS: What's that, Sally? Do you really believe so? Who? For what part? Oh, my God! ... Oxygen, oxygen, quick!

CHANCE [*seizing her by the hair and hissing*]: Me! Me! – You bitch!

PRINCESS: Sally? I'm too overwhelmed. Can I call you back later? Sally, I'll call back later. ... [*She drops phone in a daze of rapture.*] My picture has broken box-office records. In New York and L.A.!

CHANCE: Call her back, get her on the phone.

PRINCESS: Broken box-office records. The greatest comeback in the history of the industry, that's what she calls it. ...

CHANCE: You didn't mention me to her.

PRINCESS [*to herself*]: I can't appear, not yet. I'll need a week in a clinic, then a week or ten days at the Morning Star Ranch at Vegas. I'd better get Ackermann down there for a series of shots before I go on to the Coast. ...

CHANCE [*at phone*]: Come back here, call her again.

PRINCESS: I'll leave the car in New Orleans and go on by plane to, to, to – Tucson. I'd better get Strauss working on publicity for me. I'd better be sure my tracks are covered up well these last few weeks in – hell! –

CHANCE: Here. Here, get her back on this phone.

PRINCESS: Do what?

CHANCE: Talk about me and talk about Heavenly to her.

PRINCESS: Talk about a beach-boy I picked up for pleasure, distraction from panic? Now? When the nightmare is over? Involve my name, which is Alexandra Del Lago with the record of a – You've just been using me. Using me. When I needed you downstairs you shouted, 'Get her a wheel chair!' Well, I didn't need a wheel chair, I came up alone, as always. I climbed back alone up the beanstalk to the ogre's country where I live, now, alone. Chance, you've gone past something you couldn't afford to go past; your time, your youth, you've passed it. It's all you had, and you've had it.

CHANCE: Who in hell's talking! Look. [*He turns her forcibly to the mirror.*] Look in that mirror. What do you see in that mirror?

PRINCESS: I see – Alexandra Del Lago, artist and star! Now it's your turn, you look and what do you see?

CHANCE: I see – Chance Wayne. . . .

PRINCESS: The face of a Franz Albertzart, a face that tomorrow's sun will touch without mercy. Of course, you were crowned with laurel in the beginning, your gold hair was wreathed with laurel, but the gold is thinning and the laurel has withered. Face it – pitiful monster. [*She touches the crown of his head.*] . . . Of course, I know I'm one too. But one with a difference. Do you know what that difference is? No, you don't know. I'll tell you. We are two monsters, but with this difference between us. Out of the passion and torment of my existence I have created a thing that I can unveil, a sculpture, almost heroic, that I can unveil, which is true. But you? You've come back to the town you were born in, to a girl that won't see you because you put such rot in her body she had to be gutted and hung on a butcher's hook, like a chicken dressed for Sunday. . . . [*He wheels about to strike at her but his raised fist changes its course and strikes down at his own belly and he bends double with a sick cry. Palm Garden wind: whisper of the 'Lament'.*] Yes, and her brother who was one of my callers, threatens the same thing for you: castration, if you stay here.

CHANCE: That can't be done to me twice. You did that to me this morning, here on this bed, where I had the honour, where I had the great honour ...

[*Windy sound rises: they move away from each other, he to the bed, she close to her portable dressing table.*]

PRINCESS: Age does the same thing to a woman. ... [*Scrapes pearls and pillboxes off table top into handbag.*] Well ...

[*All at once her power is exhausted, her fury gone. Something uncertain appears in her face and voice betraying the fact which she probably suddenly knows, that her future course is not a progression of triumphs. She still maintains a grand air as she snatches up her platinum mink stole and tosses it about her: it slides immediately off her shoulders; she doesn't seem to notice. He picks the stole up for her, puts it about her shoulders. She grunts disdainfully, her back to him; then resolution falters; she turns to face him with great, dark eyes that are fearful, lonely, and tender.*]

PRINCESS: I am going, now, on my way. [*He nods slightly, loosening the Windsor-knot of his knitted black silk tie. Her eyes stay on him.*] Well, are you leaving or staying?

CHANCE: Staying.

PRINCESS: You can't stay here. I'll take you to the next town.

CHANCE: Thanks but no thank you, Princess.

PRINCESS [*seizing his arm*]: Come on, you've got to leave with me. My name is connected with you, we checked in here together. Whatever happens to you, my name will be dragged in with it.

CHANCE: Whatever happens to me's already happened.

PRINCESS: What are you trying to prove?

CHANCE: Something's got to mean something, don't it, Princess? I mean like your life means nothing, except that you never could make it, always almost, never quite? Well, something's still got to mean something.

PRINCESS: I'll send a boy up for my luggage. You'd better come down with my luggage.

CHANCE: I'm not part of your luggage.

PRINCESS: What else can you be?

CHANCE: Nothing ... but not part of your luggage.

[NOTE: *in this area it is very important that Chance's attitude should be self-recognition but* not *self-pity – a sort of deathbed dignity and honesty apparent in it. In both Chance and the Princess, we should return to the huddling-together of the lost, but not with sentiment, which is false, but with whatever is truthful in the moments when people share doom, face firing squads together. Because the Princess is really equally doomed. She can't turn back the clock any more than can Chance, and the clock is equally relentless to them both. For the Princess: a little, very temporary, return to, recapture of, the spurious glory. The report from Sally Powers may be and probably is a factually accurate report: but to indicate she is going on to further triumph would be to falsify her future. The* PRINCESS *makes this instinctive admission to herself when she sits down by* CHANCE *on the bed, facing the audience. Both are faced with castration, and in her heart she knows it. They sit side by side on the bed like two passengers on a train sharing a bench.*]

PRINCESS: Chance, we've got to go on.

CHANCE: Go on to where? I couldn't go past my youth, but I've gone past it.

[*The 'Lament' fades in, continues through the scene to the last curtain.*]

PRINCESS: You're still young, Chance.

CHANCE: Princess, the age of some people can only be calculated by the level of – level of – rot in them. And by that measure I'm ancient.

PRINCESS: What am I? – I know, I'm dead, as old Egypt. ... Isn't it funny? We're still sitting here together, side by side in this room, like we were occupying the same bench on a train – going on together ... Look. That little donkey's marching around and around to draw water out of a well. ... [*She points off at something as if outside a train window.*] Look, a shepherd boy's leading a flock. – What an old country, timeless. – Look –

[*The sound of a clock ticking is heard, louder and louder.*]

CHANCE: No, listen. I didn't know there was a clock in this room.

PRINCESS: I guess there's a clock in every room people live in. ...

CHANCE: It goes tick-tick, it's quieter than your heart-beat, but it's dynamite, a gradual explosion, blasting the world we lived in to burnt-out pieces. ... Time – who could beat it, who could defeat it ever? Maybe some saints and heroes, but not Chance Wayne. I lived on something, that – time?

PRINCESS: Yes, time.

CHANCE: ... Gnaws away, like a rat gnaws off its own foot caught in a trap, and then, with its foot gnawed off and the rat set free, couldn't run, couldn't go, bled and died. ...

[*The clock ticking fades away.*]

TOM JUNIOR [*offstage left*]: Miss Del Lago ...

PRINCESS: I think they're calling our – station. ...

TOM JUNIOR [*still offstage*]: Miss Del Lago, I have got a driver for you.

[*A trooper enters and waits on gallery.*

With a sort of tired grace, she rises from the bed, one hand lingering on her seat-companion's shoulder as she moves a little unsteadily to the door. When she opens it, she is confronted by TOM JUNIOR.]

PRINCESS: Come on, Chance, we're going to change trains at this station. ... So, come on, we've got to go on. ... Chance, please ...

[CHANCE *shakes his head and the* PRINCESS *gives up. She weaves out of sight with the trooper down the corridor.*

TOM JUNIOR *enters from steps, pauses, and then gives a low whistle to* SCOTTY, BUD, *and third man who enter and stand waiting.* TOM JUNIOR *comes down bedroom steps and stands on bottom step.*]

CHANCE [*rising and advancing to the forestage*]: I don't ask for your pity, but just for your understanding — not even that — no. Just for your recognition of me in you, and the enemy, time, in us all.

CURTAIN

A STREETCAR NAMED DESIRE

And so it was I entered the broken world
To trace the visionary company of love, its voice
An instant in the wind [I know not whither
    hurled]
But not for long to hold each desperate choice.

HART CRANE
The Broken Tower

THE CHARACTERS

The first London production of this play was at the
Aldwych Theatre on Wednesday, 12 October 1949,
with the following cast:

BLANCHE DuBOIS	*Vivien Leigh*
STELLA KOWALSKI	*Renee Asherson*
STANLEY KOWALSKI	*Bonar Colleano*
HAROLD MITCHELL [MITCH]	*Bernard Braden*
EUNICE HUBBEL	*Eileen Dale*
STEVE HUBBEL	*Lyn Evans*
PABLO GONZALES	*Theodore Bikel*
NEGRO WOMAN	*Bruce Howard*
A STRANGE MAN [DOCTOR]	*Sidney Monckton*
A STRANGE WOMAN [NURSE]	*Mona Lilian*
A YOUNG COLLECTOR	*John Forrest*
A MEXICAN WOMAN	*Eileen Way*

Directed by LAURENCE OLIVIER
Setting and lighting by JO MEILZINER
Costumes by BEATRICE DAWSON

SCENE ONE

The exterior of a two-storey corner building on a street in New Orleans which is named Elysian Fields and runs between the L & N tracks and the river. The section is poor but unlike corresponding sections in other American cities, it has a raffish charm. The houses are mostly white frame, weathered grey, with rickety outside stairs and galleries and quaintly ornamented gables. This building contains two flats, upstairs and down. Faded white stairs ascend to the entrances of both. It is first dark of an evening early in May. The sky that shows around the dim white building is a peculiarly tender blue, almost turquoise, which invests the scene with a kind of lyricism and gracefully attenuates the atmosphere of decay. You can almost feel the warm breath of the brown river beyond the river warehouses with their faint redolences of bananas and coffee. A corresponding air is evoked by the music of Negro entertainers at a bar-room around the corner. In this part of New Orleans you are practically always just around the corner, or a few doors down the street, from a tinny piano being played with the infatuated fluency of brown fingers. This 'blue piano' expresses the spirit of the life which goes on here.

> [*Two women, one white and one coloured, are taking the air on the steps of the building. The white woman is* EUNICE, *who occupies the upstairs flat; the coloured woman a neighbour, for New Orleans is a cosmopolitan city where there is a relatively warm and easy intermingling of races in the old part of town.*
>
> *Above the music of the 'blue piano' the voices of people on the street can be heard overlapping.*]

NEGRO WOMAN [*to* EUNICE]: ... she says St Barnabas would send out his dog to lick her and when he did she'd feel an icy cold wave all up an' down her. Well, that night when –

A MAN [*to a* SAILOR]: You keep right on going and you'll find it. You'll hear them tapping on the shutters.

SAILOR [*to* NEGRO WOMAN *and* EUNICE]: Where's the Four Deuces?

VENDOR: Red hot! Red hots!

NEGRO WOMAN: Don't waste your money in that clip joint!

SAILOR: I've got a date there.

VENDOR: Re-e-ed h-o-o-t!

NEGRO WOMAN: Don't let them sell you a Blue Moon cocktail or you won't go out on your own feet!

[*Two men come round the corner,* STANLEY KOWALSKI *and* MITCH. *They are about twenty-eight or thirty years old, roughly dressed in blue denim work clothes.* STANLEY *carries his bowling jacket and a red-stained package from a butcher's.*]

STANLEY [*to* MITCH]: Well, what did he say?

MITCH: He said he'd give us even money.

STANLEY: Naw! We gotta have odds!

[*They stop at the foot of the steps.*]

STANLEY [*bellowing*]: Hey, there! Stella, Baby!

[STELLA *comes out on the first-floor landing, a gentle young woman, about twenty-five, and of a background obviously quite different from her husband's.*]

STELLA [*mildly*]: Don't holler at me like that. Hi, Mitch.

STANLEY: Catch!

STELLA: What?

STANLEY: Meat!

[*He heaves the package at her. She cries out in protest but manages to catch it: then she laughs breathlessly. Her husband and his companion have already started back around the corner.*]

STELLA [*calling after him*]: Stanley! Where are you going?

STANLEY: Bowling!

STELLA: Can I come watch?

STANLEY: Come on. [*He goes out.*]

STELLA: Be over soon. [*To the white woman.*] Hello, Eunice. How are you?

EUNICE: I'm all right. Tell Steve to get him a poor boy's sandwich 'cause nothing's left here.

[*They all laugh; the* COLOURED WOMAN *does not stop.* STELLA *goes out.*]

COLOURED WOMAN: What was that package he th'ew at 'er? [*She rises from steps, laughing louder.*]

EUNICE: You hush, now!

NEGRO WOMAN: Catch *what!*

[*She continues to laugh.* BLANCHE *comes around the corner, carrying a valise. She looks at a slip of paper, then at the building, then again at the slip and again at the building. Her expression is one of shocked disbelief. Her appearance is incongruous to this setting. She is daintily dressed in a white suit with a fluffy bodice, necklace and ear-rings of pearl, white gloves and hat, looking as if she were arriving at a summer tea or cocktail party in the garden district. She is about five years older than* STELLA. *Her delicate beauty must avoid a strong light. There is something about her uncertain manner, as well as her white clothes, that suggests a moth.*]

EUNICE [*finally*]: What's the matter, honey? Are you lost?

BLANCHE [*with faintly hysterical humour*]: They told me to take a streetcar named Desire, and then transfer to one called Cemeteries and ride six blocks and get off at – Elysian Fields!

EUNICE: That's where you are now.

BLANCHE: At Elysian Fields?

EUNICE: This here is Elysian Fields.

BLANCHE: They mustn't have – understood – what number I wanted ...

EUNICE: What number you lookin' for?

[BLANCHE *wearily refers to the slip of paper.*]

BLANCHE: Six thirty-two.

EUNICE: You don't have to look no further.

BLANCHE [*uncomprehendingly*]: I'm looking for my sister, Stella DuBois. I mean – Mrs Stanley Kowalski.

EUNICE: That's the party. – You just did miss her, though.

BLANCHE: This – can this be – her home?

EUNICE: She's got the downstairs here and I got the up.

BLANCHE: Oh. She's – out?

EUNICE: You noticed that bowling alley around the corner?

BLANCHE: I'm – not sure I did.

EUNICE: Well, that's where she's at, watchin' her husband bowl. [*There is a pause.*] You want to leave your suitcase here an' go find her?

BLANCHE: No.

NEGRO WOMAN: I'll go tell her you come.

BLANCHE: Thanks.

NEGRO WOMAN: You welcome. [*She goes out.*]

EUNICE: She wasn't expecting you?

BLANCHE: No. No, not tonight.

EUNICE: Well, why don't you just go in and make yourself at home till they get back.

BLANCHE: How could I – do that?

EUNICE: We own this place so I can let you in.

[*She gets up and opens the downstairs door. A light goes on behind the blind, turning it light blue.* BLANCHE *slowly follows her into the downstairs flat. The surrounding areas dim out as the interior is lighted. Two rooms can be seen, not too clearly defined. The one first entered is primarily a kitchen but contains a folding bed to be used by* BLANCHE. *The room beyond this is a bedroom. Off this room is a narrow door to a bathroom.*]

EUNICE [*defensively, noticing* BLANCHE'S *look*]: It's sort of messed up right now but when it's clean it's real sweet.

BLANCHE: Is it?

EUNICE: Uh-huh, I think so. So you're Stella's sister?

BLANCHE: Yes. [*Wanting to get rid of her.*] Thanks for letting me in.

EUNICE: *Por nada*, as the Mexicans say, *por nada*! Stella spoke of you.

BLANCHE: Yes?

EUNICE: I think she said you taught school.

BLANCHE: Yes.

EUNICE: And you're from Mississippi, huh?

BLANCHE: Yes.

EUNICE: She showed me a picture of your home-place, the plantation.

BLANCHE: Belle Reve?

EUNICE: A great big place with white columns.

BLANCHE: Yes ...

EUNICE: A place like that must be awful hard to keep up.

BLANCHE: If you will excuse me, I'm just about to drop.

EUNICE: Sure, honey. Why don't you set down?

BLANCHE: What I meant was I'd like to be left alone.

EUNICE [*offended*]: Aw. I'll make myself scarce, in that case.

BLANCHE: I didn't mean to be rude, but –

EUNICE: I'll drop by the bowling alley an' hustle her up.
[*She goes out of the door.*]

> [BLANCHE *sits in a chair very stiffly with her shoulders slightly hunched and her legs pressed close together and her hands tightly clutching her purse as if she were quite cold. After a while the blind look goes out of her eyes and she begins to look slowly around. A cat screeches. She catches her breath with a startled gesture. Suddenly she notices something in a half-opened closet. She springs up and crosses to it, and removes a whisky bottle. She pours a half tumbler of whisky and tosses it down. She carefully replaces the bottle and washes out the tumbler at the sink. Then she resumes her seat in front of the table.*]

BLANCHE [*faintly to herself*]: I've got to keep hold of myself!

[STELLA *comes quickly around the corner of the building and and runs to the door of the downstairs flat.*]

STELLA [*calling out joyfully*]: *Blanche!*

[*For a moment they stare at each other. Then* BLANCHE *springs up and runs to her with a wild cry.*]

BLANCHE: Stella, oh, Stella, Stella! Stella for Star!

[*She begins to speak with feverish vivacity as if she feared for either of them to stop and think. They catch each other in a spasmodic embrace.*]

BLANCHE: Now, then, let me look at you. But don't you look at me, Stella, no, no, no, not till later, not till I've bathed and rested! And turn that over-light off! Turn that off! I won't be looked at in this merciless glare! [STELLA *laughs and complies.*] Come back here now! Oh, my baby! Stella! Stella for Star! [*She embraces her again.*] I thought you would never come back to this horrible place! What am I saying! I didn't mean to say that. I meant to be nice about it and say – Oh, what a convenient location and such – Ha-a-ha! Precious lamb! You haven't said a *word* to me.

STELLA: You haven't given me a chance to, honey! [*She laughs but her glance at* BLANCHE *is a little anxious.*]

BLANCHE: Well, now you talk. Open your pretty mouth and talk while I look around for some liquor! I know you must have some liquor on the place! Where could it be, I wonder? Oh, I spy, I spy!

[*She rushes to the closet and removes the bottle; she is shaking all over and panting for breath as she tries to laugh. The bottle nearly slips from her grasp.*]

STELLA [*noticing*]: Blanche, you sit down and let me pour the drinks. I don't know what we've got to mix with. Maybe a coke's in the icebox. Look'n see, honey, while I'm –

BLANCHE: No coke, honey, not with my nerves tonight! Where – where – where is –?

STELLA: Stanley? Bowling! He loves it. They're having a – found some soda! – tournament . . .

BLANCHE: Just water, baby, to chase it! Now don't get worried, your sister hasn't turned into a drunkard, she's just all shaken up and hot and tired and dirty! You sit down, now, and explain this place to me! What are you doing in a place like this?

STELLA: Now, Blanche –

BLANCHE: Oh, I'm not going to be hypocritical, I'm going to be honestly critical about it! Never, never, never in my worst dreams could I picture – Only Poe! Only Mr Edgar Allan Poe! – could do it justice! Out there I suppose is the ghoul-haunted woodland of Weir! [*She laughs.*]

STELLA: No, honey, those are the L & N tracks.

BLANCHE: No, now seriously, putting joking aside. Why didn't you tell me, why didn't you write me, honey, why didn't you let me know?

STELLA [*carefully, pouring herself a drink*]: Tell you what, Blanche?

BLANCHE: Why, that you had to live in these conditions!

STELLA: Aren't you being a little intense about it? It's not that bad at all! New Orleans isn't like other cities.

BLANCHE: This has got nothing to do with New Orleans. You might as well say – forgive me, blessed baby! [*She suddenly stops short.*] The subject is closed!

STELLA [*a little drily*]: Thanks.

[*During the pause,* BLANCHE *stares at her. She smiles at* BLANCHE.]

BLANCHE [*looking down at her glass, which shakes in her hand*]: You're all I've got in the world, and you're not glad to see me!

STELLA [*sincerely*]: Why, Blanche, you know that's not true.

BLANCHE: No? – I'd forgotten how quiet you were.

STELLA: You never did give me a chance to say much, Blanche. So I just got in the habit of being quiet around you.

BLANCHE [*vaguely*]: A good habit to get into ... [*then abruptly*] You haven't asked me how I happened to get away from the school before the spring term ended.

STELLA: Well, I thought you'd volunteer that information – if you wanted to tell me.

BLANCHE: You thought I'd been fired?

STELLA: No, I – thought you might have – resigned. ...

BLANCHE: I was so exhausted by all I'd been through my – nerves broke. [*Nervously tamping cigarette.*] I was on the verge of – lunacy, almost! So Mr Graves – Mr Graves is the high school superintendent – he suggested I take a leave of absence. I couldn't put all of those details into the wire. ... [*She drinks quickly.*] Oh, this buzzes right through me and feels so *good*!

STELLA: Won't you have another?

BLANCHE: No, one's my limit.

STELLA: Sure?

BLANCHE: You haven't said a word about my appearance.

STELLA: You look just fine.

BLANCHE: God love you for a liar! Daylight never exposed so total a ruin! But you – you've put on some weight, yes, you're just as plump as a little partridge! And it's so becoming to you!

STELLA: Now, Blanche –

BLANCHE: Yes, it is, it is or I wouldn't say it! You just have to watch around the hips a little. Stand up.

STELLA: Not now.

BLANCHE: You hear me? I said stand up! [STELLA *complies reluctantly.*] You messy child, you, you've spilt something on that pretty white lace collar! About your hair – you ought to have it cut in a feather bob with your dainty features. Stella, you have a maid, don't you?

STELLA: No. With only two rooms it's –

BLANCHE: What? *Two* rooms, did you say?

STELLA: This one and – [*She is embarrassed.*]

BLANCHE: The other one? [*She laughs sharply. There is an embarrassed silence.*] How quiet you are, you're so peaceful. Look how you sit there with your little hands folded like a cherub in choir!

STELLA [*uncomfortably*]: I never had anything like your energy, Blanche.

BLANCHE: Well, I never had your beautiful self-control. I am going to take just one little tiny nip more, sort of to put the stopper on, so to speak. . . . Then put the bottle away so I won't be tempted. [*She rises.*] I want you to look at *my* figure! [*She turns around.*] You know I haven't put on one ounce in ten years, Stella? I weigh what I weighed the summer you left Belle Reve. The summer Dad died and you left us . . .

STELLA [*a little wearily*]: It's just incredible, Blanche, how well you're looking.

BLANCHE: You see I still have that awful vanity about my looks even now that my looks are slipping! [*She laughs nervously and glances at* STELLA *for reassurance.*]

STELLA [*dutifully*]: They haven't slipped one particle.

BLANCHE: After all I've been through? You think I believe that story? Blessed child! [*She touches her forehead shakily.*] Stella, there's – only two rooms?

STELLA: And a bathroom.

BLANCHE: Oh, you do have a bathroom! First door to the right at the top of the stairs? [*They both laugh uncomfortably.*] But, Stella, I don't see where you're going to put me!

STELLA: We're going to put you in here.

BLANCHE: What kind of bed's this – one of those collapsible things? [*She sits on it.*]

STELLA: Does it feel all right?

BLANCHE [*dubiously*]: Wonderful, honey. I don't like a bed

that gives much. But there's no door between the two rooms, and Stanley – will it be decent?

STELLA: Stanley is Polish, you know.

BLANCHE: Oh, yes. They're something like Irish, aren't they?

STELLA: Well –

BLANCHE: Only not so – highbrow? [*They both laugh again in the same way.*] I brought some nice clothes to meet all your lovely friends in.

STELLA: I'm afraid you won't think they are lovely.

BLANCHE: What are they like?

STELLA: They're Stanley's friends.

BLANCHE: Polacks?

STELLA: They're a mixed lot, Blanche.

BLANCHE: Heterogeneous – types?

STELLA: Oh, yes. Yes, types is right!

BLANCHE: Well – anyhow – I brought nice clothes and I'll wear them. I guess you're hoping I'll say I'll put up at a hotel, but I'm not going to put up at a hotel. I want to be *near* you, got to be *with* somebody, I *can't* be *alone!* Because – as you must have noticed – I'm *not* very *well.* . . . [*Her voice drops and her look is frightened.*]

STELLA: You seem a little bit nervous or overwrought or something.

BLANCHE: Will Stanley like me, or will I be just a visiting in-law, Stella? I couldn't stand that.

STELLA: You'll get along fine together, if you'll just try not to – well – compare him with men that we went out with at home.

BLANCHE: Is he so – different?

STELLA: Yes. A different species.

BLANCHE: In what way; what's he like?

STELLA: Oh, you can't describe someone you're in love with! Here's a picture of him! [*She hands a photograph to* BLANCHE.]

BLANCHE: An officer?

STELLA: A Master Sergeant in the Engineers' Corps. Those are decorations!

BLANCHE: He had those on when you met him?

STELLA: I assure you I wasn't just blinded by all the brass.

BLANCHE: That's not what I –

STELLA: But of course there were things to adjust myself to later on.

BLANCHE: Such as his civilian background! [STELLA *laughs uncertainly.*] How did he take it when you said I was coming?

STELLA: Oh, Stanley doesn't know yet.

BLANCHE [*frightened*]: You – haven't told him?

STELLA: He's on the road a good deal.

BLANCHE: Oh. Travels?

STELLA: Yes.

BLANCHE: Good. I mean – isn't it?

STELLA [*half to herself*]: I can hardly stand it when he is away for a night. . . .

BLANCHE: Why, Stella?

STELLA: When he's away for a week I nearly go wild!

BLANCHE: Gracious!

STELLA: And when he comes back I cry on his lap like a baby. . . . [*She smiles to herself.*]

BLANCHE: I guess that is what I meant by being in love. . . . [STELLA *looks up with a radiant smile.*] Stella –

STELLA: What?

BLANCHE [*in an uneasy rush*]: I haven't asked you the things you probably thought I was going to ask. And so I'll expect you to be understanding about what *I* have to tell *you*.

STELLA: What, Blanche? [*Her face turns anxious.*]

BLANCHE: Well, Stella – you're going to reproach me, I know that you're bound to reproach me – but before you do – take into consideration – you left! I stayed and struggled! You came to New Orleans and looked out for yourself! *I* stayed at Belle Reve and tried to hold it together! I'm not meaning this in any reproachful way, but *all* the burden descended on *my* shoulders.

STELLA: The best I could do was make my own living, Blanche.

[BLANCHE *begins to shake again with intensity.*]

BLANCHE: I know, I know. But you are the one that abandoned Belle Reve, not I! I stayed and fought for it, bled for it, almost died for it!

STELLA: Stop this hysterical outburst and tell me what's happened? What do you mean fought and bled? What kind of —

BLANCHE: I knew you would, Stella. I knew you would take this attitude about it!

STELLA: About — what? — please!

BLANCHE [*slowly*]: The loss — the loss . . .

STELLA: Belle Reve? Lost, is it? No!

BLANCHE: Yes, Stella.

[*They stare at each other across the yellow-checked linoleum of the table.* BLANCHE *slowly nods her head and* STELLA *looks slowly down at her hands folded on the table. The music of the 'blue piano' grows louder.* BLANCHE *touches her handkerchief to her forehead.*]

STELLA: But how did it go? What happened?

BLANCHE [*springing up*]: You're a fine one to ask me how it went!

STELLA: Blanche!

BLANCHE: You're a fine one to sit there *accusing me* of it!

STELLA: *Blanche!*

BLANCHE: I, I, *I* took the blows in my face and my body! All of those deaths! The long parade to the graveyard! Father, mother! Margaret, that dreadful way! So big with it, it couldn't be put in a coffin! But had to be burned like rubbish! You just came home in time for the funerals, Stella. And funerals are pretty compared to deaths. Funerals are quiet, but deaths – not always. Sometimes their breathing is hoarse, and sometimes it rattles, and sometimes they even cry out to you, 'Don't let me go!' Even the old, sometimes, say, 'Don't let me go.' As if you were able to stop them! But funerals are quiet, with pretty flowers. And, oh, what gorgeous boxes they pack them away in! Unless you were there at the bed when they cried out, 'Hold me!' you'd never suspect there was the struggle for breath and bleeding. You didn't dream, but I saw! *Saw! Saw!* And now you sit there telling me with your eyes that I let the place go! How in hell do you think all that sickness and dying was paid for? Death is expensive, Miss Stella! And old Cousin Jessie's right after Margaret's, hers! Why, the Grim Reaper had put up his tent on our doorstep! ... Stella. Belle Reve was his headquarters! Honey – that's how it slipped through my fingers! Which of them left us a fortune? Which of them left a cent of insurance even? Only poor Jessie – one hundred to pay for her coffin. That was all, Stella! And I with my pitiful salary at the school. Yes, accuse me! Sit there and stare at me, thinking I let the place go! *I* let the place go? Where were *you*. In bed with your – Polak!

STELLA [*springing*]: Blanche! You be still! That's enough!
   [*She starts out.*]
BLANCHE: Where are you going?
STELLA: I'm going into the bathroom to wash my face.
BLANCHE: Oh, Stella, Stella, you're crying!
STELLA: Does that surprise you?

   [STELLA *goes into the bathroom.*
       Outside is the sound of men's voices. STANLEY, STEVE, *and* MITCH *cross to the foot of the steps.*]

STEVE: And the old lady is on her way to Mass and she's late and there's a cop standin' in front of th' church an' she comes runnin' up an' says, 'Officer – is Mass out yet?' He looks her over and says, 'No, Lady, but y'r hat's on crooked!' [*They give a hoarse bellow of laughter.*]

STEVE: Playing poker tomorrow night?

STANLEY: Yeah – at Mitch's.

MITCH: Not at my place. My mother's still sick. [*He starts off.*]

STANLEY [*calling after him*]: All right, we'll play at my place ... but you bring the beer.

EUNICE [*hollering down from above*]: Break it up down there! I made the spaghetti dish and ate it myself.

STEVE [*going upstairs*]: I told you and phoned you we was playing. [*To the men*] Jax beer!

EUNICE: You never phoned me once.

STEVE: I told you at breakfast – and phoned you at lunch ...

EUNICE: Well, never mind about that. You just get yourself home here once in a while.

STEVE: You want it in the papers?

[*More laughter and shouts of parting come from the men. STANLEY throws the screen door of the kitchen open and comes in. He is of medium height, about five feet eight or nine, and strongly, compactly built. Animal joy in his being is implicit in all his movements and attitudes. Since earliest manhood the centre of his life has been pleasure with women, the giving and taking of it, not with weak indulgence, dependently, but with the power and pride of a richly feathered male bird among hens. Branching out from this complete and satisfying centre are all the auxiliary channels of his life, such as his heartiness with men, his appreciation of rough humour, his love of good drink and food and games, his car, his radio, everything that is his, that bears his emblem of the gaudy seed-bearer. He sizes women up at a glance, with sexual classifications, crude images flashing into his mind and determining the way he smiles at them.*]

BLANCHE: [*drawing involuntarily back from his stare*] : You must be Stanley. I'm Blanche.

STANLEY: Stella's sister?

BLANCHE: Yes.

STANLEY: H'lo. Where's the little woman?

BLANCHE: In the bathroom.

STANLEY: Oh. Didn't know you were coming in town.

BLANCHE: I – uh –

STANLEY: Where you from, Blanche?

BLANCHE: Why, I – live in Laurel.

[*He has crossed to the closet and removed the whisky bottle.*]

STANLEY: In Laurel, huh? Oh, yeah, in Laurel, that's right. Not in my territory. Liquor goes fast in hot weather. [*He holds the bottle to the light to observe its depletion.*] Have a shot?

BLANCHE: No, I – rarely touch it.

STANLEY: Some people rarely touch it, but it touches them often.

BLANCHE [*faintly*]: Ha-ha.

STANLEY: My clothes're stickin' to me. Do you mind if I make myself comfortable? [*He starts to remove his shirt.*]

BLANCHE: Please, please do.

STANLEY: Be comfortable is my motto.

BLANCHE: It's mine, too. It's hard to stay looking fresh. I haven't washed or even powdered my face and – here you are!

STANLEY: You know you can catch cold sitting around in damp things, especially when you been exercising hard like bowling is. You're a teacher, aren't you?

BLANCHE: Yes.

STANLEY: What do you teach, Blanche?

BLANCHE: English.

STANLEY: I never was a very good English student. How long you here for, Blanche?

BLANCHE: I – don't know yet.

STANLEY: You going to shack up here?

BLANCHE: I thought I would if it's not inconvenient for you all.

STANLEY: Good.

BLANCHE: Travelling wears me out.

STANLEY: Well, take it easy.

[*A cat screeches near the window.* BLANCHE *springs up.*]

BLANCHE: What's that?

STANLEY: Cats. ... Hey, Stella!

STELLA [*faintly, from the bathroom*]: Yes, Stanley.

STANLEY: Haven't fallen in, have you? [*He grins at* BLANCHE. *She tries unsuccessfully to smile back. There is a silence.*] I'm afraid I'll strike you as being the unrefined type. Stella's spoke of you a good deal. You were married once, weren't you?

[*The music of the polka rises up, faint in the distance.*]

BLANCHE: Yes. When I was quite young.

STANLEY: What happened?

BLANCHE: The boy – the boy died. [*She sinks back down.*] I'm afraid I'm – going to be sick!

[*Her head falls on her arms.*]

It is six o'clock the following evening. BLANCHE _is bathing._
STELLA _is completing her toilette._ BLANCHE'S _dress, a flowered
print, is laid out on_ STELLA'S _bed._

[STANLEY _enters the kitchen from outside, leaving the door
open on the perpetual 'blue piano' around the corner._]

STANLEY: What's all this monkey doings?

STELLA: Oh, Stan! [_She jumps up and kisses him which he
accepts with lordly composure._] I'm taking Blanche to Galatoires' for supper and then to a show, because it's your
poker night.

STANLEY: How about my supper, huh? I'm not going to no
Galatoires' for supper!

STELLA: I put you a cold plate on ice.

STANLEY: Well, isn't that just dandy!

STELLA: I'm going to try to keep Blanche out till the party
breaks up because I don't know how she would take it. So
we'll go to one of the little places in the Quarter afterwards and you'd better give me some money.

STANLEY: Where is she?

STELLA: She's soaking in a hot tub to quiet her nerves.
She's terribly upset.

STANLEY: Over what?

STELLA: She's been through such an ordeal.

STANLEY: Yeah?

STELLA: Stan, we've – lost Belle Reve!

STANLEY: The place in the country?

STELLA: Yes.

STANLEY: How?

STELLA [_vaguely_]: Oh, it had to be – sacrificed or something.
[_There is a pause while_ STANLEY _considers._ STELLA _is
changing into her dress._] When she comes in be sure to say

something   nice about her appearance. And, oh! Don't
mention the baby. I haven't said anything yet, I'm waiting until she gets in a quieter condition.

STANLEY [*ominously*]: So?

STELLA: And try to understand her and be nice to her,
Stan.

BLANCHE [*singing in the bathroom*]:
      'From the land of the sky blue water,
      They brought a captive maid!'

STELLA: She wasn't expecting to find us in such a small
place. You see I'd tried to gloss things over a little in my
letters.

STANLEY: So?

STELLA: And admire her dress and tell her she's looking
wonderful. That's important with Blanche. Her little
weakness!

STANLEY: Yeah. I get the idea. Now let's skip back a
little to where you said the country place was disposed of.

STELLA: Oh! – yes . . .

STANLEY: How about that? Let's have a few more details
on that subject.

STELLA: It's best not to talk much about it until she's
calmed down.

STANLEY: So that's the deal, huh? Sister Blanche cannot
be annoyed with business details right now!

STELLA: You saw how she was last night.

STANLEY: Uh-hum, I saw how she was. Now let's have a
gander at the bill of sale.

STELLA: I haven't seen any.

STANLEY: She didn't show you no papers, no deed of sale
or nothing like that, huh?

STELLA: It seems like it wasn't sold.

STANLEY: Well, what in hell was it then, give away? To
charity?

STELLA: Shhh! She'll hear you.

STANLEY: I don't care if she hears me. Let's see the papers!

STELLA: There weren't any papers, she didn't show any papers, I don't care about papers.

STANLEY: Have you ever heard of the Napoleonic code?

STELLA: No, Stanley, I haven't heard of the Napoleonic code and if I have, I don't see what it –

STANLEY: Let me enlighten you on a point or two, baby.

STELLA: Yes?

STANLEY: In the state of Louisiana we have the Napoleonic code according to which what belongs to the wife belongs to the husband and vice versa. For instance, if I had a piece of property, or you had a piece of property –

STELLA: My head is swimming!

STANLEY: All right. I'll wait till she gets through soaking in a hot tub and then I'll inquire if *she* is acquainted with the Napoleonic code. It looks to me like you have been swindled, baby, and when you're swindled under the Napoleonic code I'm swindled *too*. And I don't like to be *swindled*.

STELLA: There's plenty of time to ask her questions later but if you do now she'll go to pieces again. I don't understand what happened to Belle Reve but you don't know how ridiculous you are being when you suggest that my sister or I or anyone of our family could have perpetrated a swindle on anyone else.

STANLEY: Then where's the money if the place was sold?

STELLA: Not sold – *lost, lost!*

[*He stalks into bedroom, and she follows him.*]

Stanley!

[*He pulls open the wardrobe trunk standing in the middle of room and jerks out an armful of dresses.*]

STANLEY: Open your eyes to this stuff! You think she got them out of a teacher's pay?

STELLA: Hush!

STANLEY: Look at these feathers and furs that she come here

to preen herself in! What's this here? A solid-gold dress, I believe! And this one! What is these here? Fox-pieces! [*He blows on them.*] Genuine fox fur-pieces, a half a mile long! Where are your fox-pieces, Stella? Bushy snow-white ones, no less! Where are your white fox-pieces?

STELLA: Those are inexpensive summer furs that Blanche has had a long time.

STANLEY: I got an acquaintance who deals in this sort of merchandise. I'll have him in here to appraise it. I'm willing to bet you there's thousands of dollars invested in this stuff here!

STELLA: Don't be such an idiot, Stanley!

[*He hurls the furs to the daybed. Then he jerks open a small drawer in the trunk and pulls up a fistful of costume jewellery.*]

STANLEY: And what have we here? The treasure chest of a pirate!

STELLA: Oh, Stanley!

STANLEY: Pearls! Ropes of them! What is this sister of yours, a deep-sea diver who brings up sunken treasures? Or is she the champion safe-cracker of all time! Bracelets of solid gold, too! Where are your pearls and gold bracelets?

STELLA: Shhh! Be still, Stanley!

STANLEY: And diamonds! A crown for an empress!

STELLA: A rhinestone tiara she wore to a costume ball.

STANLEY: What's rhinestone?

STELLA: Next door to glass.

STANLEY: Are you kidding? I have an acquaintance that works in a jewellery store. I'll have him in here to make an appraisal of this. Here's your plantation, or what was left of it, here!

STELLA: You have no idea how stupid and horrid you're being! Now close that trunk before she comes out of the bathroom!

[*He kicks the trunk partly closed and sits on the kitchen table.*]

STANLEY: The Kowalskis and the DuBois have different notions.

STELLA [*angrily*]: Indeed they have, thank heavens! – *I'm* going outside. [*She snatches up her white hat and gloves and crosses to the outside door.*] You come out with me while Blanche is getting dressed.

STANLEY: Since when do you give me orders?

STELLA: Are you going to stay here and insult her?

STANLEY: You're damn tootin' I'm going to stay here.

[STELLA *goes out on the porch.* BLANCHE *comes out of the bathroom in a red satin robe.*]

BLANCHE [*airily*]: Hello, Stanley! Here I am, all freshly bathed and scented, and feeling like a brand-new human being!

[*He lights a cigarette.*]

STANLEY: That's good.

BLANCHE [*drawing the curtains at the windows*]: Excuse me while I slip on my pretty new dress!!

STANLEY: Go right ahead, Blanche.

[*She closes the drapes between the rooms*].

BLANCHE: I understand there's to be a little card party to which we ladies are cordially *not* invited.

STANLEY [*ominously*]: Yeah?

[BLANCHE *throws off her robe and slips into a flowered print dress.*]

BLANCHE: Where's Stella?

STANLEY: Out on the porch.

BLANCHE: I'm going to ask a favour of you in a moment.

STANLEY: What could that be, I wonder?

BLANCHE: Some buttons in back! You may enter!

[*He crosses through drapes with a smouldering look.*]

How do I look?

STANLEY: You look all right.

BLANCHE: Many thanks! Now the buttons!

STANLEY: I can't do nothing with them.

BLANCHE: You men with your big clumsy fingers. May I have a drag on your cig?

STANLEY: Have one for yourself.

BLANCHE: Why, thanks! . . . It looks like my trunk has exploded.

STANLEY: Me an' Stella were helping you unpack.

BLANCHE: Well, you certainly did a fast and thorough job of it!

STANLEY: It looks like you raided some stylish shops in Paris.

BLANCHE: Ha-ha! Yes – clothes are my passion!

STANLEY: What does it cost for a string of fur-pieces like that?

BLANCHE: Why, those were a tribute from an admirer of mine!

STANLEY: He must have had a lot of – admiration!

BLANCHE: Oh, in my youth I excited some admiration. But look at me now! [*She smiles at him radiantly.*] Would you think it possible that I was once considered to be – attractive?

STANLEY: Your looks are okay.

BLANCHE: I was fishing for a compliment, Stanley.

STANLEY: I don't go in for that stuff.

BLANCHE: What – stuff?

STANLEY: Compliments to women about their looks. I never met a woman that didn't know if she was good-looking or not without being told, and some of them give themselves credit for more than they've got. I once went out with a doll who said to me, 'I am the glamorous type,

I am the glamorous type!' I said, 'So what?'

BLANCHE: And what did she say then?

STANLEY: She didn't say nothing. That shut her up like a clam.

BLANCHE: Did it end the romance?

STANLEY: It ended the conversation – that was all. Some men are took in by this Hollywood glamour stuff and some men are not.

BLANCHE: I'm sure you belong to the second category.

STANLEY: That's right.

BLANCHE: I cannot imagine any witch of a woman casting a spell over you.

STANLEY: That's – right.

BLANCHE: You're simple, straightforward and honest, a little bit on the primitive side I should think. To interest you a woman would have to – [*She pauses with an indefinite gesture.*]

STANLEY [*slowly*]: Lay ... her cards on the table.

BLANCHE [*smiling*]: Yes – yes – cards on the table. ... Well, life is too full of evasions and ambiguities, I think. I like an artist who paints in strong, bold colours, primary colours. I don't like pinks and creams and I never cared for wish-washy people. That was why, when you walked in here last night, I said to myself – 'My sister has married a man!' – Of course that was all that I could tell about you.

STANLEY [*booming*]: Now let's cut the re-bop!

BLANCHE [*pressing hands to her ears*]: Ouuuuu!

STELLA [*calling from the steps*]: Stanley! You come out here and let Blanche finish dressing!

BLANCHE: I'm through dressing, honey.

STELLA: Well, you come out, then.

STANLEY: Your sister and I are having a little talk.

BLANCHE [*lightly*]: Honey, do me a favour. Run to the drugstore and get me a lemon-coke with plenty of chipped ice in it! – Will you do that for me, Sweetie?

STELLA [*uncertainly*]: Yes. [*She goes round the corner of the building.*]

BLANCHE: The poor thing was out there listening to us, and I have an idea she doesn't understand you as well as I do.... All right; now, Mr Kowalski, let us proceed without any more double-talk. I'm ready to answer all questions. I've nothing to hide. What is it?

STANLEY: There is such a thing in this State of Louisiana as the Napoleonic code, according to which whatever belongs to my wife is also mine – and vice versa.

BLANCHE: My, but you have an impressive judicial air!

[*She sprays herself with her atomizer; then playfully sprays him with it. He seizes the atomizer and slams it down on the dresser. She throws back her head and laughs.*]

STANLEY: If I didn't know that you was my wife's sister I'd get ideas about you!

BLANCHE: Such as what?

STANLEY: Don't play so dumb. You know what! – Where's the papers?

BLANCHE: Papers?

STANLEY: Papers! That stuff people write on!

BLANCHE: Oh, papers, papers! Ha-ha! The first anniversary gift, all kinds of papers!

STANLEY: I'm talking of legal papers. Connected with the plantation.

BLANCHE: There *were* some papers.

STANLEY: You mean they're no longer existing?

BLANCHE: They probably are, somewhere.

STANLEY: But not in the trunk.

BLANCHE: Everything that I own is in that trunk.

STANLEY: Then why don't we have a look for them? [*He crosses to the trunk, shoves it roughly open, and begins to open compartments.*]

BLANCHE: What in the name of heaven are you thinking of! What's in the back of that little boy's mind of yours?

That I am absconding with something, attempting some kind of treachery on my sister? – Let me do that! It will be faster and simpler. ... [*She crosses to the trunk and takes out a box.*] I keep my papers mostly in this tin box. [*She opens it.*]

STANLEY: What's them underneath? [*He indicates another sheaf of paper.*]

BLANCHE: These are love-letters, yellowing with antiquity, all from one boy. [*He snatches them up. She speaks fiercely.*] Give those back to me!

STANLEY: I'll have a look at them first!

BLANCHE: The touch of your hands insults them!

STANLEY: Don't pull that stuff!

[*He rips off the ribbon and starts to examine them.* BLANCHE *snatches them from him, and they cascade to the floor.*]

BLANCHE: Now that you've touched them I'll burn them!

STANLEY [*staring, baffled*]: What in hell are they?

BLANCHE [*on the floor gathering them up*]: Poems a dead boy wrote. I hurt him the way that you would like to hurt me, but you can't! I'm not young and vulnerable any more. But my young husband was and I – never mind about that! Just give them back to me!

STANLEY: What do you mean by saying you'll have to burn them?

BLANCHE: I'm sorry, I must have lost my head for a moment. Everyone has something he won't let others touch because of their – intimate nature. ...

[*She now seems faint with exhaustion and she sits down with the strong box and puts on a pair of glasses and goes methodically through a large stack of papers.*]

Ambler & Ambler. Hmmmmm. ... Crabtree. ..... More Ambler & Ambler.

STANLEY: What is Ambler & Ambler?

BLANCHE: A firm that made loans on the place.

STANLEY: Then it *was* lost on a mortgage?

BLANCHE [*touching her forehead*]: That must've been what happened.

STANLEY: I don't want no ifs, ands, or buts! What's all the rest of them papers?

[*She hands him the entire box. He carries it to the table and starts to examine the papers.*]

BLANCHE [*picking up a large envelope containing more papers*]: There are thousands of papers, stretching back over hundreds of years, affecting Belle Reve as, piece by piece, our improvident grandfathers and father and uncles and brothers exchanged the land for their epic fornications – to put it plainly! [*She removes her glasses with an exhausted laugh.*] Till finally all that was left – and Stella can verify that! – was the house itself and about twenty acres of ground, including a graveyard, to which now all but Stella and I have retreated. [*She pours the contents of the envelope on the table.*] Here all of them are, all papers! I hereby endow you with them! Take them, peruse them – commit them to memory, even! I think it's wonderfully fitting that Belle Reve should finally be this bunch of old papers in your big, capable hands! ... I wonder if Stella's come back with my lemon-coke. ...

[*She leans back and closes her eyes.*]

STANLEY: I have a lawyer acquaintance who will study these out.

BLANCHE: Present them to him with a box of aspirin tablets.

STANLEY [*becoming somewhat sheepish*]: You see, under the Napoleonic code – a man has to take an interest in his wife's affairs – especially now that she's going to have a baby.

[BLANCHE *opens her eyes. The 'blue piano' sounds louder.*]

BLANCHE: Stella? Stella going to have a baby? [*Dreamily.*] I didn't know she was going to have a baby!

[*She gets up and crosses to the outside door. Stella appears around the corner with a carton from the drug-store.*
Stanley goes into the bedroom with the envelope and the box. The inner rooms fade to darkness and the outside wall of the house is visible. BLANCHE *meets* STELLA *at the foot of the steps to the sidewalk.*]

BLANCHE: Stella, Stella for Star! How lovely to have a baby! [*She embraces her sister.* STELLA *returns the embrace with a convulsive sob.* BLANCHE *speaks softly.*] Everything is all right; we thrashed it out. I feel a bit shaky, but I think I handled it nicely. I laughed and treated it all as a joke, called him a little boy and laughed – and flirted! Yes – I was flirting with your husband, Stella!

[STEVE *and* PABLO *appear carrying a case of beer.*]

The guests are gathering for the poker party.

[*The two men pass between them, and with a short, curious stare at* BLANCHE, *they enter the house.*]

STELLA: I'm sorry he did that to you.

BLANCHE: He's just not the sort that goes for jasmine perfume! But maybe he's what we need to mix with our blood now that we've lost Belle Reve and have to go on without Belle Reve to protect us. . . . How pretty the sky is! I ought to go there on a rocket that never comes down.

[*A* TAMALE VENDOR *calls out as he rounds the corner.*]

VENDOR: Red hots! Red hots!

[BLANCHE *utters a sharp, frightened cry and shrinks away; then she laughs breathlessly again.*]

BLANCHE: Which way do we – go now – Stella?

VENDOR: Re-e-d ho-o-ot!

BLANCHE: The blind are – leading the blind!

> [*They disappear around the corner,* BLANCHE'S *desperate laughter ringing out once more.*
>
> *Then there is a bellowing laugh from the interior of the flat.*
>
> *Then the 'blue piano' and the hot trumpet sound louder.*]

SCENE THREE

The Poker Night.

There is a picture of Van Gogh's of a billiard-parlour at night.
The kitchen now suggests that sort of lurid nocturnal brilliance, the
raw colours of childhood's spectrum. Over the yellow linoleum of the
kitchen table hangs an electric bulb with a vivid green glass shade.
The poker players — STANLEY, STEVE, MITCH, and PABLO —
wear coloured shirts, solid blues, a purple, a red-and-white check, a
light green, and they are men at the peak of their physical manhood,
as coarse and direct and powerful as the primary colours. There are
vivid slices of watermelon on the table, whisky bottles, and glasses.
The bedroom is relatively dim with only the light that spills between
the portières and through the wide window on the street.

[*For a moment there is absorbed silence as a hand is dealt.*]

STEVE: Anything wild this deal?

PABLO: One-eyed jacks are wild.

STEVE: Give me two cards.

PABLO: You, Mitch?

MITCH: I'm out.

PABLO: One.

MITCH: Anyone want a shot?

STANLEY: Yeah. Me.

PABLO: Why don't somebody go to the Chinaman's and
bring back a load of chop suey?

STANLEY: When I'm losing you want to eat! Ante up!
Openers? Openers! Get off the table, Mitch. Nothing
belongs on a poker table but cards, chips, and whisky.

[*He lurches up and tosses some watermelon rinds to the floor.*]

MITCH: Kind of on your high horse, ain't you?

STANLEY: How many?

STEVE: Give me three.

STANLEY: One.

MITCH: I'm out again. I oughta go home pretty soon.

STANLEY: Shut up.

MITCH: I gotta sick mother. She don't go to sleep until I come in at night.

STANLEY: Then why don't you stay home with her?

MITCH: She says to go out, so I go, but I don't enjoy it. All the while I keep wondering how she is.

STANLEY: Aw, for God's sake, go home, then!

PABLO: What've you got?

STEVE: Spade flush.

MITCH: You all are married. But I'll be alone when she goes. – I'm going to the bathroom.

STANLEY: Hurry back and we'll fix you a sugar-tit.

MITCH: Aw, lay off. [*He crosses through the bedroom into the bathroom.*]

STEVE [*dealing a hand*]: Seven card stud. [*Telling his joke as he deals.*] This ole nigger is out in back of his house sittin' down th'owing corn to the chickens when all at once he hears a loud cackle and this young hen comes lickety split around the side of the house with the rooster right behind her and gaining on her fast.

STANLEY [*impatient with the story*]: Deal!

STEVE: But when the rooster catches sight of the nigger th'owing the corn he puts on the brakes and lets the hen get away and starts pecking corn. And the old nigger says, 'Lord God, I hopes I never gits *that* hongry!'

[STEVE *and* PABLO *laugh. The sisters appear around the corner of the building.*]

STELLA: The game is still going on.

BLANCHE: How do I look?

STELLA: Lovely, Blanche.

BLANCHE: I feel so hot and frazzled. Wait till I powder before you open the door. Do I look done in?

STELLA: Why no. You are as fresh as a daisy.

BLANCHE: One that's been picked a few days.

[STELLA *opens the door and they enter.*]

STELLA: Well, well, well. I see you boys are still at it!

STANLEY: Where you been?

STELLA: Blanche and I took in a show. Blanche, this is Mr
Gonzales and Mr Hubbel.

BLANCHE: Please don't get up.

STANLEY: Nobody's going to get up, so don't be worried.

STELLA: How much longer is this game going to continue?

STANLEY: Till we get ready to quit.

BLANCHE: Poker is so fascinating. Could I kibitz?

STANLEY: You could not. Why don't you women go up and
sit with Eunice?

STELLA: Because it is nearly two-thirty. [BLANCHE *crosses
into the bedroom and partially closes the portières.*] Couldn't
you call it quits after one more hand?

[*A chair scrapes.* STANLEY *gives a loud whack of his hand on
her thigh.*]

STELLA [*sharply*]: That's not fun, Stanley.

[*The men laugh.* STELLA *goes into the bedroom.*]

STELLA: It makes me so mad when he does that in front of
people.

BLANCHE: I think I will bathe.

STELLA: Again.

BLANCHE: My nerves are in knots. Is the bathroom oc-
cupied?

STELLA: I don't know.

[BLANCHE *knocks.* MITCH *opens the door and comes out,
still wiping his hands on a towel.*]

BLANCHE: Oh! – good evening.

MITCH: Hello. [*He stares at her.*]

STELLA: Blanche, this is Harold Mitchell. My sister,
Blanche DuBois.

MITCH [*with awkward courtesy*]: How do you do, Miss DuBois.

STELLA: How is your mother now, Mitch?

MITCH: About the same, thanks. She appreciated your sending over that custard. – Excuse me, please.

[*He crosses slowly back into the kitchen, glancing back at* BLANCHE *and coughing a little shyly. He realizes he still has the towel in his hands and with an embarrassed laugh hands it to* STELLA. BLANCHE *looks after him with a certain interest.*]

BLANCHE: That one seems – superior to the others.

STELLA: Yes, he is.

BLANCHE: I thought he had a sort of sensitive look.

STELLA: His mother is sick.

BLANCHE: Is he married?

STELLA: No.

BLANCHE: Is he a wolf?

STELLA: Why, Blanche! [BLANCHE *laughs.*] I don't think he would be.

BLANCHE: What does – what does he do?

[*She is unbuttoning her blouse.*]

STELLA: He's on the precision bench in the spare parts department. At the plant Stanley travels for.

BLANCHE: Is that something much?

STELLA: No. Stanley's the only one of his crowd that's likely to get anywhere.

BLANCHE: What makes you think Stanley will?

STELLA: Look at him.

BLANCHE: I've looked at him.

STELLA: Then you should know

BLANCHE: I'm sorry, but I haven't noticed the stamp of genius even on Stanley's forehead.

[*She takes off the blouse and stands in her pink silk brassière and white skirt in the light through the portières. The game has continued in undertones.*]

STELLA: It isn't on his forehead and it isn't genius.

BLANCHE: Oh. Well, what is it, and where? I would like to know.

STELLA: It's a drive that he has. You're standing in the light, Blanche!

BLANCHE: Oh, am I!

[*She moves out of the yellow streak of light.* STELLA *has removed her dress and put on a light blue satin kimono.*]

STELLA [*with girlish laughter*]: You ought to see their wives.

BLANCHE [*laughingly*]: I can imagine. Big, beefy things, I suppose.

STELLA: You know that one upstairs? [*More laughter.*] One time [*laughing*] the plaster – [*laughing*] cracked –

STANLEY: You hens cut out that conversation in there!

STELLA: You can't hear us.

STANLEY: Well, you can hear me and I said to hush up!

STELLA: This is my house and I'll talk as much as I want to!

BLANCHE: Stella, don't start a row.

STELLA: He's half drunk! – I'll be out in a minute.

[*She goes into the bathroom.* BLANCHE *rises and crosses leisurely to a small white radio and turns it on.*]

STANLEY: Awright, Mitch, you in?

MITCH: What? Oh! – No, I'm out!

[BLANCHE *moves back into the streak of light. She raises her arms and stretches, as she moves indolently back to the chair.*

Rhumba music comes over the radio. MITCH *rises at the table.*]

STANLEY: Who turned that on in there?

BLANCHE: I did. Do you mind?

STANLEY: Turn it off!

STEVE: Aw, let the girls have their music.

PABLO: Sure, that's good, leave it on!

STEVE: Sounds like Xavier Cugat!

[STANLEY *jumps up and, crossing to the radio, turns it off. He stops short at sight of* BLANCHE *in the chair. She returns his look without flinching. Then he sits again at the poker table. Two of the men have started arguing hotly.*]

STEVE: I didn't hear you name it.

PABLO: Didn't I name it, Mitch?

MITCH: I wasn't listenin'.

PABLO: What were you doing, then?

STANLEY: He was looking through them drapes. [*He jumps up and jerks roughly at curtains to close them.*] Now deal the hand over again and let's play cards or quit. Some people get ants when they win.

[MITCH *rises as* STANLEY *returns to his seat.*]

STANLEY [*yelling*]: Sit down!

MITCH: I'm going to the 'head'. Deal me out.

PABLO: Sure he's got ants now. Seven five-dollar bills in his pants pocket folded up tight as spitballs.

STEVE: Tomorrow you'll see him at the cashier's window getting them changed into quarters.

STANLEY: And when he goes home he'll deposit them one by one in a piggy bank his mother give him for Christmas. [*Dealing.*] This game is Spit in the Ocean.

[MITCH *laughs uncomfortably and continues through the portières. He stops just inside.*]

BLANCHE [*softly*]: Hello! The Little Boys' Room is busy right now.

MITCH: We've – been drinking beer.

BLANCHE: I hate beer.

MITCH: It's – a hot weather drink.

BLANCHE: Oh, I don't think so; it always makes me warmer. Have you got any cigs? [*She has slipped on the dark red satin wrapper.*]

MITCH: Sure.

BLANCHE: What kind are they?

MITCH: Luckies.

BLANCHE: Oh, good. What a pretty case. Silver?

MITCH: Yes. Yes; read the inscription.

BLANCHE: Oh, is there an inscription? I can't make it out. [*He strikes a match and moves closer.*] Oh! [*reading with feigned difficulty*]

> 'And if God choose,
> I shall but love thee better – after death!'

Why, that's from my favourite sonnet by Mrs Browning!

MITCH: You know it?

BLANCHE: Certainly I do!

MITCH: There's a story connected with that inscription.

BLANCHE: It sounds like a romance.

MITCH: A pretty sad one.

BLANCHE: Oh?

MITCH: The girl's dead now.

BLANCHE [*in a tone of deep sympathy*]: *Oh!*

MITCH: She knew she was dying when she give me this. A very strange girl, very sweet – very!

BLANCHE: She must have been fond of you. Sick people have such deep, sincere attachments.

MITCH: That's right, they certainly do.

BLANCHE: Sorrow makes for sincerity, I think.

MITCH: It sure brings it out in people.

BLANCHE: The little there is belongs to people who have experienced some sorrow.

MITCH: I believe you are right about that.

BLANCHE: I'm positive that I am. Show me a person who hasn't known any sorrow and I'll show you a shuperficial – Listen to me! ᵧ tongue is a little – thick! You boys are responsible for it. The show let out at eleven and we couldn't come home on account of the poker game so we had to go somewhere and drink. I'm not accustomed to having more than one drink. Two is the limit – and *three!* [*She laughs.*] Tonight I had three.

STANLEY: Mitch!

MITCH: Deal me out. I'm talking to Miss –

BLANCHE: DuBois.

MITCH: Miss DuBois?

BLANCHE: It's a French name. It means woods and Blanche means white, so the two together mean white woods. Like an orchard in spring! You can remember it by that.

MITCH: You're French?

BLANCHE: We are French by extraction. Our first American ancestors were French Huguenots.

MITCH: You are Stella's sister, are you not?

BLANCHE: Yes, Stella is my precious little sister. I call her little in spite of the fact she's somewhat older than I. Just slightly. Less than a year. Will you do something for me?

MITCH: Sure. What?

BLANCHE: I bought this adorable little coloured paper lantern at a Chinese shop on Bourbon. Put it over the light bulb! Will you, please?

MITCH: Be glad to.

BLANCHE: I can't stand a naked light bulb, any more than I can a rude remark or a vulgar action.

MITCH [adjusting the lantern]: I guess we strike you as being a pretty rough bunch.

BLANCHE: I'm very adaptable – to circumstances.

MITCH: Well, that's a good thing to be. You are visiting Stanley and Stella?

BLANCHE: Stella hasn't been so well lately, and I came down to help her for a while. She's very run down.

MITCH: You're not –?

BLANCHE: Married? No, no. I'm an old maid school-teacher!

MITCH: You may teach school but you're certainly not an old maid.

BLANCHE: Thank you, sir! I appreciate your gallantry!

MITCH: So you are in the teaching profession?

BLANCHE: Yes. Ah, yes ...

MITCH: Grade school or high school or –

STANLEY [*bellowing*]: *Mitch!*

MITCH: *Coming!*

BLANCHE: Gracious, what lung-power! . . . I teach high school. In Laurel.

MITCH: What do you teach? What subject?

BLANCHE: Guess!

MITCH: I bet you teach art or music? [BLANCHE *laughs delicately.*] Of course I could be wrong. You might teach arithmetic.

BLANCHE: Never arithmetic, sir; never arithmetic! [*with a laugh*] I don't even know my multiplication tables! No, I have the misfortune of being an English instructor. I attempt to instil a bunch of bobby-soxers and drug-store Romeos with reverence for Hawthorne and Whitman and Poe!

MITCH: I guess that some of them are more interested in other things.

BLANCHE: How very right you are! Their literary heritage is not what most of them treasure above all else! But they're sweet things! And in the spring, it's touching to notice them making their first discovery of love! As if nobody had ever known it before!

[*The bathroom door opens and* STELLA *comes out.* BLANCHE *continues talking to* MITCH.]

Oh! Have you finished? Wait – I'll turn on the radio.

[*She turns the knobs on the radio and it begins to play 'Wien, Wien, nur du allein'.* BLANCHE *waltzes to the music with romantic gestures.* MITCH *is delighted and moves in awkward imitation like a dancing bear.*

STANLEY *stalks fiercely through the portières into the bedroom. He crosses to the small white radio and snatches it off the table. With a shouted oath, he tosses the instrument out of the window.*]

STELLA: *Drunk – drunk – animal thing, you!* [*She rushes through to the poker table.*] All of you – please go home! If any of you have one spark of decency in you –

BLANCHE [*wildly*]: Stella, watch out, he's –

[STANLEY *charges after* STELLA.]

MEN [*feebly*]: Take it easy, Stanley. Easy, fellow. – Let's all –

STELLA: You lay your hands on me and I'll –

[*She backs out of sight. He advances and disappears. There is the sound of a blow.* STELLA *cries out.* BLANCHE *screams and runs into the kitchen. The men rush forward and there is grappling and cursing. Something is overturned with a crash.*]

BLANCHE [*shrilly*]: My sister is going to have a baby!

MITCH: This is terrible.

BLANCHE: Lunacy, absolute lunacy!

MITCH: Get him in here, men.

[STANLEY *is forced, pinioned by the two men, into the bedroom. He nearly throws them off. Then all at once he subsides and is limp in their grasp.*

They speak quietly and lovingly to him and he leans his face on one of their shoulders.]

STELLA [*in a high, unnatural voice, out of sight*]: I want to go away, I want to go away!

MITCH: Poker shouldn't be played in a house with women.

[BLANCHE *rushes into the bedroom.*]

BLANCHE: I want my sister's clothes! We'll go to that woman's upstairs!

MITCH: Where is the clothes?

BLANCHE [*opening the closet*]: I've got them! [*She rushes through to* STELLA.] Stella, Stella, precious! Dear, dear little sister, don't be afraid!

[*With her arms around* STELLA, BLANCHE *guides her to the outside door and upstairs.*]

STANLEY [*dully*]: What's the matter; what's happened?

MITCH: You just blew your top, Stan.

PABLO: He's okay, now.

STEVE: Sure, my boy's okay!

MITCH: Put him on the bed and get a wet towel.

PABLO: I think coffee would do him a world of good, now.

STANLEY [*thickly*]: I want water.

MITCH: Put him under the shower!

[*The men talk quietly as they lead him to the bathroom.*]

STANLEY: Let go of me, you sons of bitches!

[*Sounds of blows are heard. The water goes on full tilt.*]

STEVE: Let's get quick out of here!

[*They rush to the poker table and sweep up their winnings on their way out.*]

MITCH [*sadly but firmly*]: Poker should not be played in a house with women.

[*The door closes on them and the place is still. The Negro entertainers in the bar around the corner play 'Paper Doll' slow and blue. After a moment* STANLEY *comes out of the bathroom dripping water and still in his clinging wet polka dot drawers.*]

STANLEY: Stella! [*There is a pause.*] My baby doll's left me!

[*He breaks into sobs. Then he goes to the phone and dials, still shuddering with sobs.*]

Eunice? I want my baby! [*He waits a moment; then he hangs up and dials again.*] Eunice! I'll keep on ringin' until I talk with my baby!

[*An indistinguishable shrill voice is heard. He hurls phone to floor. Dissonant brass and piano sounds as the rooms dim out to darkness and the outer walls appear in the night light. The 'blue piano' plays for a brief interval.*

Finally, STANLEY *stumbles half-dressed out to the porch*

*and down the wooden steps to the pavement before the building.
There he throws back his head like a baying hound and bellows
his wife's name: 'Stella! Stella, sweetheart! Stella!'*

STANLEY: Stell-*lahhhhh!*

EUNICE [*calling down from the door of her upper apartment*]: Quit
that howling out there an' go back to bed!

STANLEY: I want my baby down here. Stella, Stella!

EUNICE: She ain't comin' down so you quit! Or you'll git
th' law on you!

STANLEY: Stella!

EUNICE: You can't beat a woman an' then call 'er back!
She won't come! And her goin' t' have a baby! ... You
stinker! You whelp of a Polack, you! I hope they do haul
you in and turn the fire hose on you, same as the last time!

STANLEY [*humbly*]: Eunice, I want my girl to come down
with me!

EUNICE: Hah! [*She slams her door.*]

STANLEY [*with heaven-splitting violence*]: *STELLL-
AHHHHH!*

[*The low-tone clarinet moans. The door upstairs opens again.
STELLA slips down the rickety stairs in her robe. Her eyes are
glistening with tears and her hair loose about her throat and
shoulders. They stare at each other. Then they come together
with low, animal moans. He falls on his knees on the steps and
presses his face to her belly, curving a little with maternity. Her
eyes go blind with tenderness as she catches his head and raises
him level with her. He snatches the screen door open and lifts
her off her feet and bears her into the dark flat.*

    *BLANCHE comes out on the upper landing in her robe and
slips fearfully down the steps.*]

BLANCHE: Where is my little sister? Stella? Stella?

[*She stops before the dark entrance of her sister's flat. Then
catches her breath as if struck. She rushes down to the walk
before the house. She looks right and left as if for sanctuary.*

The music fades away. MITCH *appears from around the corner.*]

MITCH: Miss DuBois?

BLANCHE: Oh!

MITCH: All quiet on the Potomac now?

BLANCHE: She ran downstairs and went back in there with him.

MITCH: Sure she did.

BLANCHE: I'm terrified!

MITCH: Ho-ho! There's nothing to be scared of. They're crazy about each other.

BLANCHE: I'm not used to such –

MITCH: Naw, it's a shame this had to happen when you just got here. But don't take it serious.

BLANCHE: Violence! Is so –

MITCH: Set down on the steps and have a cigarette with me.

BLANCHE: I'm not properly dressed.

MITCH: That don't make no difference in the Quarter.

BLANCHE: Such a pretty silver case.

MITCH: I showed you the inscription, didn't I?

BLANCHE: Yes. [*During the pause, she looks up at the sky.*] There's so much – so much confusion in the world. . . . [*He coughs diffidently.*] Thank you for being so kind! I need kindness now.

SCENE FOUR

It is early the following morning. There is a confusion of street cries like a choral chant.

[STELLA *is lying down in the bedroom. Her face is serene in the early morning sunlight. One hand rests on her belly, rounding slightly with new maternity. From the other dangles a book of coloured comics. Her eyes and lips have that almost narcotized tranquillity that is in the faces of Eastern idols.*

The table is sloppy with remains of breakfast and the debris of the preceding night, and STANLEY'S *gaudy pyjamas lie across the threshold of the bathroom. The outside door is slightly ajar on a sky of summer brilliance.*

BLANCHE *appears at this door. She has spent a sleepless night and her appearance entirely contrasts with* STELLA'S. *She presses her knuckles nervously to her lips as she looks through the door, before entering.*]

BLANCHE: Stella?
STELLA [*stirring lazily*]: Hmmh?

[BLANCHE *utters a moaning cry and runs into the bedroom, throwing herself down beside* STELLA *in a rush of hysterical tenderness.*]

BLANCHE: Baby, my baby sister!
STELLA [*drawing away from her*]: Blanche, what is the matter with you?

[BLANCHE *straightens up slowly and stands beside the bed looking down at her sister with knuckles pressed to her lips.*]

BLANCHE: He's left?
STELLA: Stan? Yes.
BLANCHE: Will he be back?
STELLA: He's gone to get the car greased. Why?

BLANCHE: Why! I've been half crazy, Stella! When I found out you'd been insane enough to come back in here after what happened – I started to rush in after you!

STELLA: I'm glad you didn't.

BLANCHE: What were you thinking of? [STELLA *makes an indefinite gesture.*] Answer me! What? What?

STELLA: Please, Blanche! Sit down and stop yelling.

BLANCHE: All right, Stella. I will repeat the question quietly now. How could you come back in this place last night? Why, you must have slept with him!

[STELLA *gets up in a calm and leisurely way.*]

STELLA: Blanche, I'd forgotten how excitable you are. You're making much too much fuss about this.

BLANCHE: Am I?

STELLA: Yes, you are, Blanche. I know how it must have seemed to you and I'm awful sorry it had to happen, but it wasn't anything as serious as you seem to take it. In the first place, when men are drinking and playing poker anything can happen. It's always a powder-keg. He didn't know what he was doing. . . . He was as good as a lamb when I came back and he's really very, very ashamed of himself.

BLANCHE: And that – that makes it all right?

STELLA: No, it isn't all right for anybody to make such a terrible row, but – people do sometimes. Stanley's always smashed things. Why, on our wedding night – soon as we came in here – he snatched off one of my slippers and rushed about the place smashing the light-bulbs with it.

BLANCHE: He did – *what?*

STELLA: He smashed all the light-bulbs with the heel of my slipper! [*She laughs.*]

BLANCHE: And you – you *let* him? Didn't *run,* didn't *scream?*

STELLA: I was – sort of – thrilled by it. [*She waits for a moment.*] Eunice and you had breakfast?

BLANCHE: Do you suppose I wanted any breakfast?

STELLA: There's some coffee left on the stove.

BLANCHE: You're so – matter of fact about it, Stella.

STELLA: What other can I be? He's taken the radio to get it fixed. It didn't land on the pavement so only one tube was smashed.

BLANCHE: And you are standing there smiling!

STELLA: What do you want me to do?

BLANCHE: Pull yourself together and face the facts.

STELLA: What are they, in your opinion?

BLANCHE: In my opinion? You're married to a madman!

STELLA: No!

BLANCHE: Yes, you are, your fix is worse than mine is! Only you're not being sensible about it. I'm going to *do* something. Get hold of myself and make myself a new life!

STELLA: Yes?

BLANCHE: But you've given in. And that isn't right, you're not old! You can get out.

STELLA [*slowly and emphatically*]: I'm not in anything I want to get out of.

BLANCHE [*incredulously*]: What – Stella?

STELLA: I said I am not in anything that I have a desire to get out of. Look at the mess in this room! And those empty bottles! They went through two cases last night! He promised this morning that he was going to quit having these poker parties, but you know how long such a promise is going to keep. Oh, well, it's his pleasure, like mine is movies and bridge. People have got to tolerate each other's habits, I guess.

BLANCHE: I don't understand you. [STELLA *turns toward her.*] I don't understand your indifference. Is this a Chinese philosophy you've – cultivated?

STELLA: Is what – what?

BLANCHE: This – shuffling about and mumbling – 'One tube smashed – beer-bottles – mess in the kitchen' – as if nothing out of the ordinary has happened! [STELLA *laughs uncertainly and, picking up the broom, twirls it in her hands.*]

BLANCHE: Are you deliberately shaking that thing in my face?

STELLA: No.

BLANCHE: Stop it. Let go of that broom. I won't have you cleaning up for him!

STELLA: Then who's going to do it? Are you?

BLANCHE: I? I!

STELLA: No, I didn't think so.

BLANCHE: Oh, let me think, if only my mind would function! We've got to get hold of some money, that's the way out!

STELLA: I guess that money is always nice to get hold of.

BLANCHE: Listen to me. I have an idea of some kind. [*Shakily she twists a cigarette into her holder.*] Do you remember Shep Huntleigh? [STELLA *shakes her head.*] Of course you remember Shep Huntleigh. I went out with him at college and wore his pin for a while. Well –

STELLA: Well?

BLANCHE: I ran into him last winter. You know I went to Miami during the Christmas holidays?

STELLA: No.

BLANCHE: Well, I did. I took the trip as an investment, thinking I'd meet someone with a million dollars.

STELLA: Did you?

BLANCHE: Yes. I ran into Shep Huntleigh – I ran into him on Biscayne Boulevard, on Christmas Eve, about dusk . . . getting into his car – Cadillac convertible; must have been a block long!

STELLA: I should think it would have been – inconvenient in traffic!

BLANCHE: You've heard of oil-wells?

STELLA: Yes – remotely.

BLANCHE: He has them, all over Texas. Texas is literally spouting gold in his pockets.

STELLA: My, my.

BLANCHE: Y'know how indifferent I am to money. I think of money in terms of what it does for you. But he could do it, he could certainly do it!

STELLA: Do what, Blanche?

BLANCHE: Why – set us up in a – shop!

STELLA: What kind of a shop?

BLANCHE: Oh, a – shop of some kind! He could do it with half what his wife throws away at the races.

STELLA: He's married?

BLANCHE: Honey, would I be here if the man weren't married? [STELLA *laughs a little.* BLANCHE *suddenly springs up and crosses to phone. She speaks shrilly.*] How do I get Western Union? Operator! Western Union!

STELLA: That's a dial phone, honey.

BLANCHE: I can't dial, I'm too –

STELLA: Just dial O.

BLANCHE: O?

STELLA: Yes, 'O' for Operator! [BLANCHE *considers a moment; then she puts the phone down.*]

BLANCHE: Give me a pencil. Where is a slip of paper? I've got to write it down first – the message, I mean. . . .

[*She goes to the dressing-table, and grabs up a sheet of Kleenex and an eyebrow pencil for writing equipment.*]

Let me see now . . . [*She bites the pencil.*] 'Darling Shep. Sister and I in desperate situation.'

STELLA: I beg your pardon!

BLANCHE: 'Sister and I in desperate situation. Will explain details later. Would you be interested in –?' [*She bites the pencil again.*] 'Would you be – interested – in . . .' [*She smashes the pencil on the table and springs up.*] You never get anywhere with direct appeals!

STELLA [*with a laugh*]: Don't be so ridiculous, darling!

BLANCHE: But I'll think of something, I've *got* to think of – *some*thing! Don't, don't laugh at me, Stella! Please, please

don't – I – I want you to look at the contents of my purse!
Here's what's in it! [*She snatches her purse open.*] Sixty-five
measly cents in coin of the realm!

STELLA [*crossing to bureau*]: Stanley doesn't give me a regular
allowance, he likes to pay bills himself, but – this morning
he gave me ten dollars to smooth things over. You take
five of it, Blanche, and I'll keep the rest.

BLANCHE: Oh, no. No, Stella.

STELLA [*insisting*]: I know how it helps your morale just
having a little pocket-money on you.

BLANCHE: No, thank you – I'll take to the streets!

STELLA: Talk sense! How did you happen to get so low on
funds?

BLANCHE: Money just goes – it goes places. [*She rubs her forehead.*] Sometime today I've got to get hold of a bromo!

STELLA: I'll fix you one now.

BLANCHE: Not yet – I've got to keep thinking!

STELLA: I wish you'd just let things go, at least for a –
while . . .

BLANCHE: Stella, I can't live with him! You can, he's your
husband. But how could I stay here with him, after last
night, with just those curtains between us?

STELLA: Blanche, you saw him at his worst last night.

BLANCHE: On the contrary, I saw him at his best! What
such a man has to offer is animal force and he gave a
wonderful exhibition of that! But the only way to live
with such a man is to – go to bed with him! And that's
your job – not mine!

STELLA: After you've rested a little, you'll see it's going to
work out. You don't have to worry about anything while
you're here. I mean – expenses . . .

BLANCHE: I have to plan for us both, to get us both –
out!

STELLA: You take it for granted that I am in something that
I want to get out of.

BLANCHE: I take it for granted that you still have sufficient memory of Belle Reve to find this place and these poker players impossible to live with.

STELLA: Well, you're taking entirely too much for granted.

BLANCHE: I can't believe you're in earnest.

STELLA: No?

BLANCHE: I understand how it happened – a little. You saw him in uniform, an officer, not here but –

STELLA: I'm not sure it would have made any difference where I saw him.

BLANCHE: Now don't say it was one of those mysterious electric things between people! If you do I'll laugh in your face.

STELLA: I am not going to say anything more at all about it!

BLANCHE: All right, then, don't!

STELLA: But there are things that happen between a man and a woman in the dark – that sort of make everything else seem – unimportant. [*Pause.*]

BLANCHE: What you are talking about is brutal desire – just – Desire! – the name of that rattle-trap street-car that bangs through the Quarter, up one old narrow street and down another . . .

STELLA: Haven't you ever ridden on that street-car?

BLANCHE: It brought me here. – Where I'm not wanted and where I'm ashamed to be . . .

STELLA: Then don't you think your superior attitude is a bit out of place?

BLANCHE: I am not being or feeling at all superior, Stella. Believe me I'm not! It's just this. This is how I look at it. A man like that is someone to go out with – once – twice – three times when the devil is in you. But live with! Have a child by?

STELLA: I have told you I love him.

BLANCHE: Then I *tremble* for you! I just – *tremble* for you. . . .

STELLA: I can't help your trembling if you insist on trembling!

[*There is a pause.*]

BLANCHE: May I – speak – *plainly?*

STELLA: Yes, do. Go ahead. As plainly as you want to.

[*Outside a train approaches. They are silent till the noise subsides. They are both in the bedroom.*

Under cover of the train's noise STANLEY *enters from outside. He stands unseen by the women, holding some packages in his arms, and overhears their following conversation. He wears an undershirt and grease-stained seersucker pants.*]

BLANCHE: Well – if you'll forgive me – he's *common!*

STELLA: Why, yes, I suppose he is.

BLANCHE: Suppose! You can't have forgotten that much of our bringing up, Stella, that you just *suppose* that any part of a gentleman's in his nature! *Not one particle, no!* Oh, if he was just – *ordinary!* Just *plain* – but good and wholesome, but – *no*. There's something downright – *bestial* – about him! You're hating me saying this, aren't you?

STELLA [*coldly*]: Go on and say it all, Blanche.

BLANCHE: He acts like an animal, has an animal's habits! Eats like one, moves like one, talks like one! There's even something – sub-human – something not quite to the stage of humanity yet! Yes, something – ape-like about him, like one of those pictures I've seen in – anthropological studies! Thousands and thousands of years have passed him right by, and there he is – Stanley Kowalski – survivor of the Stone Age! Bearing the raw meat home from the kill in the jungle! And you – *you* here – *waiting* for him! Maybe he'll strike you or maybe grunt and kiss you! That is, if kisses have been discovered yet! Night falls and the other apes gather! There in the front of the cave, all grunting like him, and swilling and gnawing and hulking! His poker night! – you call it – this party of apes! Somebody growls – some creature snatches at something – the fight is on! *God!* Maybe we are a long way from being made in God's image, but Stella – my sister – there has been *some* progress since then! Such things as art – as poetry and music – such kinds of new light have come into the world since then! In some kinds of people some tenderer feelings have had some little beginning! That we have got to make *grow!* And *cling* to, and hold as our flag! In this dark march toward whatever it is we're approaching. . . . *Don't – don't hang back with the brutes!*

[*Another train passes outside.* STANLEY *hesitates, licking his lips. Then suddenly he turns stealthily about and withdraws through the front door. The women are still unaware of his presence. When the train has passed he calls through the closed front door.*]

STANLEY: Hey! Hey! Stella!
STELLA [*who has listened gravely to* BLANCHE]: Stanley!
BLANCHE: Stell, I –

[*But* STELLA *has gone to the front door.* STANLEY *enters casually with his packages.*]

STANLEY: Hiyuh, Stella, Blanche back?
STELLA: Yes, she's back.
STANLEY: Hiyuh, Blanche. [*He grins at her.*]
STELLA: You must've got under the car.
STANLEY: Them darn mechanics at Fritz's don't know their can from third base!

[STELLA *has embraced him with both arms, fiercely, and full in the view of* BLANCHE. *He laughs and clasps her head to him. Over her head he grins through the curtains at* BLANCHE.
  As the lights fade away, with a lingering brightness on their embrace, the music of the 'blue piano' and trumpet and drums is heard.]

SCENE FIVE

BLANCHE *is seated in the bedroom fanning herself with a palm leaf as she reads over a just completed letter. Suddenly she bursts into a peal of laughter.* STELLA *is dressing in the bedroom.*

STELLA: What are you laughing at, honey?

BLANCHE: Myself, myself, for being such a liar! I'm writing a letter to Shep. [*She picks up the letter.*] 'Darling Shep. I am spending the summer on the wing, making flying visits here and there. And who knows, perhaps I shall take a sudden notion to *swoop* down on *Dallas!* How would you feel about that? Ha-ha! [*She laughs nervously and brightly, touching her throat as if actually talking to* SHEP.] Forewarned is forearmed, as they say!' – How does that sound?

STELLA: Uh-huh ...

BLANCHE [*going on nervously*]: 'Most of my sister's friends go north in the summer but some have homes on the Gulf and there has been a continued round of entertainments, teas, cocktails, and luncheons –'

[*A disturbance is heard upstairs at the* HUBBELS' *apartment.*]

STELLA [*crossing to the door*]: Eunice seems to be having some trouble with Steve.

[EUNICE'S *voice shouts in terrible wrath.*]

EUNICE: I heard about you and that blonde!

STEVE: That's a damn lie!

EUNICE: You ain't pulling the wool over my eyes! I wouldn't mind if you'd stay down at the Four Deuces, but you always going up.

STEVE: Who ever seen me up?

EUNICE: I seen you chasing her 'round the balcony – I'm gonna call the vice squad!

STEVE: Don't you throw that at me!

EUNICE [*shrieking*]: You hit me! I'm gonna call the police!

[*A clatter of aluminium striking a wall is heard, followed by a man's angry roar, shouts, and overturned furniture. There is a crash; then a relative hush.*]

BLANCHE [*brightly*]: Did he *kill* her?

[EUNICE *appears on the steps in daemonic disorder.*]

STELLA: No! She's coming downstairs.

EUNICE: Call the police, I'm going to call the police! [*She rushes around the corner.*]

STELLA [*returning from the door*]: Some of your sister's friends have stayed in the city.

[*They laugh lightly.* STANLEY *comes around the corner in his green and scarlet silk bowling shirt. He trots up the steps and bangs into the kitchen.* BLANCHE *registers his entrance with nervous gestures.*]

STANLEY: What's a matter with Eun-uss?

STELLA: She and Steve had a row. Has she got the police?

STANLEY: Naw. She's gettin' a drink.

STELLA: That's much more practical!

[STEVE *comes down nursing a bruise on his forehead and looks in the door.*]

STEVE: *She here?*

STANLEY: Naw, naw. At the Four Deuces.

STEVE: That hunk! [*He looks around the corner a bit timidly, then turns with affected boldness and runs after her.*]

BLANCHE: I must jot that down in my notebook. Ha-ha! I'm compiling a notebook of quaint little words and phrases I've picked up here.

STANLEY: You won't pick up nothing here you ain't heard before.

BLANCHE: Can I count on that?

STANLEY: You can count on it up to five hundred.

BLANCHE: That's a mighty high number. [*He jerks open the bureau drawer, slams it shut, and throws shoes in a corner. At each noise* BLANCHE *winces slightly. Finally she speaks.*] What sign were you born under?

STANLEY [*while he is dressing*]: Sign?

BLANCHE: Astrological sign. I bet you were born under Aries. Aries people are forceful and dynamic. They dote on noise! They love to bang things around! You must have had lots of banging around in the army, and now that you're out, you make up for it by treating inanimate objects with such a fury!

[STELLA *has been going in and out of closet during this scene. Now she pops her head out of the closet.*]

STELLA: Stanley was born just five minutes after Christmas.

BLANCHE: Capricorn – the Goat!

STANLEY: What sign were *you* born under?

BLANCHE: Oh, my birthday's next month, the fifteenth of September, that's under Virgo.

STANLEY: What's Virgo?

BLANCHE: Virgo is the Virgin.

STANLEY [*contemptuously*]: Hah! [*He advances a little as he knots his tie.*] Say, do you happen to know somebody named Shaw?

[*Her face expresses a faint shock. She reaches for the cologne bottle and dampens her handkerchief as she answers carefully.*]

BLANCHE: Why, everybody knows somebody named Shaw!

STANLEY: Well, this somebody named Shaw is under the impression he met you in Laurel, but I figure he must have got you mixed up with some other party because this other party is someone he met at a hotel called the Flamingo.

[BLANCHE *laughs breathlessly as she touches the cologne-dampened handkerchief to her temples.*]

BLANCHE: I'm afraid he does have me mixed up with this 'other party'. The Hotel Flamingo is not the sort of establishment I would dare to be seen in!

STANLEY: You know of it?

BLANCHE: Yes, I've seen it and smelled it.

STANLEY: You must've got pretty close if you could smell it.

BLANCHE: The odour of cheap perfume is penetrating.

STANLEY: That stuff you use is expensive?

BLANCHE: Twenty-five dollars an ounce! I'm nearly out. That's just a hint if you want to remember my birthday! [*She speaks lightly but her voice has a note of fear.*]

STANLEY: Shaw must've got you mixed up. He goes in and out of Laurel all the time, so he can check on it and clear up any mistake.

[*He turns away and crosses to the portières.* BLANCHE *closes her eyes as if faint. Her hand trembles as she lifts the handkerchief again to her forehead.*

STEVE *and* EUNICE *come around the corner.* STEVE'S *arm is around* EUNICE'S *shoulder and she is sobbing luxuriously and he is cooing love-words. There is a murmur of thunder as they go slowly upstairs in a tight embrace.*]

STANLEY [*to* STELLA]: I'll wait for you at the Four Deuces!

STELLA: Hey! Don't I rate one kiss?

STANLEY: Not in front of your sister.

[*He goes out.* BLANCHE *rises from her chair. She seems faint; looks about her with an expression of almost panic.*]

BLANCHE: Stella! What have you heard about me?

STELLA: Huh?

BLANCHE: What have people been telling you about me?

STELLA: Telling?

BLANCHE: You haven't heard any – unkind – gossip about me?

STELLA: Why, no, Blanche, of course not!

BLANCHE: Honey, there was – a good deal of talk in Laurel.

STELLA: About *you*, Blanche?

BLANCHE: I wasn't so good the last two years or so, after Belle Reve had started to slip through my fingers.

STELLA: All of us do things we –

BLANCHE: I never was hard or self-sufficient enough. When people are soft – soft people have got to court the favour of hard ones, Stella. Have got to be seductive – put on soft colours, the colours of butterfly wings, and glow – make a little – temporary magic just in order to pay for – one night's shelter! That's why I've been – not so awf'ly good lately. I've run for protection, Stella, from under one leaky roof to another leaky roof – because it was storm – all storm, and I was – caught in the centre. . . . People don't see you – *men* don't – don't even admit your existence unless they are making love to you. And you've got to have your existence admitted by someone, if you're going to have someone's protection. And so the soft people have got to – shimmer and glow – put a – paper lantern over the light. . . . But I'm scared now – awf'ly scared. I don't know how much longer I can turn the trick. It isn't enough to be soft. You've got to be soft *and attractive*. And I – I'm fading now!

[*The afternoon has faded to dusk.* STELLA *goes into the bedroom and turns on the light under the paper lantern. She holds a bottled soft drink in her hand.*]

Have you been listening to me?

STELLA: I don't listen to you when you are being morbid! [*She advances with the bottled coke.*]

BLANCHE [*with abrupt change to gaiety*]: Is that coke for me?

STELLA: Not for anyone else!

BLANCHE: Why, you precious thing, you! Is it just coke?

STELLA [*turning*]: You mean you want a shot in it!

BLANCHE: Well, honey, a shot never does a coke any harm! Let me? You mustn't wait on me!

STELLA: I like to wait on you, Blanche. It makes it seem more like home. [*She goes into the kitchen, finds a glass, and pours a shot of whisky into it.*]

BLANCHE: I have to admit I love to be waited on. . . .

[*She rushes into the bedroom.* STELLA *goes to her with the glass.* BLANCHE *suddenly clutches* STELLA'S *free hand with a moaning sound and presses the hand to her lips.* STELLA *is embarrassed by her show of emotion.* BLANCHE *speaks in a choked voice.*]

You're – you're – so *good* to me! And I –

STELLA: Blanche.

BLANCHE: I know, I won't! You hate me to talk senti-mental. But honey, *believe* I feel things more than I *tell* you! I *won't* stay long! I won't, I *promise* I –

STELLA: Blanche!

BLANCHE [*hysterically*]: I won't, I promise, *I'll* go! Go *soon!* I will *really!* I *won't* hang around until he – throws me out. . . .

STELLA: Now will you stop talking foolish?

BLANCHE: Yes, honey. Watch how you pour – that fizzy stuff foams over!

[BLANCHE *laughs shrilly and grabs the glass, but her hand shakes so it almost slips from her grasp.* STELLA *pours the coke into the glass. It foams over and spills.* BLANCHE *gives a piercing cry.*]

STELLA [*shocked by the cry*]: Heavens!

BLANCHE: Right on my pretty white skirt!

STELLA: Oh. . . . Use my hanky. Blot gently.

BLANCHE [*slowly recovering*]: I know – gently – gently . . .

STELLA: Did it stain?

BLANCHE: Not a bit. Ha-ha! Isn't that lucky? [*She sits down shakily, taking a grateful drink. She holds the glass in both hands and continues to laugh a little.*]

STELLA: Why did you scream like that?

BLANCHE: I don't know why I screamed! [*Continuing nervously.*] Mitch – Mitch is coming at seven. I guess I am just feeling nervous about our relations. [*She begins to talk rapidly and breathlessly.*] He hasn't gotten a thing but a good-night kiss, that's all I have given him, Stella. I want his respect. And men don't want anything they get too easy. But on the other hand men lose interest quickly. Especially when the girl is over – thirty. They think a girl over thirty ought to – the vulgar term is – 'put out'. . . . And I – I'm not 'putting out'. Of course he – he doesn't know – I mean I haven't informed him – of my real age!

STELLA: Why are you sensitive about your age?

BLANCHE: Because of hard knocks my vanity's been given. What I mean is – he thinks I'm sort of – prim and proper, you know! [*She laughs out sharply.*] I want to *deceive* him enough to make him – want me. . . .

STELLA: Blanche, do you want *him?*

BLANCHE: I want to *rest!* I want to breathe quietly again! Yes – I *want* Mitch . . . *very badly!* Just think! If it happens! I can leave here and not be anyone's problem. . . .

[STANLEY *comes round the corner with a drink under his belt.*]

STANLEY [*bawling*]: Hey, Steve! Hey, Eunice! Hey, Stella!

[*There are joyous calls from above. Trumpet and drums are heard from around the corner.*]

STELLA [*kissing* BLANCHE *impulsively*]: It *will* happen!

BLANCHE [*doubtfully*]: It will?

STELLA: It *will!* [*She goes across into the kitchen, looking back at* BLANCHE.] It will, honey, *it will.* . . . But don't take another drink! [*Her voice catches as she goes out of the door to meet her husband.*]

> [BLANCHE *sinks faintly back in her chair with her drink.* EUNICE *shrieks with laughter and runs down the steps.* STEVE *bounds after her with goat-like screeches and chases her around corner.* STANLEY *and* STELLA *twine arms as they follow, laughing.*
>
> *Dusk settles deeper. The music from the Four Deuces is slow and blue.*]

BLANCHE: Ah, me, ah, me, ah, me . . .

> [*Her eyes fall shut and the palm leaf drops from her fingers. She slaps her hand on the chair arm a couple of times; then she raises herself wearily to her feet and picks up the hand mirror.*
>
> *There is a little glimmer of lightning about the building.*
>
> *The* NEGRO WOMAN, *cackling hysterically, swaying drunkenly, comes around the corner from the Four Deuces. At the same time, a* YOUNG MAN *enters from the opposite direction. The* NEGRO WOMAN *snaps her fingers before his belt.*]

NEGRO WOMAN: Hey! Sugar!

> [*She says something indistinguishable. The* YOUNG MAN *shakes his head violently and edges hastily up the steps. He rings the bell.* BLANCHE *puts down the mirror. The* NEGRO WOMAN *has wandered down the street.*]

BLANCHE: Come in.

> [*The* YOUNG MAN *appears through the portières. She regards him with interest.*]

BLANCHE: Well, well! What can I do for *you?*
YOUNG MAN: I'm collecting for the *Evening Star.*
BLANCHE: I didn't know that stars took up collections.
YOUNG MAN: It's the paper.

BLANCHE: I know, I was joking – feebly ! Will you – have a drink?

YOUNG MAN: No, ma'am. No, thank you. I can't drink on the job.

BLANCHE: Oh, well, now, let's see. . . . No, I don't have a dime ! I'm not the lady of the house. I'm her sister from Mississippi. I'm one of those poor relations you've heard about.

YOUNG MAN: That's all right. I'll drop by later. [*He starts to go out. She approaches a little.*]

BLANCHE: Hey ! [*He turns back shyly. She puts a cigarette in a long holder.*] Could you give me a light? [*She crosses toward him. They meet at the door between the two rooms.*]

YOUNG MAN: Sure. [*He takes out a lighter.*] This doesn't always work.

BLANCHE: It's temperamental? [*It flares.*] Ah ! Thank you.

YOUNG MAN: Thank *you!* [*He starts away again.*]

BLANCHE: Hey ! [*He turns again, still more uncertainly. She goes close to him.*] What time is it?

YOUNG MAN: Fifteen of seven.

BLANCHE: So late? Don't you just love these long rainy afternoons in New Orleans when an hour isn't just an hour – but a little bit of Eternity dropped in your hands – and who knows what to do with it?

YOUNG MAN: Yes, ma'am.

[*In the ensuing pause, the 'blue piano' is heard. It continues through the rest of this scene and the opening of the next. The* YOUNG MAN *clears his throat and looks glancingly at the door.*]

BLANCHE: You – uh – didn't get wet in the shower?

YOUNG MAN: No, ma'am. I stepped inside.

BLANCHE: In a drug-store? And had a soda?

YOUNG MAN: Uhhuh.

BLANCHE: Chocolate?

YOUNG MAN: No, ma'am. Cherry.

BLANCHE: Mmmm!

YOUNG MAN: A cherry soda!

BLANCHE: You make my mouth water.

YOUNG MAN: Well, I'd better be –

BLANCHE: Young man! Young, young, young, young –
man! Has anyone ever told you that you look like a young
prince out of the Arabian Nights?

YOUNG MAN: No, ma'am.

[*The* YOUNG MAN *laughs uncomfortably and stands like a
bashful kid.* BLANCHE *speaks softly to him.*]

BLANCHE: Well, you do, honey lamb. Come here! Come
on over here like I told you! I want to kiss you – just
once – softly and sweetly on your mouth. [*Without waiting
for him to accept, she crosses quickly to him and presses her lips to
his.*] Run along now! It would be nice to keep you, but
I've got to be good and keep my hands off children.
Adios!

YOUNG MAN: Huh?

[*He stares at her a moment. She opens the door for him and
blows a kiss to him as he goes down the steps with a dazed look.
She stands there a little dreamily after he has disappeared.
Then* MITCH *appears around the corner with a bunch of
roses.*]

BLANCHE: Look who's coming! My Rosenkavalier! Bow to
me first! Now present them.

[*He does so. She curtsies low.*]

Ahhh! Merciiii!

SCENE SIX

It is about two a.m. the same night. The outer wall of the building is visible. BLANCHE *and* MITCH *come in. The utter exhaustion which only a neurasthenic personality can know is evident in* BLANCHE'S *voice and manner.* MITCH *is stolid but depressed. They have probably been out to the amusement park on Lake Pontchartrain, for* MITCH *is bearing, upside down, a plaster statuette of Mae West, the sort of prize won at shooting-galleries and carnival games of chance.*

BLANCHE [*stopping lifelessly at the steps*]: Well –

[MITCH *laughs uneasily.*]

Well ...

MITCH: I guess it must be pretty late – and you're tired.

BLANCHE: Even the hot tamale man has deserted the street, and he hangs on till the end. [MITCH *laughs uneasily again.*] How will you get home?

MITCH: I'll walk over to Bourbon and catch an owl-car.

BLANCHE [*laughing grimly*]: Is that streetcar named Desire still grinding along the tracks at this hour?

MITCH [*heavily*]: I'm afraid you haven't gotten much fun out of this evening, Blanche.

BLANCHE: I spoiled it for *you*.

MITCH: No, you didn't, but I felt all the time that I wasn't giving you much – entertainment.

BLANCHE: I simply couldn't rise to the occasion. That was all. I don't think I've ever tried so hard to be gay and made such a dismal mess of it. I get ten points for trying ! – I *did* try.

MITCH: Why did you try if you didn't feel like it, Blanche?

BLANCHE: I was just obeying the law of nature.

MITCH: Which law is that?

BLANCHE: The one that says the lady must entertain the

gentleman – or no dice ! See if you can locate my door-key in this purse. When I'm so tired my fingers are all thumbs !

MITCH [*rooting in her purse*]: This it?

BLANCHE: No, honey, that's the key to my trunk which I must soon be packing.

MITCH: You mean you are leaving here soon?

BLANCHE: I've outstayed my welcome.

MITCH: This it?

[*The music fades away.*]

BLANCHE: Eureka ! Honey, you open the door while I take a last look at the sky [*She leans on the porch rail. He opens the door and stands awkwardly behind her.*] I'm looking for the Pleiades, the Seven Sisters, but these girls are not out to-night. Oh, yes they are, there they are ! God bless them ! All in a bunch going home from their little bridge party. . . . Y' get the door open? Good boy ! I guess you – want to go now . . .

[*He shuffles and coughs a little.*]

MITCH: Can I – uh – kiss you – good-night?

BLANCHE: Why do you always ask me if you may?

MITCH: I don't know whether you want me to or not.

BLANCHE: Why should you be so doubtful?

MITCH: That night when we parked by the lake and I kissed you, you –

BLANCHE: Honey, it wasn't the kiss I objected to. I liked the kiss very much. It was the other little – familiarity – that I – felt obliged to – discourage. . . . I didn't resent it ! Not a bit in the world ! In fact, I was somewhat flattered that you – desired me ! But, honey, you know as well as I do that a single girl, a girl alone in the world, has got to keep a firm hold on her emotions or she'll be lost !

MITCH [*solemnly*]: Lost?

BLANCHE: I guess you are used to girls that like to be lost.

The kind that get lost immediately, on the first date!

MITCH: I like you to be exactly the way that you are, because in all my – experience – I have never known anyone like you.

[BLANCHE *looks at him gravely; then she bursts into laughter and then claps a hand to her mouth.*]

MITCH: Are you laughing at me?

BLANCHE: No, honey. The lord and lady of the house have not yet returned, so come in. We'll have a night-cap. Let's leave the lights off. Shall we?

MITCH: You just – do what you want to.

[BLANCHE *precedes him into the kitchen. The outer wall of the building disappears and the interiors of the two rooms can be dimly seen.*]

BLANCHE [*remaining in the first room*]: The other room's more comfortable – go on in. This crashing around in the dark is my search for some liquor.

MITCH: You want a drink?

BLANCHE: I want *you* to have a drink! You have been so anxious and solemn all evening, and so have I; we have both been anxious and solemn and now for these few last remaining moments of our lives together – I want to create – *joie de vivre!* I'm lighting a candle.

MITCH: That's good.

BLANCHE: We are going to be very Bohemian. We are going to pretend that we are sitting in a little artists' café on the Left Bank in Paris! [*She lights a candle stub and puts it in a bottle.*] *Je suis la Dame aux Camellias! Vous êtes – Armand!* Understand French?

MITCH [*heavily*]: Naw. Naw, I –

BLANCHE: *Voulez-vous couchez avec moi ce soir? Vous ne comprenez pas? Ah, quel dommage!* – I mean it's a damned good thing. ... I've found some liquor! Just enough for two shots without any dividends, honey ...

MITCH [*heavily*]: That's – good.

[*She enters the bedroom with the drinks and the candle.*]

BLANCHE: Sit down! Why don't you take off your coat and loosen your collar?

MITCH: I better leave it on.

BLANCHE: No. I want you to be comfortable.

MITCH: I am ashamed of the way I perspire. My shirt is sticking to me.

BLANCHE: Perspiration is healthy. If people didn't perspire they would die in five minutes. [*She takes his coat from him.*] This is a nice coat. What kind of material is it?

MITCH: They call that stuff alpaca.

BLANCHE: Oh. Alpaca.

MITCH: It's very light-weight alpaca.

BLANCHE: Oh. Light-weight alpaca.

MITCH: I don't like to wear a wash-coat even in summer because I sweat through it.

BLANCHE: Oh.

MITCH: And it don't look neat on me. A man with a heavy build has got to be careful of what he puts on him so he don't look too clumsy.

BLANCHE: You are not too heavy.

MITCH: You don't think I am?

BLANCHE: You are not the delicate type. You have a massive bone-structure and a very imposing physique.

MITCH: Thank you. Last Christmas I was given a membership to the New Orleans Athletic Club.

BLANCHE: Oh, good.

MITCH: It was the finest present I ever was given. I work out there with the weights and I swim and I keep myself fit. When I started there, I was getting soft in the belly but now my belly is hard. It is so hard that now a man can punch me in the belly and it don't hurt me. Punch me! Go on! See? [*She pokes lightly at him.*]

BLANCHE: Gracious. [*Her hand touches her chest.*]

MITCH: Guess how much I weigh, Blanche?

BLANCHE: Oh, I'd say in the vicinity of – one hundred and eighty?

MITCH: Guess again.

BLANCHE: Not that much?

MITCH: No. More.

BLANCHE: Well, you're a tall man and you can carry a good deal of weight without looking awkward.

MITCH: I weigh two hundred and seven pounds and I'm six feet one and a half inches tall in my bare feet – without shoes on. And that is what I weigh stripped.

BLANCHE: Oh, my goodness, me! It's awe-inspiring.

MITCH [*embarrassed*]: My weight is not a very interesting subject to talk about. [*He hesitates for a moment.*] What's yours?

BLANCHE: My weight?

MITCH: Yes.

BLANCHE: Guess!

MITCH: Let me lift you.

BLANCHE: Samson! Go on, lift me. [*He comes behind her and puts his hands on her waist and raises her lightly off the ground.*] Well?

MITCH: You are light as a feather.

BLANCHE: Ha-ha! [*He lowers her but keeps his hands on her waist.* BLANCHE *speaks with an affectation of demureness.*] You may release me now.

MITCH: Huh?

BLANCHE [*gaily*]: I said unhand me, sir. [*He fumblingly embraces her. Her voice sounds gently reproving.*] Now, Mitch. Just because Stanley and Stella aren't at home is no reason why you shouldn't behave like a gentleman.

MITCH: Just give me a slap whenever I step out of bounds.

BLANCHE: That won't be necessary. You're a natural gentleman, one of the very few that are left in the world. I don't want you to think that I am severe and old maid school-teacherish or anything like that. It's just – well –

MITCH: Huh?

BLANCHE: I guess it is just that I have – old-fashioned ideals! [*She rolls her eyes, knowing he cannot see her face.* MITCH *goes to the front door. There is a considerable silence between them.* BLANCHE *sighs and* MITCH *coughs self-consciously.*]

MITCH [*finally*]: Where's Stanley and Stella tonight?

BLANCHE: They have gone out. With Mr and Mrs Hubbel upstairs.

MITCH: Where did they go?

BLANCHE: I think they were planning to go to a midnight preview at Loew's State.

MITCH: We should all go out together some night.

BLANCHE: No. That wouldn't be a good plan.

MITCH: Why not?

BLANCHE: You are an old friend of Stanley's?

MITCH: We was together in the Two-forty-first.

BLANCHE: I guess he talks to you frankly?

MITCH: Sure.

BLANCHE: Has he talked to you about me?

MITCH: Oh – not very much.

BLANCHE: The way you say that, I suspect that he has.

MITCH: No, he hasn't said much.

BLANCHE: But what he *has* said. What would you say his attitude toward me was?

MITCH: Why do you want to ask that?

BLANCHE: Well –

MITCH: Don't you get along with him?

BLANCHE: What do you think?

MITCH: I don't think he understands you.

BLANCHE: That is putting it mildly. If it weren't for Stella about to have a baby, I wouldn't be able to endure things here.

MITCH: He isn't – nice to you?

BLANCHE: He is insufferably rude. Goes out of his way to offend me.

MITCH: In what way, Blanche?

BLANCHE: Why, in every conceivable way.

MITCH: I'm surprised to hear that.

BLANCHE: Are you?

MITCH: Well, I – don't see how anybody could be rude to you.

BLANCHE: It's really a pretty frightful situation. You see, there's no privacy here. There's just these portières between the two rooms at night. He stalks through the rooms in his underwear at night. And I have to ask him to close the bathroom door. That sort of commonness isn't necessary. You probably wonder why I don't move out. Well, I'll tell you frankly. A teacher's salary is barely sufficient for her living-expenses. I didn't save a penny last year and so I had to come here for the summer. That's why I have to put up with my sister's husband. And he has to put up with me, apparently so much against his wishes. . . . Surely he must have told you how much he hates me!

MITCH: I don't think he hates you.

BLANCHE: He hates me. Or why would he insult me? Of course there is such a thing as the hostility of – perhaps in some perverse kind of way he – No! To think of it makes me . . . [She makes a gesture of revulsion. Then she finishes her drink. A pause follows.]

MITCH: Blanche –

BLANCHE: Yes, honey?

MITCH: Can I ask you a question?

BLANCHE: Yes. What?

MITCH: How old are you?

[She makes a nervous gesture.]

BLANCHE: Why do you want to know?

MITCH: I talked to my mother about you and she said, 'How old is Blanche?' And I wasn't able to tell her. [There is another pause.]

BLANCHE: You talked to your mother about me?

MITCH: Yes.

BLANCHE: Why?

MITCH: I told my mother how nice you were, and I liked you.

BLANCHE: Were you sincere about that?

MITCH: You know I was.

BLANCHE: Why did your mother want to know my age?

MITCH: Mother is sick.

BLANCHE: I'm sorry to hear it. Badly?

MITCH: She won't live long. Maybe just a few months.

BLANCHE: Oh.

MITCH: She worries because I'm not settled.

BLANCHE: Oh.

MITCH: She wants me to be settled down before she – [*His voice is hoarse and he clears his throat twice, shuffling nervously around with his hands in and out of his pockets.*]

BLANCHE: You love her very much, don't you?

MITCH: Yes.

BLANCHE: I think you have a great capacity for devotion. You will be lonely when she passes on, won't you? [MITCH *clears his throat and nods.*] I understand what that is.

MITCH: To be lonely?

BLANCHE: I loved someone, too, and the person I loved I lost.

MITCH: Dead? [*She crosses to the window and sits on the sill, looking out. She pours herself another drink.*] A man?

BLANCHE: He was a boy, just a boy, when I was a very young girl. When I was sixteen, I made the discovery – love. All at once and much, much too completely. It was like you suddenly turned a blinding light on something that had always been half in shadow, that's how it struck the world for me. But I was unlucky. Deluded. There was something different about the boy, a nervousness, a softness and tenderness which wasn't like a man's, although he wasn't the least bit effeminate-looking – still – that thing was there. ... He came to me for help. I didn't know that. I didn't find out anything till after our marriage when we'd run away and come back and all I knew was I'd failed him in some mysterious way and wasn't able to give the help he needed but couldn't speak of! He was in the quicksands and clutching at me – but I wasn't holding him out, I was slipping in with him! I didn't know that. I didn't know anything except I loved him unendurably but without being able to help him or help myself. Then I found out. In the worst of all possible ways. By coming suddenly into a room that I thought was empty – which wasn't empty, but had two people in it ...

[*A locomotive is heard approaching outside. She claps her hands to her ears and crouches over. The headlight of the locomotive glares into the room as it thunders past. As the noise recedes she straightens slowly and continues speaking.*]

Afterwards we pretended that nothing had been discovered. Yes, the three of us drove out to Moon Lake Casino, very drunk and laughing all the way.

[*Polka music sounds, in a minor key faint with distance.*]

We danced the Varsouviana! Suddenly in the middle of the dance the boy I had married broke away from me and ran out of the casino. A few moments later – a shot!

[*The polka stops abruptly.*
    BLANCHE *rises stiffly. Then the polka resumes in a major key.*]

I ran out – all did – all ran and gathered about the terrible thing at the edge of the lake! I couldn't get near for the crowding. Then somebody caught my arm. 'Don't go any closer! Come back! You don't want to see!' See? See what! Then I heard voices say – Allan! Allan! The Grey

boy! He'd stuck the revolver into his mouth, and fired –
so that the back of his head had been – blown away!

[*She sways and covers her face.*]

It was because – on the dance-floor – unable to stop myself – I'd suddenly said – 'I know! I know! You disgust
me ...' And then the searchlight which had been turned
on the world was turned off again and never for one
moment since has there been any light that's stronger
than this – kitchen – candle. ...

[MITCH *gets up awkwardly and moves towards her a little.
The polka music increases.* MITCH *stands beside her.*]

MITCH [*drawing her slowly into his arms*]: You need somebody.
And I need somebody, too. Could it be – you and me,
Blanche?

[*She stares at him vacantly for a moment. Then with a soft cry
huddles in his embrace. She makes a sobbing effort to speak but
the words won't come. He kisses her forehead and her eyes and
finally her lips. The polka tune fades out. Her breath is drawn
and released in long, grateful sobs.*]

BLANCHE: Sometimes – there's God – so quickly!

SCENE SEVEN

It is late afternoon in mid-September.

The portières are open and a table is set for a birthday supper, with cake and flowers.

[STELLA *is completing the decorations as* STANLEY *comes in.*]

STANLEY: What's all this stuff for?

STELLA: Honey, it's Blanche's birthday.

STANLEY: She here?

STELLA: In the bathroom.

STANLEY [*mimicking*]: 'Washing out some things'?

STELLA: I reckon so.

STANLEY: How long she been in there?

STELLA: All afternoon.

STANLEY [*mimicking*]: 'Soaking in a hot tub'?

STELLA: Yes.

STANLEY: Temperature 100 on the nose, and she soaks herself in a hot tub.

STELLA: She says it cools her off for the evening.

STANLEY: And you run out an' get her cokes, I suppose? And serve 'em to Her Majesty in the tub? [STELLA *shrugs.*] Set down here a minute.

STELLA: Stanley, I've got things to do.

STANLEY: Set down! I've got th' dope on your big sister, Stella.

STELLA: Stanley, stop picking on Blanche.

STANLEY: That girl calls *me* common!

STELLA: Lately you have been doing all you can think of to rub her the wrong way, Stanley, and Blanche is sensitive and you've got to realize that Blanche and I grew up under very different circumstances than you did.

STANLEY: So I been told. And told and told and told!

You know she's been feeding us a pack of lies here?

STELLA: No, I don't, and –

STANLEY: Well, she has, however. But now the cat's out of the bag! I found out some things!

STELLA: What – things?

STANLEY: Things I already suspected. But now I got proof from the most reliable sources – which I have checked on!

[BLANCHE *is singing in the bathroom a saccharine popular ballad which is used contrapuntally with* STANLEY'S *speech.*]

STELLA [*to* STANLEY]: Lower your voice!

STANLEY: Some canary-bird, huh!

STELLA: Now please tell me quietly what you think you've found out about my sister.

STANLEY: Lie Number One: All this squeamishness she puts on! You should just know the line she's been feeding to Mitch. He thought she had never been more than kissed by a fellow! But Sister Blanche is no lily! Ha-ha! Some lily she is!

STELLA: What have you heard and who from?

STANLEY: Our supply-man down at the plant has been going through Laurel for years and he knows all about her and everybody else in the town of Laurel knows all about her. She is as famous in Laurel as if she was the President of the United States, only she is not respected by any party! This supply-man stops at a hotel called the Flamingo.

BLANCHE [*singing blithely*]:

'Say, it's only a paper moon, Sailing over a cardboard sea – But it wouldn't be make-believe If you believed in me!'

STELLA: What about the – Flamingo?

STANLEY: She stayed there, too.

STELLA: My sister lived at Belle Reve.

STANLEY: This is after the home-place had slipped through her lily-white fingers! She moved to the Flamingo! A

second-class hotel which has the advantage of not interfering in the private social life of the personalities there!
The Flamingo is used to all kinds of goings-on. But even
the management of the Flamingo was impressed by
Dame Blanche! In fact they were so impressed by Dame
Blanche that they requested her to turn in her room-key –
for permanently! This happened a couple of weeks before
she showed here.

BLANCHE [*singing*]:

'It's a Barnum and Bailey world, Just as phony as it can
be – But it wouldn't be make-believe If you believed in
me!'

STELLA: What – contemptible – lies!

STANLEY: Sure, I can see how you would be upset by this.
She pulled the wool over your eyes as much as Mitch's!

STELLA: It's pure invention! There's not a word of truth in
it and if I were a man and this creature had dared to invent such things in my presence–

BLANCHE [*singing*]:

'Without your love,
It's a honky-tonk parade!
Without your love,
It's a melody played In a penny arcade. ...'

STANLEY: Honey, I told you I thoroughly checked on these
stories! Now wait till I finish. The trouble with Dame
Blanche was that she couldn't put on her act any more in
Laurel! They got wised up after two or three dates with
her and then they quit, and she goes on to another, the
same old lines, same old act, same old hooey! But the
town was too small for this to go on for ever! And as time
went by she became a town character. Regarded as not
just different but downright loco – nuts.

[STELLA *draws back*.]

And for the last year or two she has been washed up like
poison. That's why she's here this summer, visiting

royalty, putting on all this act – because she's practically told by the mayor to get out of town! Yes, did you know there was an army camp near Laurel and your sister's was one of the places called 'Out-of-Bounds'?

BLANCHE:

'It's only a paper moon, Just as phony as it can be – But it wouldn't be make-believe If you believed in me!'

STANLEY: Well, so much for her being such a refined and particular type of girl. Which brings us to Lie Number Two.

STELLA: I don't want to hear any more!

STANLEY: She's not going back to teach school! In fact I am willing to bet you that she never had no idea of returning to Laurel! She didn't resign temporarily from the high school because of her nerves! No, siree, Bob! She didn't. They kicked her out of that high school before the spring term ended – and I hate to tell you the reason that step was taken! A seventeen-year-old boy – she'd gotten mixed up with!

BLANCHE:

'It's a Barnum and Bailey world, Just as phony as it can be –'

[*In the bathroom the water goes on loud; little breathless cries and peals of laughter are heard as if a child were frolicking in the tub.*]

STELLA: This is making me – sick!

STANLEY: The boy's dad learned about it and got in touch with the high school superintendent. Boy, oh, boy, I'd like to have been in that office when Dame Blanche was called on the carpet! I'd like to have seen her trying to squirm out of that one! But they had her on the hook good and proper that time and she knew that the jig was all up! They told her she better move on to some fresh territory. Yep, it was practickly a town ordinance passed against her!

[*The bathroom door is opened and* BLANCHE *thrusts her head out holding a towel about her hair.*]

BLANCHE: Stella!

STELLA [*faintly*]: Yes, Blanche?

BLANCHE: Give me another bath-towel to dry my hair with. I've just washed it.

STELLA: Yes, Blanche. [*She crosses in a dazed way from the kitchen to the bathroom door with a towel.*]

BLANCHE: What's the matter, honey?

STELLA: Matter? Why?

BLANCHE: You have such a strange expression on your face!

STELLA: Oh – [*She tries to laugh.*] I guess I'm a little tired!

BLANCHE: Why don't you bathe, too, soon as I get out?

STANLEY [*calling fron the kitchen*]: How soon is that going to be?

BLANCHE: Not so terribly long! Possess your soul in patience!

STANLEY: It's not my soul I'm worried about!

[BLANCHE *slams the door.* STANLEY *laughs harshly.* STELLA *comes slowly back into the kitchen.*]

STANLEY: Well, what do you think of it?

STELLA: I don't believe all of those stories and I think your supply-man was mean and rotten to tell them. It's possible that some of the things he said are partly true. There are things about my sister I don't approve of – things that caused sorrow at home. She was always – flighty!

STANLEY: Flighty is some word for it!

STELLA: But when she was young, very young, she had an experience that – killed her illusions!

STANLEY: What experience was that?

STELLA: I mean her marriage, when she was – almost a child! She married a boy who wrote poetry. . . . He was extremely good-looking. I think Blanche didn't just love

him but worshipped the ground he walked on! Adored
him and thought him almost too fine to be human! But
then she found out –

STANLEY: What?

STELLA: This beautiful and talented young man was a
degenerate. Didn't your supply-man give you that information?

STANLEY: All we discussed was recent history. That must
have been a pretty long time ago.

STELLA: Yes, it was – a pretty long time ago. ...

[STANLEY *comes up and takes her by the shoulders rather
gently. She gently withdraws from him. Automatically she
starts sticking little pink candles in the birthday cake.*]

STANLEY: How many candles you putting in that cake?

STELLA: I'll stop at twenty-five.

STANLEY: Is company expected?

STELLA: We asked Mitch to come over for cake and ice-
cream.

[STANLEY *looks a little uncomfortable. He lights a cigarette
from the one he has just finished.*]

STANLEY: I wouldn't be expecting Mitch over tonight.

[STELLA *pauses in her occupation with candles and looks
slowly around at* STANLEY.]

STELLA: *Why?*

STANLEY: Mitch is a buddy of mine. We were in the same
outfit together – Two-forty-first Engineers. We work in
the same plant and now on the same bowling team. You
think I could face him if –

STELLA: Stanley Kowalski, did you – did you repeat what
that –?

STANLEY: You're goddam right I told him! I'd have that
on my conscience the rest of my life if I knew all that stuff
and let my best friend get caught!

STELLA: Is Mitch through with her?

STANLEY: Wouldn't you be if –?

STELLA: I said, *Is Mitch through with her?*

[BLANCHE'S *voice is lifted again, serenely as a bell. She sings 'But it wouldn't be make-believe If you believed in me.'*]

STANLEY: No, I don't think he's necessarily through with her – just wised up!

STELLA: Stanley, she thought Mitch was – going to – going to marry her. I was hoping so, too.

STANLEY: Well, he's not going to marry her. Maybe he *was*, but he's not going to jump in a tank with a school of sharks – now! [*He rises*]: Blanche! Oh, Blanche! Can I please get in my bathroom? [*There is a pause.*]

BLANCHE: Yes, indeed, sir! Can you wait one second while I dry?

STANLEY: Having waited one hour I guess one second ought to pass in a hurry.

STELLA: And she hasn't got her job? Well, what will she do!

STANLEY: She's not stayin' here after Tuesday. You know that, don't you? Just to make sure I bought her ticket myself. A bus-ticket!

STELLA: In the first place, Blanche wouldn't go on a bus.

STANLEY: She'll go on a bus and like it.

STELLA: No, she won't, no, she won't, Stanley!

STANLEY: *She'll go!* Period. P.S. She'll go *Tuesday*!

STELLA [*slowly*]: What'll – she – do? What on earth will she – *do!*

STANLEY: Her future is mapped out for her.

STELLA: What do you mean?

[BLANCHE *sings.*]

STANLEY: Hey, canary bird! Toots! Get *OUT* of the *BATHROOM!* Must I speak more plainly?

[*The bathroom door flies open and* BLANCHE *emerges with a gay peal of laughter, but as* STANLEY *crosses past her, a frightened look appears in her face, almost a look of panic. He doesn't look at her but slams the bathroom door shut as he goes in.*]

BLANCHE [*snatching up a hair-brush*]: Oh, I feel so good after my long, hot bath, I feel so good and cool and – rested!

STELLA [*sadly and doubtfully from the kitchen*]: Do you, Blanche?

BLANCHE [*brushing her hair vigorously*]: Yes, I do, so refreshed. [*She tinkles her highball glass.*] A hot bath and a long, cold drink always gives me a brand-new outlook on life! [*She looks through the portières at* STELLA, *standing between them, and slowly stops brushing.*] Something has happened! – What is it?

STELLA [*turning quickly away*]: Why, nothing has happened, Blanche.

BLANCHE: You're lying! Something has!

[*She stares fearfully at* STELLA, *who pretends to be busy at the table. The distant piano goes into a hectic breakdown.*]

Three-quarters of an hour later.

The view through the big windows is fading gradually into a still-golden dusk. A torch of sunlight blazes on the side of a big water-tank or oil-drum across the empty lot toward the business district which is now pierced by pin-points of lighted windows or windows reflecting the sunset.

[*The three people are completing a dismal birthday supper.* STANLEY *looks sullen.* STELLA *is embarrassed and sad.*

BLANCHE *has a tight, artificial smile on her drawn face. There is a fourth place at the table which is left vacant.*]

BLANCHE [*suddenly*]: Stanley, tell us a joke, tell us a funny story to make us all laugh. I don't know what's the matter, we're all so solemn. Is it because I've been stood up by my beau?

[STELLA *laughs feebly.*]

It's the first time in my entire experience with men, and I've had a good deal of all sorts, that I've actually been stood up by anybody! Ha-ha! I don't know how to take it. . . . Tell us a funny little story, Stanley! Something to help us out.

STANLEY: I didn't think you liked my stories, Blanche.

BLANCHE: I like them when they're amusing but not indecent.

STANLEY: I don't know any refined enough for your taste.

BLANCHE: Then let me tell one.

STELLA: Yes, you tell one, Blanche. You used to know lots of good stories.

[*The music fades.*]

BLANCHE: Let me see, now. . . . I must run through my

repertoire! Oh, yes – I love parrot stories! Do you all like parrot stories? Well, this one's about the old maid and the parrot. This old maid, she had a parrot that cursed a blue streak and knew more vulgar expressions than Mr Kowalski!

STANLEY: Huh.

BLANCHE: And the only way to hush the parrot up was to put the cover back on its cage so it would think it was night and go back to sleep. Well, one morning the old maid had just uncovered the parrot for the day – when who should she see coming up the front walk but the preacher! Well, she rushed back to the parrot and slipped the cover back on the cage and then she let in the preacher. And the parrot was perfectly still, just as quiet as a mouse, but just as she was asking the preacher how much sugar he wanted in his coffee – the parrot broke the silence with a loud – (*she whistles*) – and said – 'God *damn*, but that was a short day!'

[*She throws back her head and laughs.* STELLA *also makes an ineffectual effort to seem amused.* STANLEY *pays no attention to the story but reaches way over the table to spear his fork into the remaining chop which he eats with his fingers.*]

BLANCHE: Apparently Mr Kowalski was not amused.

STELLA: Mr Kowalski is too busy making a pig of himself to think of anything else!

STANLEY: That's right, baby.

STELLA: Your face and your fingers are disgustingly greasy. Go and wash up and then help me clear the table.

[*He hurls a plate to the floor.*]

STANLEY: That's how I'll clear the table! [*He seizes her arm.*] Don't ever talk that way to me! 'Pig – Polack – disgusting – vulgar – greasy!' – them kind of words have been on your tongue and your sister's too much around here! What do you two think you are? A pair of queens?

Remember what Huey Long said – 'Every Man is a King!' And I am the king around here, so don't forget it! [*He hurls a cup and saucer to the floor.*] My place is cleared! You want me to clear your places?

[STELLA *begins to cry weakly.* STANLEY *stalks out on the porch and lights a cigarette.*

The Negro entertainers around the corner are heard.]

BLANCHE: What happened while I was bathing? What did he tell you, Stella?

STELLA: Nothing, nothing, nothing!

BLANCHE: I think he told you something about Mitch and me! You know why Mitch didn't come but you won't tell me! [STELLA *shakes her head helplessly.*] I'm going to call him!

STELLA: I wouldn't call him, Blanche.

BLANCHE: I am, I'm going to call him on the phone.

STELLA [*miserably*]: I wish you wouldn't.

BLANCHE: I intend to be given some explanation from someone!

[*She rushes to the phone in the bedroom.* STELLA *goes out on the porch and stares reproachfully at her husband. He grunts and turns away from her.*]

STELLA: I hope you're pleased with your doings. I never had so much trouble swallowing food in my life, looking at the girl's face and the empty chair. [*She cries quietly.*]

BLANCHE [*at the phone*]: Hello. Mr Mitchell, please.... Oh. ... I would like to leave a number if I may. Magnolia 9047. And say it's important to call. ... Yes, very important. ... Thank you. [*She remains by the phone with a lost, frightened look.*]

[STANLEY *turns slowly back towards his wife and takes her clumsily in his arms.*]

STANLEY: Stell, it's gonna be all right after she goes and

after you've had the baby. It's gonna be all right again between you and me the way that it was. You remember that way that it was? Them nights we had together? God, honey, it's gonna be sweet when we can make noise in the night the way that we used to and get the coloured lights going with nobody's sister behind the curtains to hear us!

[*Their upstairs neighbours are heard in bellowing laughter at something.* STANLEY *chuckles.*]

Steve an' Eunice ...

STELLA: Come on back in. [*She returns to the kitchen and starts lighting the candles on the white cake.*] Blanche?

BLANCHE: Yes. [*She returns from the bedroom to the table in the kitchen.*] Oh, those pretty, pretty little candles! Oh, don't burn them, Stella.

STELLA: I certainly will.

[STANLEY *comes back in.*]

BLANCHE: You ought to save them for baby's birthdays. Oh, I hope candles are going to glow in his life and I hope that his eyes are going to be like candles, like two blue candles lighted in a white cake!

STANLEY [*sitting down*]: What poetry!

BLANCHE: His Auntie knows candles aren't safe, that candles burn out in little boys' and girls' eyes, or wind blows them out and after that happens, electric light bulbs go on and you see too plainly ... [*She pauses reflectively for a moment.*] I shouldn't have called him.

STELLA: There's lots of things could have happened.

BLANCHE: There's no excuse for it, Stella. I don't have to put up with insults. I won't be taken for granted.

STANLEY: Goddamn, it's hot in here with the steam from the bathroom.

BLANCHE: I've said I was sorry three times. [*The piano fades out.*] I take hot baths for my nerves. Hydro-therapy, they call it. You healthy Polack, without a nerve in your body, of course you don't know what anxiety feels like!

STANLEY: I am not a Polack. People from Poland are Poles, not Polacks. But what I am is a one hundred per cent American, born and raised in the greatest country on earth and proud as hell of it, so don't ever call me a Polack.

[*The phone rings.* BLANCHE *rises expectantly.*]

BLANCHE: Oh, that's for me, I'm sure.

STANLEY: *I'm* not sure. Keep your seat. [*He crosses leisurely to phone.*] H'lo. Aw, yeh, hello, Mac.

[*He leans against wall, staring insultingly in at* BLANCHE. *She sinks back in her chair with a frightened look.* STELLA *leans over and touches her shoulder.*]

BLANCHE: Oh, keep your hands off me, Stella. What is the matter with you? Why do you look at me with that pitying look?

STANLEY [*bawling*]: QUIET IN THERE! – We've got a noisy woman on the place. – Go on, Mac. At Rileys? No, I don't wanta bowl at Riley's. I had a little trouble with Riley last week. I'm the team-captain, ain't I? All right, then, we're not gonna bowl at Riley's, we're gonna bowl at the West Side or the Gala! All right, Mac. See you!

[*He hangs up and returns to the table.* BLANCHE *fiercely controls herself, drinking quietly from her tumbler of water. He doesn't look at her but reaches in a pocket. Then he speaks slowly and with false amiability.*]

Sister Blanche, I've got a little birthday remembrance for you.

BLANCHE: Oh, have you, Stanley? I wasn't expecting any, I – I don't know why Stella wants to observe my birthday! I'd much rather forget it – when you – reach twenty-seven! Well – age is a subject that you'd prefer to – ignore!

STANLEY: Twenty-seven!

BLANCHE [*quickly*]: What is it? Is it for *me?*

[*He is holding a little envelope towards her.*]

STANLEY: Yes, I hope you like it!

BLANCHE: Why, why – Why, it's a –

STANLEY: Ticket! Back to Laurel! On the Greyhound! Tuesday!

[*The Varsouviana music steals in softly and continues playing.* STELLA *rises abruptly and turns her back.* BLANCHE *tries to smile. Then she tries to laugh. Then she gives both up and springs from the table and runs into the next room. She clutches her throat and then runs into the bathroom. Coughing, gagging sounds are heard.*]

Well!

STELLA: You didn't need to do that.

STANLEY: Don't forget all that I took off her.

STELLA: You needn't have been so cruel to someone alone as she is.

STANLEY: Delicate piece she is.

STELLA: She is. She was. You didn't know Blanche as a girl. Nobody, nobody, was tender and trusting as she was. But people like you abused her, and forced her to change.

[*He crosses into the bedroom, ripping off his shirt, and changes into a brilliant silk bowling shirt. She follows him.*]

Do you think you're going bowling now?

STANLEY: Sure.

STELLA: You're not going bowling. [*She catches hold of his shirt.*] Why did you do this to her?

STANLEY: I done nothing to no one. Let go of my shirt. You've torn it.

STELLA: I want to know why. Tell me why.

STANLEY: When we first met, me and you, you thought I was common. How right you was, baby. I was common as dirt. You showed me the snapshot of the place with the columns. I pulled you down off them columns and how you loved it, having them coloured lights going! And wasn't we happy together, wasn't it all okay till she showed here?

[STELLA *makes a slight movement. Her look goes suddenly inward as if some interior voice had called her name. She begins a slow, shuffling progress from the bedroom to the kitchen, leaning and resting on the back of the chair and then on the edge of a table with a blind look and listening expression.* STANLEY, *finishing with his shirt, is unaware of her reaction.*]

And wasn't we happy together? Wasn't it all okay? Till she showed here. Hoity-toity, describing me as an ape. [*He suddenly notices the change in* STELLA.] Hey, what is it, Stell? [*He crosses to her.*]

STELLA [*quietly*]: Take me to the hospital.

[*He is with her now, supporting her with his arm, murmuring indistinguishably as they go outside. The 'Varsouviana' is heard, its music rising with sinister rapidity as the bathroom door opens slightly.* BLANCHE *comes out twisting a washcloth. She begins to whisper the words as the light fades slowly.*]

BLANCHE: *El pan de mais, el pan de mais,*
　　　　　El pan de mais sin sal.
　　　　　El pan de mais, el pan de mais,
　　　　　El pan de mais sin sal ...

SCENE NINE

A while later that evening. BLANCHE *is seated in a tense hunched position in a bedroom chair that she has re-covered with diagonal green and white stripes. She has on her scarlet satin robe. On the table beside chair is a bottle of liquor and a glass. The rapid, feverish polka tune, the 'Varsouviana', is heard. The music is in her mind; she is drinking to escape it and the sense of disaster closing in on her, and she seems to whisper the words of the song. An electric fan is turning back and forth across her.*

> [MITCH *comes around the corner in work clothes: blue denim shirt and pants. He is unshaven. He climbs the steps to the door and rings.*
>
> BLANCHE *is startled.*]

BLANCHE: Who is it, please?
MITCH [*hoarsely*]: Me. Mitch.

> [*The polka tune stops.*]

BLANCHE: Mitch! – Just a minute.

> [*She rushes about frantically, hiding the bottle in a closet, crouching at the mirror and dabbing her face with cologne and powder. She is so excited that her breath is audible as she dashes about. At last she rushes to the door in the kitchen and lets him in.*]

Mitch! – Y'know, I really shouldn't let you in after the treatment I have received from you this evening! So utterly uncavalier! But hello, beautiful!

> [*She offers him her lips. He ignores it and pushes past her into the flat. She looks fearfully after him as he stalks into the bedroom.*]

My, my, what a cold shoulder! And a face like a

thundercloud! And such uncouth apparel! Why, you haven't even shaved! The unforgivable insult to a lady! But I forgive you. I forgive you because it's such a relief to see you. You've stopped that polka tune that I had caught in my head. Have you ever had anything caught in your head? Some words, a piece of music? That goes relentlessly on and on in your head? No, of course you haven't, you dumb angel-puss, you'd never get anything awful caught in your head!

[*He stares at her while she follows him while she talks. It is obvious that he has had a few drinks on the way over.*]

MITCH: Do we have to have that fan on?

BLANCHE: No!

MITCH: I don't like fans.

BLANCHE: Then let's turn it off, honey. I'm not partial to them!

[*She presses the switch and the fan nods slowly off. She clears her throat uneasily as* MITCH *plumps himself down on the bed in the bedroom and lights a cigarette.*]

I don't know what there is to drink. I – haven't investigated.

MITCH: I don't want Stan's liquor.

BLANCHE: It isn't Stan's. Everything here isn't Stan's. Some things on the premises are actually mine! How is your mother? Isn't your mother well?

MITCH: Why?

BLANCHE: Something's the matter tonight, but never mind. I won't cross-examine the witness. I'll just – [*She touches her forehead vaguely. The polka tune starts up again.*] – pretend I don't notice anything different about you! That – music again ...

MITCH: What music?

BLANCHE: The 'Varsouviana'? The polka tune they were playing when Allan – Wait!

[*A distant revolver shot is heard,* BLANCHE *seems relieved.*]

There now, the shot! It always stops after that.

[*The polka music dies out again.*]

Yes, now it's stopped.

MITCH: Are you boxed out of your mind?

BLANCHE: I'll go and see what I can find in the way of – [*She crosses into the closet, pretending to search for the bottle.*] Oh, by the way, excuse me for not being dressed. But I'd practically given you up! Had you forgotten your invitation to supper?

MITCH: I wasn't going to see you any more.

BLANCHE: Wait a minute. I can't hear what you're saying and you talk so little that when you do say something, I don't want to miss a single syllable of it. . . . What am I looking around here for? Oh, yes – liquor! We've had so much excitement around here this evening that I *am* boxed out of my mind! [*She pretends suddenly to find the bottle. He draws his foot up on the bed and stares at her contemptuously.*] Here's something. Southern Comfort! What is that I wonder?

MITCH: If you don't know, it must belong to Stan.

BLANCHE: Take your foot off the bed. It has a light cover on it. Of course you boys don't notice things like that. I've done so much with this place since I've been here.

MITCH: I bet you have.

BLANCHE: You saw it before I came. Well, look at it now! This room is almost – dainty! I want to keep it that way. I wonder if this stuff ought to be mixed with something? Ummm, it's sweet, so sweet! It's terribly, terribly sweet! Why, it's a *liqueur*, I believe! Yes, that's what it *is*, a liqueur! [MITCH *grunts.*] I'm afraid you won't like it, but try it, and maybe you will.

MITCH: I told you already I don't want none of his liquor and I mean it. You ought to lay off his liquor. He says you been lapping it up all summer like a wild-cat!

BLANCHE: What a fantastic statement! Fantastic of him to say it, fantastic of you to repeat it! I won't descend to the level of such cheap accusations to answer them, even!

MITCH: Huh.

BLANCHE: What's in your mind? I see something in your eyes!

MITCH [*getting up*]: It's dark in here.

BLANCHE: I like it dark. The dark is comforting to me.

MITCH: I don't think I ever seen you in the light. [BLANCHE *laughs breathlessly*.] That's a fact!

BLANCHE: Is it?

MITCH: I've never seen you in the afternoon.

BLANCHE: Whose fault is that?

MITCH: You never want to go out in the afternoon.

BLANCHE: Why, Mitch, you're at the plant in the afternoon!

MITCH: Not Sunday afternoon. I've asked you to go out with me sometimes on Sundays but you always make an excuse. You never want to go out till after six and then it's always some place that's not lighted much.

BLANCHE: There is some obscure meaning in this but I fail to catch it.

MITCH: What it means is I've never had a real good look at you, Blanche.

BLANCHE: What are you leading up to?

MITCH: Let's turn the light on here.

BLANCHE [*fearfully*]: Light? Which light? What for?

MITCH: This one with the paper thing on it. [*He tears the paper lantern off the light bulb. She utters a frightened gasp.*]

BLANCHE: What did you do that for?

MITCH: So I can take a look at you good and plain!

BLANCHE: Of course you don't really mean to be insulting!

MITCH: No, just realistic.

BLANCHE: I don't want realism.

MITCH: Naw, I guess not.

BLANCHE: I'll tell you what I want. Magic! [MITCH *laughs.*] Yes, yes, magic! I try to give that to people. I misrepresent things to them. I don't tell the truth. I tell what *ought* to be truth. And if that is sinful, then let me be damned for it! – *Don't turn the light on!*

[MITCH *crosses to the switch. He turns the light on and stares at her. She cries out and covers her face. He turns the light off again.*]

MITCH [*slowly and bitterly*]: I don't mind you being older than what I thought. But all the rest of it – God! That pitch about your ideals being so old-fashioned and all the malarkey that you've dished out all summer. Oh, I knew you weren't sixteen any more. But I was a fool enough to believe you was straight.

BLANCHE: Who told you I wasn't – 'straight'? My loving brother-in-law. And you believed him.

MITCH: I called him a liar at first. And then I checked on the story. First I asked our supply-man who travels through Laurel. And then I talked directly over long-distance to this merchant.

BLANCHE: Who is the merchant?

MITCH: Kiefaber.

BLANCHE: The merchant Kiefaber of Laurel! I know the man. He whistled at me. I put him in his place. So now for revenge he makes up stories about me.

MITCH: Three people, Kiefaber, Stanley, and Shaw, swore to them!

BLANCHE: Rub-a-dub-dub, three men in a tub! And such a filthy tub!

MITCH: Didn't you stay at a hotel called The Flamingo?

BLANCHE: Flamingo? No! Tarantula was the name of it! I stayed at a hotel called The Tarantula Arms!

MITCH [*stupidly*]: Tarantula?

BLANCHE: Yes, a big spider! That's where I brought my victims. [*She pours herself another drink.*] Yes, I had many intimacies with strangers. After the death of Allan – intimacies with strangers was all I seemed able to fill my empty heart with. . . . I think it was panic, just panic, that drove me from one to another, hunting for some protection – here and there, in the most – unlikely places – even, at last, in a seventeen-year-old boy but – somebody wrote the superintendent about it – 'This woman is morally unfit for her position!'

[*She throws back her head with convulsive, sobbing laughter. Then she repeats the statement, gasps, and drinks.*]

True? Yes, I suppose – unfit somehow – anyway. . . . So I came here. There was nowhere else I could go. I was played out. You know what played out is? My youth was suddenly gone up the water-spout, and – I met you. You said you needed somebody. Well, I needed somebody, too. I thanked God for you, because you seemed to be gentle – a cleft in the rock of the world that I could hide in! The poor man's Paradise – is a little peace. . . . But I guess I was asking, hoping – too much! Kiefaber, Stanley, and Shaw have tied an old tin can to the tail of the kite.

[*There is a pause.* MITCH *stares at her dumbly.*]

MITCH: You lied to me, Blanche.
BLANCHE: Don't say I lied to you.
MITCH: Lies, lies, inside and out, all lies.
BLANCHE: Never inside, I didn't lie in my heart. . . .

[*A Vendor comes around the corner. She is a blind* MEXICAN WOMAN *in a dark shawl, carrying bunches of those gaudy tin flowers that lower-class Mexicans display at funerals and other festive occasions. She is calling barely audibly. Her figure is only faintly visible outside the building.*]

MEXICAN WOMAN: *Flores. Flores. Flores para los muertos. Flores. Flores.*
BLANCHE: What? Oh! Somebody outside. . . . I – lived in a

house where dying old women remembered their dead
men . . .

MEXICAN WOMAN: *Flores. Flores para los muertos* . . .

[*The polka tune fades in.*]

BLANCHE [*as if to herself*]: Crumble and fade and – regrets –
recriminations . . . 'If you'd done this, it wouldn't've cost
me that!'

MEXICAN WOMAN: *Corones para los muertos. Corones* . . .

BLANCHE: Legacies! Huh . . . And other things such as
blood-stained pillow-slips – 'Her linen needs changing' –
'Yes, Mother. But couldn't we get a coloured girl to do
it?' No, we couldn't of course. Everything gone but the –

MEXICAN WOMAN: *Flores.*

BLANCHE: Death – I used to sit here and she used to sit
over there and death was as close as you are. . . . We didn't
dare even admit we had ever heard of it!

MEXICAN WOMAN: *Flores para los muertos, flores – flores* . . .

BLANCHE: The opposite is desire. So do you wonder? How
could you possibly wonder! Not far from Belle Reve,
before we had lost Belle Reve, was a camp where they
trained young soldiers. On Saturday nights they would go
in town to get drunk –

MEXICAN WOMAN [*softly*]: *Corones* . . .

BLANCHE: – and on the way back they would stagger on to
my lawn and call – 'Blanche! Blanche!' – The deaf old
lady remaining suspected nothing. But sometimes I
slipped outside to answer their calls. . . . Later the paddy-
wagon would gather them up like daisies . . . the long way
home . . .

[*The* MEXICAN WOMAN *turns slowly and drifts back off
with her soft mournful cries.* BLANCHE *goes to the dresser and
leans forward on it. After a moment,* MITCH *rises and follows
her purposefully. The polka music fades away. He places his
hands on her waist and tries to turn her about.*]

BLANCHE: What do you want?

MITCH [*fumbling to embrace her*]: What I been missing all summer.

BLANCHE: Then marry me, Mitch!

MITCH: I don't think I want to marry you any more.

BLANCHE: No?

MITCH [*dropping his hands from her waist*]: You're not clean enough to bring in the house with my mother.

BLANCHE: Go away, then. [*He stares at her.*] Get out of here quick before I start screaming fire! [*Her throat is tightening with hysteria.*] Get out of here quick before I start screaming fire.

[*He still remains staring. She suddenly rushes to the big window with its pale blue square of the soft summer light and cries wildly.*]

Fire! Fire! Fire!

[*With a startled gasp,* MITCH *turns and goes out of the outer door, clatters awkwardly down the steps and around the corner of the building.* BLANCHE *staggers back from the window and falls to her knees. The distant piano is slow and blue.*]

SCENE TEN

It is a few hours later that night.

   BLANCHE *has been drinking fairly steadily since* MITCH *left.*
She has dragged her wardrobe trunk into the centre of the bedroom. It
hangs open with flowery dresses thrown across it. As the drinking
and packing went on, a mood of hysterical exhilaration came into her
and she has decked herself out in a somewhat soiled and crumpled
white satin evening gown and a pair of scuffed silver slippers with
brilliants set in their heels.

   [*Now she is placing the rhinestone tiara on her head before the*
   mirror of the dressing-table and murmuring excitedly as if to a
   group of spectral admirers.]

BLANCHE: How about taking a swim, a moonlight swim at
   the old rock-quarry? If anyone's sober enough to drive
   a car! Ha-Ha! Best way in the world to stop your head
   buzzing! Only you've got to be careful to dive where the
   deep pool is – if you hit a rock you don't come up till tomorrow. . . .

   [*Tremblingly she lifts the hand mirror for a closer inspection.*
   She catches her breath and slams the mirror face down with
   such violence that the glass cracks. She moans a little and
   attempts to rise.

   STANLEY *appears around the corner of the building. He*
   still has on the vivid green silk bowling shirt. As he rounds the
   corner the honky-tonk music is heard. It continues softly
   throughout the scene.

   He enters the kitchen, slamming the door. As he peers in at
   BLANCHE, *he gives a low whistle. He has had a few drinks*
   on the way and has brought some quart beer bottles home with
   him.]

BLANCHE: How is my sister?

STANLEY: She is doing okay.

BLANCHE: And how is the baby?

STANLEY [*grinning amiably*]: The baby won't come before morning so they told me to go home and get a little shut-eye.

BLANCHE: Does that mean we are to be alone in here?

STANLEY: Yep. Just me and you, Blanche. Unless you got somebody hid under the bed. What've you got on those fine feathers for?

BLANCHE: Oh, that's right. You left before my wire came.

STANLEY: You got a wire?

BLANCHE: I received a telegram from an old admirer of mine.

STANLEY: Anything good?

BLANCHE: I think so. An invitation.

STANLEY: What to? A fireman's ball?

BLANCHE [*throwing back her head*]: A cruise of the Caribbean on a yacht!

STANLEY: Well, well. What do you know?

BLANCHE: I have never been so surprised in my life.

STANLEY: I guess not.

BLANCHE: It came like a bolt from the blue!

STANLEY: Who did you say it was from?

BLANCHE: An old beau of mine.

STANLEY: The one that give you the white fox-pieces!

BLANCHE: Mr Shep Huntleigh. I wore his ATO pin my last year at college. I hadn't seen him again until last Christmas. I ran in to him on Biscayne Boulevard. Then – just now – this wire – inviting me on a cruise of the Caribbean! The problem is clothes. I tore into my trunk to see what I have that's suitable for the tropics!

STANLEY: And come up with that – gorgeous – diamond – tiara?

BLANCHE: This old relic! Ha-ha! It's only rhinestones.

STANLEY: Gosh. I thought it was Tiffany diamonds. [*He unbuttons his shirt.*]

BLANCHE: Well, anyhow, I shall be entertained in style.

STANLEY: Uh-huh. It goes to show, you never know what is coming.

BLANCHE: Just when I thought my luck had begun to fail me —

STANLEY: Into the picture pops this Miami millionaire.

BLANCHE: This man is not from Miami. This man is from Dallas.

STANLEY: This man is from Dallas?

BLANCHE: Yes, this man is from Dallas where gold spouts out of the ground!

STANLEY: Well, just so he's from somewhere! [*He starts removing his shirt.*]

BLANCHE: Close the curtains before you undress any further.

STANLEY [*amiably*]: This is all I'm going to undress right now. [*He rips the sack off a quart beer-bottle.*] Seen a bottle-opener?

> [*She moves slowly towards the dresser, where she stands with her hands knotted together.*]

I used to have a cousin who could open a beer-bottle with his teeth. [*Pounding the bottle cap on the corner of table.*] That was his only accomplishment, all he could do — he was just a human bottle-opener. And then one time, at a wedding party, he broke his front teeth off! After that he was so ashamed of himself he used t' sneak out of the house when company came . . .

> [*The bottle cap pops off and a geyser of foam shoots up.* STANLEY *laughs happily, holding up the bottle over his head.*]

Ha-ha! Rain from heaven! [*He extends the bottle towards her.*] Shall we bury the hatchet and make it a loving-cup? Huh?

BLANCHE: No, thank you.

STANLEY: Well, it's a red-letter night for us both. You having an oil-millionaire and me having a baby.

[*He goes to the bureau in the bedroom and crouches to remove something from the bottom drawer.*]

BLANCHE [*drawing back*]: What are you doing in here?

STANLEY: Here's something I always break out on special occasions like this! The silk pyjamas I wore on my wedding night!

BLANCHE: Oh.

STANLEY: When the telephone rings and they say, 'You've got a son!' I'll tear this off and wave it like a flag! [*He shakes out a brilliant pyjama coat.*] I guess we are both entitled to put on the dog. [*He goes back to the kitchen with the coat over his arm.*]

BLANCHE: When I think of how divine it is going to be to have such a thing as privacy once more – I could weep with joy!

STANLEY: This millionaire from Dallas is not going to interfere with your privacy any?

BLANCHE: It won't be the sort of thing you have in mind. This man is a gentleman and he respects me. [*Improvising feverishly.*] What he wants is my companionship. Having great wealth sometimes makes people lonely!

STANLEY: I wouldn't know about that.

BLANCHE: A cultivated woman, a woman of intelligence and breeding, can enrich a man's life – immeasurably! I have those things to offer, and this doesn't take them away. Physical beauty is passing. A transitory possession. But beauty of the mind and richness of the spirit and tenderness of the heart – and I have all of those things – aren't taken away, but grow! Increase with the years! How strange that I should be called a destitute woman! When I have all of these treasures locked in my heart. [*A choked sob comes from her.*] I think of myself as a very, very rich woman! But I have been foolish – casting my pearls before swine!

STANLEY: Swine, huh?

BLANCHE: Yes, swine! Swine! And I'm thinking not only of you but of your friend, Mr Mitchell. He came to see me tonight. He dared to come here in his work-clothes! And to repeat slander to me, vicious stories that he had gotten from you! I gave him his walking papers ...

STANLEY: You did, huh?

BLANCHE: But then he came back. He returned with a box of roses to beg my forgiveness! He implored my forgiveness. But some things are not forgivable. Deliberate cruelty is not forgivable. It is the one unforgivable thing in my opinion and it is the one thing of which I have never, never been guilty. And so I told him, I said to him, Thank you, but it was foolish of me to think that we could ever adapt ourselves to each other. Our ways of life are too different. Our attitudes and our backgrounds are incompatible. We have to be realistic about such things. So farewell, my friend! And let there be no hard feelings ...

STANLEY: Was this before or after the telegram came from the Texas oil millionaire?

BLANCHE: What telegram? No! No, after! As a matter of fact, the wire came just as –

STANLEY: As a matter of fact there wasn't no wire at all!

BLANCHE: Oh, oh!

STANLEY: There isn't no millionaire! And Mitch didn't come back with roses 'cause I know where he is –

BLANCHE: Oh!

STANLEY: There isn't a goddam thing but imagination!

BLANCHE: Oh!

STANLEY: And lies and conceit and tricks!

BLANCHE: Oh!

STANLEY: And look at yourself! Take a look at yourself in that worn-out Mardi Gras outfit, rented for fifty cents

from some rag-picker! And with the crazy crown on!
What queen do you think you are!

BLANCHE: Oh – God . . .

STANLEY: I've been on to you from the start! Not once did
you pull any wool over this boy's eyes! You come in here
and sprinkle the place with powder and spray perfume
and cover the light-bulb with a paper lantern, and lo and
behold the place has turned into Egypt and you are the
Queen of the Nile! Sitting on your throne and swilling
down my liquor! I say – *Ha – Ha!* Do you hear me? *Ha –
ha – ha!* [*He walks into the bedroom.*]

BLANCHE: Don't come in here!

> [*Lurid reflections appear on the walls around* BLANCHE. *The
> shadows are of a grotesque and menacing form. She catches her
> breath, crosses to the phone, and jiggles the hook.* STANLEY
> goes into the bathroom and closes the door.*]

Operator, operator! Give me long-distance, please. . . . I
want to get in touch with Mr Shep Huntleigh of Dallas.
He's so well known he doesn't require any address. Just
ask anybody who – Wait! – No, I couldn't find it right
now. . . . Please understand, I – No! No, wait! . . . One
moment! Someone is – Nothing! Hold on, please!

> [*She sets the phone down and crosses warily into the kitchen.*
> *The night is filled with inhuman voices like cries in a jungle.*
> *The shadows and lurid reflections move sinuously as flames
> along the wall spaces.*
> *Through the back wall of the rooms, which have become
> transparent, can be seen the sidewalk. A prostitute has rolled a
> drunkard. He pursues her along the walk, overtakes her, and
> there is a struggle. A policeman's whistle breaks it up. The
> figures disappear.*
> *Some moments later the* NEGRO WOMAN *appears around
> the corner with a sequined bag which the prostitute had dropped
> on the walk. She is rooting excitedly through it.*

[*BLANCHE presses her knuckles to her lips and returns slowly to the phone. She speaks in a hoarse whisper.*]

Operator! Operator! Never mind long-distance. Get Western Union. There isn't time to be – Western – Western Union.

[*She waits anxiously.*]

Western Union? Yes! I – want to – Take down this message! 'In desperate, desperate circumstances! Help me! Caught in a trap. Caught in –' *Oh!*

[*The bathroom door is thrown open and* STANLEY *comes out in the brilliant silk pyjamas. He grins at her as he knots the tasselled sash about his waist. She gasps and backs away from the phone. He stares at her for a count of ten. Then a clicking becomes audible from the telephone, steady and rasping.*]

STANLEY: You left th' phone off th' hook.

[*He crosses to it deliberately and sets it back on the hook. After he has replaced it, he stares at her again, his mouth slowly curving into a grin, as he waits between* BLANCHE *and the outer door.*

The barely audible 'blue piano' begins to drum up louder. The sound of it turns into the roar of an approaching locomotive. BLANCHE *crouches, pressing her fists to her ears until it has gone by.*]

BLANCHE [*finally straightening*]: Let me – let me get by you!

STANLEY: Get by me? Sure. Go ahead. [*He moves back a pace in the doorway.*]

BLANCHE: You – you stand over there! [*She indicates a further position.*]

STANLEY [*grinning*]: You got plenty of room to walk by me now.

BLANCHE: Not with you there! But I've got to get out somehow!

STANLEY: You think I'll interfere with you? Ha-ha!

[*The 'blue piano' goes softly. She turns confusedly and makes a faint gesture. The inhuman jungle voices rise up. He takes a step towards her, biting his tongue which protrudes between his lips.*]

STANLEY [*softly*]: Come to think of it – maybe you wouldn't be bad to – interfere with . . .

[BLANCHE *moves backward through the door into the bedroom.*]

BLANCHE: Stay back! Don't you come towards me another step or I'll –

STANLEY: What?

BLANCHE: Some awful thing will happen! It will!

STANLEY: What are you putting on now?

[*They are now both inside the bedroom.*]

BLANCHE: I warn you, don't, I'm in danger!

[*He takes another step. She smashes a bottle on the table and faces him, clutching the broken top.*]

STANLEY: What did you do that for?

BLANCHE: So I could twist the broken end in your face!

STANLEY: I bet you would do that!

BLANCHE: I would: I will if you –

STANLEY: Oh! So you want some rough-house! All right, let's have some rough-house!

[*He springs towards her, overturning the table. She cries out and strikes at him with the bottle top but he catches her wrist.*]

Tiger – tiger! Drop the bottle-top! Drop it! We've had this date with each other from the beginning!

[*She moans. The bottle-top falls. She sinks to her knees. He picks up her inert figure and carries her to the bed. The hot trumpet and drums from the Four Deuces sound loudly.*]

SCENE ELEVEN

It is some weeks later. STELLA *is packing* BLANCHE'S *things. Sound of water can be heard running in the bathroom.*

The portières are partly open on the poker players – STANLEY, STEVE, MITCH, *and* PABLO – *who sit around the table in the kitchen. The atmosphere of the kitchen is now the same raw, lurid one of the disastrous poker night.*

The building is framed by the sky of turquoise. STELLA *has been crying as she arranges the flowery dresses in the open trunk.*

[EUNICE *comes down the steps from her flat above and enters the kitchen. There is another burst from the poker table.*]

STANLEY: Drew to an inside straight and made it, by God.

PABLO: *Maldita sea tu suerto!*

STANLEY: Put it in English, greaseball.

PABLO: I am cursing your goddam luck.

STANLEY [*prodigiously elated*]: You know what luck is? Luck is believing you're lucky. Take at Salerno. I believed I was lucky. I figured that 4 out of 5 would not come through but I would ... and I did. I put that down as a rule. To hold front position in this rat-race you've got to believe you are lucky.

MITCH: You ... you ... you. ... Brag ... brag ... bull ... bull.

[STELLA *goes into the bedroom and starts folding a dress.*]

STANLEY: What's the matter with him?

EUNICE [*walking past the table*]: I always did say that men are callous things with no feelings, but this does beat anything. Making pigs of yourselves. [*She comes through the portières into the bedroom.*]

STANLEY: What's the matter with her?

STELLA: How is my baby?

EUNICE: Sleeping like a little angel. Brought you some grapes. [*She puts them on a stool and lowers her voice.*] Blanche?

STELLA: Bathing.

EUNICE: How is she?

STELLA: She wouldn't eat anything but asked for a drink.

EUNICE: What did you tell her?

STELLA: I – just told her that – we'd made arrangements for her to rest in the country. She's got it mixed in her mind with Shep Huntleigh.

[BLANCHE *opens the bathroom door slightly.*]

BLANCHE: Stella.

STELLA: Yes, Blanche?

BLANCHE: If anyone calls while I'm bathing take the number and tell them I'll call right back.

STELLA: Yes.

BLANCHE: That cool yellow silk – the bouclé. See if it's crushed. If it's not too crushed I'll wear it and on the lapel that silver and turquoise pin in the shape of a seahorse. You will find them in the heart-shaped box I keep my accessories in. And Stella ... Try and locate a bunch of artificial violets in that box, too, to pin with the seahorse on the lapel of the jacket.

[*She closes the door.* STELLA *turns to* EUNICE.]

STELLA: I don't know if I did the right thing.

EUNICE: What else could you do?

STELLA: I couldn't believe her story and go on living with Stanley.

EUNICE: Don't ever believe it. Life has got to go on. No matter what happens, you've got to keep on going.

[*The bathroom door opens a little.*]

BLANCHE [*looking out*]: Is the coast clear?

STELLA: Yes, Blanche. [*To* EUNICE.] Tell her how well she's looking.

BLANCHE: Please close the curtains before I come out.

STELLA: They're closed.

STANLEY: – How many for you.

PABLO: Two. –

STEVE: – Three.

[BLANCHE *appears in the amber light of the door. She has a tragic radiance in her red satin robe following the sculptural lines of her body. The 'Varsouviana' rises audibly as* BLANCHE *enters the bedroom.*]

BLANCHE [*with faintly hysterical vivacity*]: I have just washed my hair.

STELLA: Did you?

BLANCHE: I'm not sure I got the soap out.

EUNICE: Such fine hair!

BLANCHE [*accepting the compliment*]: It's a problem. Didn't I get a call?

STELLA: Who from, Blanche?

BLANCHE: Shep Huntleigh ...

STELLA: Why, not yet, honey!

BLANCHE: How strange! I –

[*At the sound of* BLANCHE'S *voice* MITCH'S *arm supporting his cards has sagged and his gaze is dissolved into space.* STANLEY *slaps him on the shoulder.*]

STANLEY: Hey, Mitch, come to!

[*The sound of this new voice shocks* BLANCHE. *She makes a shocked gesture, forming his name with her lips.* STELLA *nods and looks quickly away.* BLANCHE *stands quite still for some moments – the silver-backed mirror in her hand and a look of sorrowful perplexity as though all human experience shows on her face.* BLANCHE *finally speaks with sudden hysteria.*]

BLANCHE: What's going on here?

[*She turns from* STELLA *to* EUNICE *and back to* STELLA. *Her rising voice penetrates the concentration of the game.*

MITCH *ducks his head lower but* STANLEY *shoves back his chair as if about to rise.* STEVE *places a restraining hand on his arm.*]

BLANCHE [*continuing*]: What's happened here? I want an explanation of what's happened here.

STELLA [*agonizingly*]: Hush! Hush!

EUNICE: Hush! Hush! Honey.

STELLA: Please, Blanche.

BLANCHE: Why are you looking at me like that? Is something wrong with me?

EUNICE: You look wonderful, Blanche. Don't she look wonderful?

STELLA: Yes.

EUNICE: I understand you are going on a trip.

STELLA: Yes, Blanche *is*. She's going on vacation.

EUNICE: I'm green with envy.

BLANCHE: Help me, help me get dressed!

STELLA [*handing her dress*]: Is this what you —

BLANCHE: Yes, it will do! I'm anxious to get out of here — this place is a trap!

EUNICE: What a pretty blue jacket.

STELLA: It's lilac coloured.

BLANCHE: You're both mistaken. It's Della Robbia blue. The blue of the robe in the old Madonna pictures. Are these grapes washed?

[*She fingers the bunch of grapes which* EUNICE *has brought in.*]

EUNICE: Huh?

BLANCHE: Washed, I said. Are they washed?

EUNICE: They're from the French Market.

BLANCHE: That doesn't mean they've been washed. [*The cathedral bells chime.*] Those cathedral bells — they're the only clean thing in the Quarter. Well, I'm going now. I'm ready to go.

EUNICE [*whispering*]: She's going to walk out before they get here.

STELLA: Wait, Blanche.

BLANCHE: I don't want to pass in front of those men.

EUNICE: Then wait'll the game breaks up.

STELLA: Sit down and ...

[BLANCHE *turns weakly, hesitantly about. She lets them push her into a chair.*]

BLANCHE: I can smell the sea air. The rest of my time I'm going to spend on the sea. And when I die, I'm going to die on the sea. You know what I shall die of? [*She plucks a grape.*] I shall die of eating an unwashed grape one day out on the ocean. I will die – with my hand in the hand of some nice-looking ship's doctor, a very young one with a small blond moustache and a big silver watch. 'Poor lady,' they'll say, 'the quinine did her no good. That unwashed grape has transported her soul to heaven.' [*The cathedral chimes are heard.*] And I'll be buried at sea sewn up in a clean white sack and dropped overboard – at noon – in the blaze of summer – and into an ocean as blue as [*chimes again*] my first lover's eyes!

[*A* DOCTOR *and a* MATRON *have appeared around the corner of the building and climbed the steps to the porch. The gravity of their profession is exaggerated – the unmistakable aura of the state institution with its cynical detachment. The* DOCTOR *rings the doorbell. The murmur of the game is interrupted.*]

EUNICE [*whispering to* STELLA]: That must be them.

[STELLA *presses her fist to her lips.*]

BLANCHE [*rising slowly*]: What is it?

EUNICE [*affectedly casual*]: Excuse me while I see who's at the door.

STELLA: Yes.

[EUNICE *goes into the kitchen.*]

BLANCHE [*tensely*]: I wonder if it's for me.

[*A whispered colloquy takes place at the door.*]

EUNICE [*returning, brightly*]: Someone is calling for Blanche.

BLANCHE: It *is* for me, then! [*She looks fearfully from one to the other and then to the portières. The 'Varsouviana' faintly plays.*] Is it the gentleman I was expecting from Dallas?

EUNICE: I think it is, Blanche.

BLANCHE: I'm not quite ready.

STELLA: Ask him to wait outside.

BLANCHE: I . . .

[EUNICE *goes back to the portières. Drums sound very softly.*]

STELLA: Everything packed?

BLANCHE: My silver toilet articles are still out.

STELLA: Ah!

EUNICE [*returning*]: They're waiting in front of the house.

BLANCHE: They! Who's 'they'?

EUNICE: There's a lady with him.

BLANCHE: I cannot imagine who this 'lady' could be! How is she dressed?

EUNICE: Just – just a sort of a – plain-tailored outfit.

BLANCHE: Possibly she's – [*Her voice dies out nervously.*]

STELLA: Shall we go, Blanche?

BLANCHE: Must we go through that room?

STELLA: I will go with you.

BLANCHE: How do I look?

STELLA: Lovely.

EUNICE [*echoing*]: Lovely.

[BLANCHE *moves fearfully to the portières.* EUNICE *draws them open for her.* BLANCHE *goes into the kitchen.*]

BLANCHE [*to the men*]: Please don't get up. I'm only passing through.

[*She crosses quickly to outside door.* STELLA *and* EUNICE *follow. The poker players stand awkwardly at the table – all except* MITCH, *who remains seated, looking at the table.* BLANCHE *steps out on a small porch at the side of the door. She stops short and catches her breath.*]

DOCTOR: How do you do?

BLANCHE: You are not the gentleman I was expecting. [*She suddenly gasps and starts back up the steps. She stops by* STELLA, *who stands just outside the door, and speaks in a frightened whisper.*] That man isn't Shep Huntleigh.

[*The 'Varsouviana' is playing distantly.*

STELLA *stares back at* BLANCHE. EUNICE *is holding* STELLA'S *arm. There is a moment of silence – no sound but that of* STANLEY *steadily shuffling the cards.*

BLANCHE *catches her breath again and slips back into the flat. She enters the flat with a peculiar smile, her eyes wide and brilliant. As soon as her sister goes past her,* STELLA *closes her eyes and clenches her hands.* EUNICE *throws her arms comfortingly about her. Then she starts up to her flat.* BLANCHE *stops just inside the door.* MITCH *keeps staring down at his hands on the table, but the other men look at her curiously. At last she starts around the table towards the bedroom. As she does,* STANLEY *suddenly pushes back his chair and rises as if to block her way. The* MATRON *follows her into the flat.*]

STANLEY: Did you forget something?

BLANCHE [*shrilly*]: Yes! Yes, I forgot something!

[*She rushes past him into the bedroom. Lurid reflections appear on the walls in odd, sinuous shapes. The 'Varsouviana' is filtered into weird distortion, accompanied by the cries and noises of the jungle.* BLANCHE *seizes the back of a chair as if to defend herself.*]

STANLEY: Doc, you better go in.

DOCTOR [*motioning to the* MATRON]: Nurse, bring her out.

[*The* MATRON *advances on one side,* STANLEY *on the other. Divested of all the softer properties of womanhood, the* MATRON *is a peculiarly sinister figure in her severe dress. Her voice is bold and toneless as a fire-bell.*]

MATRON: Hello, Blanche.

[*The greeting is echoed and re-echoed by other mysterious voices behind the walls, as if reverberated through a canyon of rock.*]

STANLEY: She says that she forgot something.

[*The echo sounds in threatening whispers.*]

MATRON: That's all right.
STANLEY: What did you forget, Blanche?
BLANCHE: I – I –
MATRON: It don't matter. We can pick it up later.
STANLEY: Sure. We can send it along with the trunk.
BLANCHE [*retreating in panic*]: I don't know you – I don't know you. I want to be – left alone – please!
MATRON: Now, Blanche!
ECHOES [*rising and falling*]: Now, Blanche – now, Blanche – now, Blanche!
STANLEY: You left nothing here but spilt talcum and old empty perfume bottles – unless it's the paper lantern you want to take with you. You want the lantern?

[*He crosses to dressing-table and seizes the paper lantern, tearing it off the light bulb, and extends it towards her. She cries out as if the lantern was herself. The* MATRON *steps boldly towards her. She screams and tries to break past the* MATRON. *All the men spring to their feet.* STELLA *runs out to the porch, with* EUNICE *following to comfort her, simultaneously with the confused voices of the men in the kitchen.* STELLA *rushes into* EUNICE'S *embrace on the porch.*]

STELLA: Oh, my God, Eunice, help me! Don't let them do

that to her, don't let them hurt her! Oh, God, oh, please God, don't hurt her! What are they doing to her? What are they doing? [*She tries to break from* EUNICE's *arms.*]

EUNICE: No, honey, no, no, honey. Stay here. Don't go back in there. Stay with me and don't look.

STELLA: What have I done to my sister? Oh, God, what have I done to my sister?

EUNICE: You done the right thing, the only thing you could do. She couldn't stay here; there wasn't no other place for her to go.

[*While* STELLA *and* EUNICE *are speaking on the porch the voices of the men in the kitchen overlap them.*]

STANLEY [*running in from the bedroom*]: Hey! Hey! Doctor! Doctor, you better go in!

DOCTOR: Too bad, too bad. I always like to avoid it.

PABLO: This is a very bad thing.

STEVE: This is no way to do it. She should've been told.

PABLO: *Madre de Dios! Cosa mala, muy, muy mala!*

[MITCH *has started towards the bedroom.* STANLEY *crosses to block him.*]

MITCH [*wildly*]: You! You done this, all o' your God damn interfering with things you –

STANLEY: Quit the blubber! [*He pushes him aside.*]

MITCH: I'll kill you! [*He lunges and strikes at* STANLEY.]

STANLEY: Hold this bone-headed cry-baby!

STEVE [*grasping* MITCH]: Stop it, Mitch.

PABLO: Yeah, yeah, take it easy!

[MITCH *collapses at the table, sobbing.*
    During the preceding scenes, the MATRON *catches hold of* BLANCHE's *arm and prevents her flight.* BLANCHE *turns wildly and scratches at the* MATRON. *The heavy woman pinions her arms.* BLANCHE *cries out hoarsely and slips to her knees.*]

MATRON: These fingernails have to be trimmed. [*The* DOCTOR *comes into the room and she looks at him.*] Jacket, Doctor?

DOCTOR: Not unless necessary.

[*He takes off his hat and now becomes personalized. The unhuman quality goes. His voice is gentle and reassuring as he crosses to* BLANCHE *and crouches in front of her. As he speaks her name, her terror subsides a little. The lurid reflections fade from the walls, the inhuman cries and noises die out and her own hoarse crying is calmed.*]

DOCTOR: Miss DuBois.

[*She turns her face to him and stares at him with desperate pleading. He smiles; then he speaks to the* MATRON.]

It won't be necessary.

BLANCHE [*faintly*]: Ask her to let go of me.

DOCTOR [*to the* MATRON]: Let go.

[*The* MATRON *releases her.* BLANCHE *extends her hands towards the* DOCTOR. *He draws her up gently and supports her with his arm and leads her through the portières.*]

BLANCHE [*holding tight to his arm*]: Whoever you are – I have always depended on the kindness of strangers.

[*The poker players stand back as* BLANCHE *and the* DOCTOR *cross the kitchen to the front door. She allows him to lead her as if she were blind. As they go out on the porch,* STELLA *cries out her sister's name from where she is crouched a few steps upon the stairs.*

STELLA: Blanche! Blanche, Blanche!

[BLANCHE *walks on without turning, followed by the* DOCTOR *and the* MATRON. *They go around the corner of the building.*

EUNICE *descends to* STELLA *and places the child in her arms. It is wrapped in a pale blue blanket.* STELLA *accepts the child, sobbingly.* EUNICE *continues downstairs and enters the kitchen where the men except for* STANLEY, *are returning silently to their places about the table.* STANLEY *has gone out on the porch and stands at the foot of the steps looking at* STELLA.]

STANLEY [*a bit uncertainly*]: Stella?

[*She sobs with inhuman abandon. There is something luxurious in her complete surrender to crying now that her sister is gone.*]

STANLEY [*voluptuously, soothingly*]: Now, honey. Now, love. Now, now love. [*He kneels beside her and his fingers find the opening of her blouse.*] Now, now, love. Now, love. . . .

[*The luxurious sobbing, the sensual murmur fade away under the swelling music of the 'blue piano' and the muted trumpet.*

STEVE: This game is seven-card stud.

CURTAIN

THE GLASS MENAGERIE

THE CHARACTERS

AMANDA WINGFIELD [*the mother*]: A little woman of great but confused vitality clinging frantically to another time and place. Her characterization must be carefully created, not copied from type. She is not paranoiac, but her life is paranoia. There is much to admire in Amanda, and as much to love and pity as there is to laugh at. Certainly she has endurance and a kind of heroism, and though her foolishness makes her unwittingly cruel at times, there is tenderness in her slight person.

LAURA WINGFIELD [*her daughter*]: Amanda, having failed to establish contact with reality, continues to live vitally in her illusions, but Laura's situation is even graver. A childhood illness has left her crippled, one leg slightly shorter than the other, and held in a brace. This defect need not be more than suggested on the stage. Stemming from this, Laura's separation increases till she is like a piece of her own glass collection, too exquisitely fragile to move from the shelf.

TOM WINGFIELD [*her son, and the narrator of the play*]: A poet with a job in a warehouse. His nature is not remorseless, but to escape from a trap he has to act without pity.

JIM O'CONNOR [*the gentleman caller*]: A nice, ordinary, young man.

PRODUCTION NOTES

Being a 'memory play', *The Glass Menagerie* can be presented with unusual freedom from convention. Because of its considerably delicate or tenuous material, atmospheric touches and subtleties of direction play a particularly important part. Expressionism and all other unconventional techniques in drama have only one valid aim, and that is a closer approach to truth. When a play employs unconventional techniques, it is not, or certainly shouldn't be, trying to escape its responsibility of dealing with reality, or interpreting experience, but is actually or should be attempting to find a closer approach, a more penetrating and vivid expression of things as they are. The straight realistic play with its genuine frigidaire and authentic ice-cubes, its characters that speak exactly as its audience speaks, corresponds to the academic landscape and has the same virtue of a photographic likeness. Everyone should know nowadays the unimportance of the photographic in art: that truth, life, or reality is an organic thing which the poetic imagination can represent or suggest, in essence, only through transformation, through changing into other forms than those which were merely present in appearance.

These remarks are not meant as a preface only to this particular play. They have to do with a conception of a new, plastic theatre which must take the place of the exhausted theatre of realistic conventions if the theatre is to resume vitality as a part of our culture.

THE SCREEN DEVICE

There is *only one important difference between the original and acting version of the play* and that is the *omission* in the latter of the device which I tentatively included in my *original* script. This device was the use of a screen on which were projected magic-lantern slides bearing images or titles. I do not regret the omission of this device from the present Broadway production. The extraordinary power of Miss Taylor's performance made it suitable to have the utmost simplicity in the physical production. But I think it may be interesting to some readers to see how this device was conceived. So I am putting it into the published manuscript. These images and legends, projected from behind, were cast on a section of wall between the front room and the dining-room areas, which should be indistinguishable from the rest when not in use.

The purpose of this will probably be apparent. It is to give accent to certain values in each scene. Each scene contains a particular point (or several) which is structurally the most important. In an episodic play, such as this, the basic structure or narrative line may be obscured from the audience; the effect may seem fragmentary rather than architectural. This may not be the fault of the play so much as a lack of attention in the audience. The legend or image upon the screen will strengthen the effect of what is merely illusion in the writing and allow the primary point to be made more simply and lightly than if the entire responsibility were on the spoken lines. Aside from this structural value, I think the screen will have a definite emotional appeal, less definable but just as important. An imaginative producer or director may invent many other uses for this device than those indicated in the present script. In fact the possibilities of the device seem much larger to me than the instance of this play can possibly utilize.

THE MUSIC

Another extra-literary accent in this play is provided by the use of music. A single recurring tune, 'The Glass Menagerie', is used to give emotional emphasis to suitable passages. This tune is like circus music, not when you are on the grounds or in the immediate vicinity of the parade, but when you are at some distance and very likely thinking of something else. It seems under those circumstances to

continue almost interminably and it weaves in and out of
your preoccupied consciousness; then it is the lightest, most
delicate music in the world and perhaps the saddest. It
expresses the surface vivacity of life with the underlying
strain of immutable and inexpressible sorrow. When you
look at a piece of delicately spun glass you think of two
things: how beautiful it is and how easily it can be broken.
Both of those ideas should be woven into the recurring tune,
which dips in and out of the play as if it were carried on a
wind that changes. It serves as a thread of connexion and
allusion between the narrator with his separate point in
time and space and the subject of his story. Between each
episode it returns as reference to the emotion, nostalgia,
which is the first condition of the play. It is primarily
LAURA's music and therefore comes out most clearly when
the play focuses upon her and the lovely fragility of glass
which is her image.

THE LIGHTING

The lighting in the play is not realistic. In keeping with the
atmosphere of memory, the stage is dim. Shafts of light are
focused on selected areas or actors, sometimes in contradis-
tinction to what is the apparent centre. For instance, in the
quarrel scene between TOM and AMANDA, in which
LAURA has no active part, the clearest pool of light is on
her figure. This is also true of the supper scene, when her
silent figure on the sofa should remain the visual centre.
The light upon LAURA should be distinct from the others,
having a peculiar pristine clarity such as light used in early
religious portraits of female saints or madonnas. A certain
correspondence to light in religious paintings, such as El
Greco's, where the figures are radiant in atmosphere that
is relatively dusky, could be effectively used throughout the
play. [It will also permit a more effective use of the screen.]
A free, imaginative use of light can be of enormous value
in giving a mobile, plastic quality to plays of a more or less
static nature.   T.W.

THE GLASS MENAGERIE

This play was first presented in London at the
Theatre Royal, Haymarket, on 28 July 1948 with
the following cast:

AMANDA WINGFIELD	*Helen Hayes*
LAURA, her daughter	*Frances Heflin*
TOM, her son	*Phil Brown*
THE GENTLEMAN CALLER	*Hugh McDermott*

The play directed by John Gielgud
Setting by Jo Mielziner. Original music composed
by Paul Bowles.
Dance music arranged by Leslie Bridgewater

Scene: An alley in St Louis
PART 1: Preparation for a Gentleman Caller
PART 2: The Gentleman Calls

Time: Now and the Past

SCENE ONE

The Wingfield apartment is in the rear of the building, one of those vast hive-like conglomerations of cellular living-units that flower as warty growths in overcrowded urban centres of lower-middle-class population and are symptomatic of the impulse of this largest and fundamentally enslaved section of American society to avoid fluidity and differentiation and to exist and function as one interfused mass of automatism.

The apartment faces an alley and is entered by a fire-escape, a structure whose name is a touch of accidental poetic truth, for all of these huge buildings are always burning with the slow and implacable fires of human desperation. The fire-escape is included in the set – that is, the landing of it and steps descending from it.

The scene is memory and is therefore non-realistic. Memory takes a lot of poetic licence. It omits some details; others are exaggerated, according to the emotional value of the articles it touches, for memory is seated predominantly in the heart. The interior is therefore rather dim and poetic.

[*At the rise of the curtain, the audience is faced with the dark, grim rear wall of the Wingfield tenement. This building, which runs parallel to the footlights, is flanked on both sides by dark, narrow alleys which run into murky canyons of tangled clothes-lines, garbage cans, and the sinister lattice-work of neighbouring fire-escapes. It is up and down these side alleys that exterior entrances and exits are made, during the play. At the end of* TOM'S *opening commentary, the dark tenement wall slowly reveals (by means of a transparency) the interior of the ground floor Wingfield apartment.*

Downstage is the living-room, which also serves as a sleeping-room for LAURA, *the sofa unfolding to make her bed. Upstage, centre, and divided by a wide arch or second proscenium with transparent faded portières (or second curtain), is the dining-room. In an old-fashioned what-not in the living-room are seen scores of transparent glass animals. A blown-up photograph of the father hangs on the wall of the living-room, facing the audience, to the left of the archway. It is the face of a very handsome young man in a doughboy's First World War cap. He is gallantly smiling, ineluctably smiling, as if to say 'I will be smiling for ever'.*

The audience hears and sees the opening scene in the dining-room through both the transparent fourth wall of the building and the transparent gauze portières of the dining-room arch. It is during this revealing scene that the fourth wall slowly ascends out of sight. This transparent exterior wall is not brought down again until the very end of the play, during TOM'S *final speech.*

The narrator is an undisguised convention of the play. He takes whatever licence with dramatic convention is convenient to his purposes.

TOM *enters dressed as a merchant sailor from alley, stage left, and strolls across the front of the stage to the fire-escape. There he stops and lights a cigarette. He addresses the audience.*]

TOM: Yes, I have tricks in my pocket, I have things up my sleeve. But I am the opposite of a stage magician. He gives you illusion that has the appearance of truth. I give you truth in the pleasant disguise of illusion.

To begin with, I turn back time. I reverse it to that quaint period, the thirties, when the huge middle class of America was matriculating in a school for the blind. Their eyes had failed them, or they had failed their eyes, and so they were having their fingers pressed forcibly down on the fiery Braille alphabet of a dissolving economy.

In Spain there was revolution. Here there was only shouting and confusion.

In Spain there was Guernica. Here there were dis-turbances of labour, sometimes pretty violent, in otherwise peaceful cities such as Chicago, Cleveland, Saint Louis. . . .

This is the social background of the play.

[MUSIC]

The play is memory.

Being a memory play, it is dimly lighted, it is sentimental, it is not realistic.

In memory everything seems to happen to music. That explains the fiddle in the wings.

I am the narrator of the play, and also a character in it. The other characters are my mother Amanda, my sister Laura, and a gentleman caller who appears in the final scenes.

He is the most realistic character in the play, being an emissary from a world of reality that we were somehow set apart from.

But since I have a poet's weakness for symbols, I am using this character also as a symbol; he is the long-delayed but always expected something that we live for.

There is a fifth character in the play who doesn't appear except in this larger-than-life-size photograph over the mantel.

This is our father who left us a long time ago.

He was a telephone man who fell in love with long distances; he gave up his job with the telephone company and skipped the light fantastic out of town. . . .

The last we heard of him was a picture postcard from Mazatlan, on the Pacific coast of Mexico, containing a message of two words –

'Hello – Good-bye!' and no address.

I think the rest of the play will explain itself. . . .

[AMANDA'S *voice becomes audible through the portières.*
LEGEND ON SCREEN: 'OÙ SONT LES NEIGES'.
He divides the portières and enters the upstage area.

> AMANDA *and* LAURA *are seated at a drop-leaf table.*
> *Eating is indicated by gestures without food or utensils.*
> AMANDA *faces the audience.* TOM *and* LAURA *are seated*
> *in profile.*
>
> *The interior has lit up softly and through the scrim we see*
> AMANDA *and* LAURA *seated at the table in the upstage*
> *area.*]

AMANDA [*calling*]: Tom?

TOM: Yes, Mother.

AMANDA: We can't say grace until you come to the table!

TOM: Coming, Mother. [*He bows slightly and withdraws, re-appearing a few moments later in his place at the table.*]

AMANDA [*to her son*]: Honey, don't *push* with your *fingers*. If you have to push with something, the thing to push with is a crust of bread. And chew – chew! Animals have sections in their stomachs which enable them to digest food without mastication, but human beings are supposed to chew their food before they swallow it down. Eat food leisurely, son, and really enjoy it. A well-cooked meal has lots of delicate flavours that have to be held in the mouth for appreciation. So chew your food and give your salivary glands a chance to function!

> [TOM *deliberately lays his imaginary fork down and pushes his chair back from the table.*]

TOM: I haven't enjoyed one bite of this dinner because of your constant directions on how to eat it. It's you that makes me rush through meals with your hawk-like attention to every bite I take. Sickening – spoils my appetite – all this discussion of – animals' secretion – salivary glands – mastication!

AMANDA [*lightly*]: Temperament like a Metropolitan star! [*He rises and crosses downstage.*] You're not excused from the table.

TOM: I'm getting a cigarette.

AMANDA: You smoke too much.

[LAURA *rises*.]

LAURA: I'll bring in the blancmange.

[*He remains standing with his cigarette by the portières during the following.*]

AMANDA [*rising*]: No, sister, no, sister — you be the lady this time and I'll be the darkey.

LAURA: I'm already up.

AMANDA: Resume your seat, little sister — I want you to stay fresh and pretty — for gentleman callers!

LAURA: I'm not expecting any gentleman callers.

AMANDA [*crossing out to kitchenette. Airily*]: Sometimes they come when they are least expected! Why, I remember one Sunday afternoon in Blue Mountain — [*Enters kitchenette.*]

TOM: I know what's coming!

LAURA: Yes. But let her tell it.

TOM: Again?

LAURA: She loves to tell it.

[AMANDA *returns with bowl of dessert.*]

AMANDA: One Sunday afternoon in Blue Mountain — your mother received — *seventeen!* — gentlemen callers! Why, sometimes there weren't chairs enough to accommodate them all. We had to send the nigger over to bring in folding chairs from the parish house.

TOM [*remaining at portières*]: How did you entertain those gentleman callers?

AMANDA: I understood the art of conversation!

TOM: I bet you could talk.

AMANDA: Girls in those days *knew* how to talk, I can tell you.

TOM: Yes?

[IMAGE: AMANDA AS A GIRL ON A PORCH, GREET-
ING CALLERS.]

AMANDA: They knew how to entertain their gentlemen
callers. It wasn't enough for a girl to be possessed of a
pretty face and a graceful figure – although I wasn't
slighted in either respect. She also needed to have a
nimble wit and a tongue to meet all occasions.

TOM: What did you talk about?

AMANDA: Things of importance going on in the world!
Never anything coarse or common or vulgar. [*She
addresses* TOM *as though he were seated in the vacant chair at the
table though he remains by portières. He plays this scene as
though he held the book.*] My callers were gentleman – all!
Among my callers were some of the most prominent
young planters of the Mississippi Delta – planters and
sons of planters!

[TOM *motions for music and a spot of light on* AMANDA.
  *Her eyes lift, her face glows, her voice becomes rich and
elegiac.*
SCREEN LEGEND: 'OÙ SONT LES NEIGES'.]

There was young Champ Laughlin who later became
vice-president of the Delta Planters Bank.
Hadley Stevenson who was drowned in Moon Lake and
left his widow one hundred and fifty thousand in Govern-
ment bonds.
There were the Cutrere brothers, Wesley and Bates. Bates
was one of my bright particular beaux! He got in a
quarrel with that wild Wainwright boy. They shot it out
on the floor of Moon Lake Casino. Bates was shot through
the stomach. Died in the ambulance on his way to
Memphis. His widow was also well provided for, came
into eight or ten thousand acres, that's all. She married
him on the rebound – never loved her – carried my picture on him the night he died!

And there was that boy that every girl in the Delta had
set her cap for! That brilliant, brilliant young Fitzhugh
boy from Greene County!

TOM: What did he leave his widow?

AMANDA: He never married! Gracious, you talk as though
all of my old admirers had turned up their toes to the
daisies!

TOM: Isn't this the first you've mentioned that still survives?

AMANDA: That Fitzhugh boy went North and made a fortune – came to be known as the Wolf of Wall Street! He
had the Midas touch, whatever he touched turned to
gold!

And I could have been Mrs Duncan J. Fitzhugh, mind
you! But – I picked your *father*!

LAURA [*rising*]: Mother, let me clear the table.

AMANDA: No, dear, you go in front and study your typewriter chart. Or practise your shorthand a little. Stay
fresh and pretty! – It's almost time for our gentlemen
callers to start arriving. [*She flounces girlishly toward the
kitchenette.*] How many do you suppose we're going to
entertain this afternoon?

[TOM *throws down the paper and jumps up with a groan.*]

LAURA [*alone in the dining-room*]: I don't believe we're going
to receive any, Mother.

AMANDA [*reappearing, airily*]: What? No one – not one?
You must be joking! [LAURA *nervously echoes her laugh.
She slips in a fugitive manner through the half-open portières and
draws them in gently behind her. A shaft of very clear light is
thrown on her face against the faded tapestry of the curtains.*]

[MUSIC: 'THE GLASS MENAGERIE' UNDER FAINTLY.
Lightly.]

Not one gentleman caller? It can't be true! There must
be a flood, there must have been a tornado!

LAURA: It isn't a flood, it's not a tornado, Mother. I'm just not popular like you were in Blue Mountain. ... [TOM *utters another groan.* LAURA *glances at him with a faint, apologetic smile. Her voice catching a little.*] Mother's afraid I'm going to be an old maid.

THE SCENE DIMS OUT WITH 'GLASS MENAGERIE' MUSIC

SCENE TWO

'*Laura, Haven't you Ever Liked Some Boy?*'
  On the dark stage the screen is lighted with the image of blue roses.

[*Gradually* LAURA'S *figure becomes apparent and the screen goes out.*

  The music subsides.

  LAURA *is seated in the delicate ivory chair at the small claw-foot table.*

  She wears a dress of soft violet material for a kimono – her hair tied back from her forehead with a ribbon.

  She is washing and polishing her collection of glass.

  AMANDA *appears on the fire-escape steps. At the sound of her ascent,* LAURA *catches her breath, thrusts the bowl of ornaments away and seats herself stiffly before the diagram of the typewriter keyboard as though it held her spellbound.*

  Something has happened to AMANDA. *It is written in her face as she climbs to the landing: a look that is grim and hopeless and a little absurd.*

  She has on one of those cheap or imitation velvety-looking cloth coats with imitation fur collar. Her hat is five or six years old, one of those dreadful cloche hats that were worn in the late twenties and she is clasping an enormous black patent-leather pocketbook with nickel clasps and initials. This is her full-dress outfit, the one she usually wears to the D.A.R.

  Before entering she looks through the door.

  She purses her lips, opens her eyes very wide, rolls them upward, and shakes her head.

  Then she slowly lets herself in the door. Seeing her mother's expression LAURA *touches her lips with a nervous gesture.*]

LAURA: Hello, Mother, I was – [*She makes a nervous gesture toward the chart on the wall.* AMANDA *leans against the shut door and stares at* LAURA *with a martyred look.*]

AMANDA: Deception? Deception? [*She slowly removes her hat and gloves, continuing the sweet suffering stare. She lets the hat and gloves fall on the floor – a bit of acting.*]

LAURA [*shakily*]: How was the D.A.R. meeting? [AMANDA *slowly opens her purse and removes a dainty white handkerchief which she shakes out delicately and delicately touches to her lips and nostrils.*] Didn't you go to the D.A.R. meeting, Mother?

AMANDA [*faintly, almost inaudibly*]: – No. – No. [*Then more forcibly.*] I did not have the strength – to go to the D.A.R. In fact, I did not have the courage! I wanted to find a hole in the ground and hide myself in it for ever! [*She crosses slowly to the wall and removes the diagram of the typewriter keyboard. She holds it in front of her for a second, staring at it sweetly and sorrowfully – then bites her lips and tears it into two pieces.*]

LAURA [*faintly*]: Why did you do that, Mother? [AMANDA *repeats the same procedure with the chart of the Gregg alphabet.*] Why are you –?

AMANDA: Why? Why? How old are you, Laura?

LAURA: Mother, you know my age.

AMANDA: I thought that you were an adult; it seems that I was mistaken. [*She crosses slowly to the sofa and sinks down and stares at* LAURA.]

LAURA: Please don't stare at me, Mother.

[AMANDA *closes her eyes and lowers her head. Count ten.*]

AMANDA: What are we going to do, what is going to become of us, what is the future?

[*Count ten.*]

LAURA: Has something happened, Mother? [AMANDA *draws a long breath and takes out the handkerchief again. Dabbing process.*] Mother, has – something happened?

AMANDA: I'll be all right in a minute, I'm just bewildered – [*Count five.*] – by life. . . .

LAURA: Mother, I wish that you would tell me what's happened!

AMANDA: As you know, I was supposed to be inducted into my office at the D.A.R. this afternoon. [IMAGE: A SWARM OF TYPEWRITERS.] But I stopped off at Rubicam's business college to speak to your teachers about your having a cold and ask them what progress they thought you were making down there.

LAURA: Oh. . . .

AMANDA: I went to the typing instructor and introduced myself as your mother. She didn't know who you were. Wingfield, she said. We don't have any such student enrolled at the school!

I assured her she did, that you had been going to classes since early in January.

'I wonder,' she said, 'if you could be talking about that terribly shy little girl who dropped out of school after only a few days' attendance?'

'No,' I said, 'Laura, my daughter, has been going to school every day for the past six weeks!'

'Excuse me,' she said. She took the attendance book out and there was your name, unmistakably printed, and all the dates you were absent until they decided that you had dropped out of school.

I still said, 'No, there must have been some mistake! There must have been some mix-up in the records!'

And she said, 'No – I remember her perfectly now. Her hands shook so that she couldn't hit the right keys! The first time we gave a speed-test, she broke down completely – was sick at the stomach and almost had to be carried into the wash-room! After that morning she never showed up any more. We phoned the house but never got any answer' – while I was working at Famous and Barr, I suppose, demonstrating those – Oh!

I felt so weak I could barely keep on my feet!

I had to sit down while they got me a glass of water!

Fifty dollars' tuition, all of our plans – my hopes and ambition for you – just gone up the spout, just gone up the spout like that. [LAURA *draws a long breath and gets awkwardly to her feet. She crosses to the victrola and winds it up.*]

What are you doing?

LAURA: Oh! [*She releases the handle and returns to her seat.*]

AMANDA: Laura, where have you been going when you've gone on pretending that you were going to business college?

LAURA: I've just been going out walking.

AMANDA: That's not true.

LAURA: It is. I just went walking.

AMANDA: Walking? Walking? In winter? Deliberately courting pneumonia in that light coat? Where did you walk to, Laura?

LAURA: All sorts of places – mostly in the park.

AMANDA: Even after you'd started catching that cold?

LAURA: It was the lesser of two evils, Mother. [IMAGE: WINTER SCENE IN PARK.] I couldn't go back up. I – threw up – on the floor!

AMANDA: From half past seven till after five every day you mean to tell me you walked around in the park, because you wanted to make me think that you were still going to Rubicam's Business College?

LAURA: It wasn't as bad as it sounds. I went inside places to get warmed up.

AMANDA: Inside where?

LAURA: I went in the art museum and the bird-houses at the Zoo. I visited the penguins every day! Sometimes I did without lunch and went to the movies. Lately I've been spending most of my afternoons in the Jewel-box, that big glass-house where they raise the tropical flowers.

AMANDA: You did all this to deceive me, just for deception? [LAURA *looks down.*] Why?

LAURA: Mother, when you're disappointed, you get that awful suffering look on your face, like the picture of Jesus' mother in the museum!

AMANDA: Hush!

LAURA: I couldn't face it.

> [*Pause. A whisper of strings.*
>   LEGEND: 'THE CRUST OF HUMILITY'.]

AMANDA [*hopelessly fingering the huge pocketbook*]: So what are we going to do the rest of our lives? Stay home and watch the parades go by? Amuse ourselves with the glass menagerie, darling? Eternally play those worn-out phonograph records your father left as a painful reminder of him? We won't have a business career – we've given that up because it gave us nervous indigestion! [*Laughs wearily.*] What is there left but dependency all our lives? I know so well what becomes of unmarried women who aren't prepared to occupy a position. I've seen such pitiful cases in the South – barely tolerated spinsters living upon the grudging patronage of sister's husband or brother's wife! – stuck away in some little mousetrap of a room – encouraged by one in-law to visit another – little birdlike women without any nest – eating the crust of humility all their life!
Is that the future that we've mapped out for ourselves? I swear it's the only alternative I can think of!
It isn't a very pleasant alternative, is it?
Of course – some girls *do marry*.

> [LAURA *twists her hands nervously.*]

Haven't you ever liked some boy?

LAURA: Yes. I liked one once. [*Rises.*] I came across his picture a while ago.

AMANDA [*with some interest*]: He gave you his picture?

LAURA: No, it's in the year-book.

AMANDA: [*disappointed*]: Oh – a high-school boy.

[SCREEN IMAGE: JIM AS HIGH-SCHOOL HERO BEAR-
ING A SILVER CUP.]

LAURA: Yes. His name was Jim. [LAURA *lifts the heavy
annual from the claw-foot table*.] Here he is in *The Pirates of
Penzance*.

AMANDA [*absently*]: The what?

LAURA: The operetta the senior class put on. He had a wonderful voice and we sat across the aisle from each other
Mondays, Wednesdays, and Fridays in the Aud. Here he
is with the silver cup for debating! See his grin?

AMANDA [*absently*]: He must have had a jolly disposition.

LAURA: He used to call me – Blue Roses.

[IMAGE: BLUE ROSES.]

AMANDA: Why did he call you such a name as that?

LAURA: When I had that attack of pleurosis – he asked me
what was the matter when I came back. I said pleurosis –
he thought that I said Blue Roses! So that's what he
always called me after that. Whenever he saw me, he'd
holler, 'Hello, Blue Roses!' I didn't care for the girl that
he went out with. Emily Meisenbach. Emily was the best-
dressed girl at Soldan. She never struck me, though, as
being sincere. . . . It says in the Personal Section – they're
engaged. That's – six years ago! They must be married by
now.

AMANDA: Girls that aren't cut out for business careers
usually wind up married to some nice man. [*Gets up with a
spark of revival*.] Sister, that's what you'll do!

[LAURA *utters a startled, doubtful laugh. She reaches quickly
for a piece of glass*.]

LAURA: But, Mother –

AMANDA: Yes? [*Crossing to photograph*.]

LAURA [*in a tone of frightened apology*]: I'm – crippled!

[IMAGE: SCREEN.]

AMANDA: Nonsense! Laura, I've told you never, never to use that word. Why, you're not crippled, you just have a little defect – hardly noticeable, even! When people have some slight disadvantage like that, they cultivate other things to make up for it – develop charm – and vivacity – and – *charm!* That's all you have to do! [*She turns again to the photograph.*] One thing your father had *plenty of* – was *charm!*

[TOM *motions to the fiddle in the wings.*]

THE SCENE FADES OUT WITH MUSIC

SCENE THREE

LEGEND ON SCREEN: 'AFTER THE FIASCO —'

[TOM *speaks from the fire-escape landing.*]

TOM: After the fiasco at Rubicam's Business College, the idea of getting a gentleman caller for Laura began to play a more and more important part in Mother's calculations. It became an obsession. Like some archetype of the universal unconscious, the image of the gentleman caller haunted our small apartment. ...

[IMAGE: YOUNG MAN AT DOOR WITH FLOWERS.]

An evening at home rarely passed without some allusion to this image, this spectre, this hope. ...
Even when he wasn't mentioned, his presence hung in Mother's preoccupied look and in my sister's frightened, apologetic manner – hung like a sentence passed upon the Wingfields !
Mother was a woman of action as well as words.
She began to take logical steps in the planned direction. Late that winter and in the early spring – realizing that extra money would be needed to properly feather the nest and plume the bird – she conducted a vigorous campaign on the telephone, roping in subscribers to one of those magazines for matrons called *The Home-maker's Companion*, the type of journal that features the serialized sublimations of ladies of letters who think in terms of delicate cup-like breasts, slim, tapering waists, rich, creamy thighs, eyes like wood-smoke in autumn, fingers that soothe and caress like strains of music, bodies as powerful as Etruscan sculpture.

[SCREEN IMAGE: GLAMOUR MAGAZINE COVER.]

[AMANDA *enters with phone on long extension cord. She is spotted in the dim stage.*]

AMANDA: Ida Scott? This is Amanda Wingfield!
We *missed* you at the D.A.R. last Monday!
I said to myself: She's probably suffering with that sinus condition! How is that sinus condition?
Horrors! Heaven have mercy! – You're a Christian martyr, yes, that's what you are, a Christian martyr!
Well, I just have happened to notice that your subscription to the *Companion*'s about to expire! Yes, it expires with the next issue, honey! – just when that wonderful new serial by Bessie Mae Hopper is getting off to such an exciting start. Oh, honey, it's something that you can't miss! You remember how *Gone With the Wind* took everybody by storm? You simply couldn't go out if you hadn't read it. All everybody *talked* was Scarlet O'Hara. Well, this is a book that critics already compare to *Gone With the Wind*. It's the *Gone With the Wind* of the post-World War generation! – What? – Burning! – Oh, honey, don't let them burn, go take a look in the oven and I'll hold the wire! Heavens – I think she's hung up!

[DIM OUT]

[LEGEND ON SCREEN: 'YOU THINK I'M IN LOVE WITH CONTINENTAL SHOEMAKERS?']

[*Before the stage is lighted, the violent voices of* TOM *and* AMANDA *are heard.*
The are quarrelling behind the portières. In front of them stands LAURA *with clenched hands and panicky expression.*
A clear pool of light on her figure throughout this scene.]

TOM: What in Christ's name am I –
AMANDA [*shrilly*]: Don't you use that –
TOM: Supposed to do!
AMANDA: Expression! Not in my –

TOM: Ohhh!

AMANDA: Presence! Have you gone out of your senses?

TOM: I have, that's true, *driven* out!

AMANDA: What is the matter with you, you – big – big IDIOT!

TOM: Look! – I've got *no thing*, no single thing –

AMANDA: Lower your voice!

TOM: In my life here that I can call my OWN! Everything is –

AMANDA: Stop that shouting!

TOM: Yesterday you confiscated my books! You had the nerve to –

AMANDA: I took that horrible novel back to the library – yes! That hideous book by that insane Mr Lawrence. [TOM *laughs wildly.*] I cannot control the output of diseased minds or people who cater to them – [TOM *laughs still more wildly.*] BUT I WON'T ALLOW SUCH FILTH BROUGHT INTO MY HOUSE! No, no, no, no, no!

TOM: House, house! Who pays rent on it, who makes a slave of himself to –

AMANDA [*fairly screeching*]: Don't you D A R E to –

TOM: No, no, *I* mustn't say things! *I've* got to just –

AMANDA: Let me tell you –

TOM: I don't want to hear any more! [*He tears the portières open. The upstage area is lit with a turgid smoky red glow.*]

> [AMANDA'S *hair is in metal curlers and she wears a very old bathrobe, much too large for her slight figure, a relic of the faithless Mr Wingfield. An upright typewriter and a wild disarray of manuscripts are on the drop-leaf table. The quarrel was probably precipitated by* AMANDA'S *interruption of his creative labour. A chair lying overthrown on the floor.*
>
> *Their gesticulating shadows are cast on the ceiling by the fiery glow.*]

AMANDA: You *will* hear more, you –

TOM: No, I won't hear more, I'm going out!

AMANDA: You come right back in —

TOM: Out, out, out! Because I'm —

AMANDA: Come back here, Tom Wingfield! I'm not through talking to you!

TOM: Oh, go —

LAURA [*desperately*]: — Tom!

AMANDA: You're going to listen, and no more insolence from you! I'm at the end of my patience!

[*He comes back toward her.*]

TOM: What do you think I'm at? Aren't I supposed to have any patience to reach the end of, Mother? I know, I know. It seems unimportant to you, what I'm *doing* — what I *want* to do — having a little *difference* between them! You don't think that —

AMANDA: I think you've been doing things that you're ashamed of. That's why you act like this. I don't believe that you go every night to the movies. Nobody goes to the movies night after night. Nobody in their right mind goes to the movies as often as you pretend to. People don't go to the movies at nearly midnight, and movies don't let out at two a.m. Come in stumbling. Muttering to yourself like a maniac! You get three hours' sleep and then go to work. Oh, I can picture the way you're doing down there. Moping, doping, because you're in no condition.

TOM [*wildly*]: No, I'm in no condition!

AMANDA: What right have you got to jeopardize your job? Jeopardize the security of us all? How do you think we'd manage if you were —

TOM: Listen! You think I'm crazy about the *warehouse*? [*He bends fiercely toward her slight figure.*] You think I'm in love with the Continental Shoemakers? You think I want to spend fifty-five *years* down there in that — *celotex interior*! with — *fluorescent* — *tubes*! Look! I'd rather somebody picked up a crowbar and battered out my brains — than go back mornings! I *go*! Every time you come in yelling that God damn '*Rise and Shine!*' '*Rise and Shine!*' I say to myself, 'How *lucky dead* people are!' But I get up. I *go!* For sixty-five dollars a month I give up all that I dream of doing and being *ever!* And you say self – *self*'s' all I ever think of. Why, listen, if self is what I thought of, Mother, I'd be where he is – GONE! [*Pointing to father's picture.*] As far as the system of transportation reaches! [*He starts past her. She grabs his arm.*] Don't grab at me, Mother!

AMANDA: Where are you going?

TOM: I'm going to the *movies!*

AMANDA: I don't believe that lie!

TOM [*crouching toward her, overtowering her tiny figure. She backs away, gasping*]: I'm going to opium dens! Yes, opium dens, dens of vice and criminals' hang-outs, Mother. I've joined the Hogan gang, I'm a hired assassin, I carry a tommy-gun in a violin case! I run a string of cat-houses in the Valley! They call me Killer, Killer Wingfield, I'm leading a double-life, a simple, honest warehouse worker by day, by night a dynamic *tsar* of the *underworld, Mother.* I go to gambling casinos, I spin away fortunes on the roulette table! I wear a patch over one eye and a false moustache, sometimes I put on green whiskers. On those occasions they call me – *El Diablo!* Oh, I could tell you things to make you sleepless! My enemies plan to dynamite this place. They're going to blow us all sky-high some night! I'll be glad, very happy, and so will you! You'll go up, up on a broomstick, over Blue Mountain with seventeen gentlemen callers! You ugly – babbling old – *witch.* ... [*He goes through a series of violent, clumsy movements, seizing his overcoat, lunging to the door, pulling it fiercely open. The women watch him, aghast. His arm catches in the sleeve of the coat as he struggles to pull it on. For a moment he is pinioned by the bulky garment. With an outraged groan he tears the coat off again, splitting the shoulder of it, and hurls it across the room. It strikes against the shelf of* LAURA'*s glass collection, there is a tinkle of shattering glass.* LAURA *cries out as if wounded.*]

[MUSIC. LEGEND: 'THE GLASS MENAGERIE'.]

LAURA [*shrilly*]: *My glass!* – menagerie. . . . [*She covers her face and turns away.*]

[*But* AMANDA *is still stunned and stupefied by the 'ugly witch' so that she barely notices this occurrence. Now she recovers her speech.*]

AMANDA [*in an awful voice*]: I won't speak to you – until you apologize ! [*She crosses through portières and draws them together behind her.* TOM *is left with* LAURA. LAURA *clings weakly to the mantel with her face averted.* TOM *stares at her stupidly for a moment. Then he crosses to shelf. Drops awkwardly on his knees to collect the fallen glass, glancing at* LAURA *as if he would speak but couldn't.*]

'*The Glass Menagerie*' *steals in as*

THE SCENE DIMS OUT

SCENE FOUR

The interior is dark. Faint light in the alley.

A deep-voiced bell in a church is tolling the hour of five as the scene commences.

[TOM *appears at the top of the alley. After each solemn boom of the bell in the tower, he shakes a little noise-maker or rattle as if to express the tiny spasm of man in contrast to the sustained power and dignity of the Almighty. This and the unsteadiness of his advance make it evident that he has been drinking.*

As he climbs the few steps to the fire-escape landing light steals up inside. LAURA *appears in night-dress, observing* TOM's *empty bed in the front room.*

TOM *fishes in his pockets for door-key, removing a motley assortment of articles in the search, including a perfect shower of movie-ticket stubs and an empty bottle. At last he finds the key, but just as he is about to insert it, it slips from his fingers. He strikes a match and crouches below the door.*]

TOM [*bitterly*]: One crack – and it falls through!

[LAURA *opens the door.*]

LAURA: Tom! Tom, what are you doing?
TOM: Looking for a door-key.
LAURA: Where have you been all this time?
TOM: I have been to the movies.
LAURA: All this time at the movies?
TOM: There was a very long programme. There was a Garbo picture and a Mickey Mouse and a travelogue and a newsreel and a preview of coming attractions. And there was an organ solo and a collection for the milk-fund – simultaneously – which ended up in a terrible fight between a fat lady and an usher!

LAURA [*innocently*]: Did you have to stay through everything?

TOM: Of course! And, oh, I forgot! There was a big stage show! The headliner on this stage show was Malvolio the Magician. He performed wonderful tricks, many of them, such as pouring water back and forth between pitchers. First it turned to wine and then it turned to beer and then it turned to whisky. I knew it was whisky it finally turned into because he needed somebody to come up out of the audience to help him, and I came up – both shows! It was Kentucky Straight Bourbon. A very generous fellow, he gave souvenirs. [*He pulls from his back pocket a shimmering rainbow-coloured scarf.*] He gave me this. This is his magic scarf. You can have it, Laura. You wave it over a canary cage and you get a bowl of gold-fish. You wave it over the gold-fish bowl and they fly away canaries. . . . But the wonderfullest trick of all was the coffin trick. We nailed him into a coffin and he got out of the coffin without removing one nail. [*He has come inside.*] There is a trick that would come in handy for me – get me out of this 2 by 4 situation! [*Flops on to a bed and starts removing shoes.*]

LAURA: Tom – Shhh!

TOM: What're you shushing me for?

LAURA: You'll wake up mother.

TOM: Goody, goody! Pay 'er back for all those 'Rise an' Shines'. [*Lies down, groaning.*] You know it don't take much intelligence to get yourself into a nailed-up coffin, Laura. But who in hell ever got himself out of one without removing one nail?

[*As if in answer, the father's grinning photograph lights up.*]

[SCENE DIMS OUT.]

[*Immediately following: The church bell is heard striking six. At the sixth stroke the alarm clock goes off in* AMANDA's *room, and after a few moments we hear her calling 'Rise and:*

Shine! Rise and Shine! Laura, go tell your brother to rise and shine!*]

TOM [*sitting up slowly*]: I'll rise – but I won't shine.

[*The light increases.*]

AMANDA: Laura, tell your brother his coffee is ready.

[LAURA *slips into front room.*]

LAURA: Tom! – It's nearly seven. Don't make mother nervous. [*He stares at her stupidly. Beseechingly.*] Tom, speak to mother this morning. Make up with her, apologize, speak to her!

TOM: She won't to me. It's her that started not speaking.

LAURA: If you just say you're sorry she'll start speaking.

TOM: Her not speaking – is that such a tragedy?

LAURA: Please – please!

AMANDA [*calling from kitchenette*]: Laura, are you going to do what I asked you to do, or do I have to get dressed and go out myself?

LAURA: Going, going – soon as I get on my coat! [*She pulls on a shapeless felt hat with nervous, jerky movement, pleadingly glancing at* TOM. *Rushes awkwardly for coat. The coat is one of* AMANDA'S, *inaccurately made-over, the sleeves too short for* LAURA.] Butter and what else?

AMANDA [*entering upstage*]: Just butter. Tell them to charge it.

LAURA: Mother, they make such faces when I do that.

AMANDA: Sticks and stones can break our bones, but the expression on Mr Garfinkel's face won't harm us! Tell your brother his coffee is getting cold.

LAURA [*at door*]: Do what I asked you, will you, will you, Tom?

[*He looks sullenly away.*]

AMANDA: Laura, go now or just don't go at all!

LAURA [*rushing out*]: Going – going! [*A second later she cries out.* TOM *springs up and crosses to door.* AMANDA *rushes anxiously in.* TOM *opens the door.*]

TOM: Laura?

LAURA: I'm all right. I slipped, but I'm all right.

AMANDA [*peering anxiously after her*]: If anyone breaks a leg on those fire-escape steps, the landlord ought to be sued for every cent he possesses! [*She shuts door. Remembers she isn't speaking and returns to other room.*]

[*As* TOM *enters listlessly for his coffee, she turns her back to him and stands rigidly facing the window on the gloomy grey vault of the areaway. Its light on her face with its aged but childish features is cruelly sharp, satirical as a Daumier print.*

MUSIC UNDER: 'AVE MARIA'.

TOM *glances sheepishly but sullenly at her averted figure and slumps at the table. The coffee is scalding hot; he sips it and gasps and spits it back in the cup. At his gasp,* AMANDA *catches her breath and half turns. Then catches herself and turns back to window.*

TOM *blows on his coffee, glancing sidewise at his mother. She clears her throat.* TOM *clears his. He starts to rise. Sinks back down again, scratches his head, clears his throat again.* AMANDA *coughs.* TOM *raises his cup in both hands to blow on it, his eyes staring over the rim of it at his mother for several moments. Then he slowly sets the cup down and awkwardly and hesitantly rises from the chair.*]

TOM [*hoarsely*]: Mother. I – I apologize, Mother. [AMANDA *draws a quick, shuddering breath. Her face works grotesquely. She breaks into childlike tears.*] I'm sorry for what I said, for everything that I said; I didn't mean it.

AMANDA [*sobbingly*]: My devotion has made me a witch and so I make myself hateful to my children!

TOM: *No*, you *don't*.

AMANDA: I worry so much, don't sleep, it makes me nervous!

TOM [*gently*]: I understand that.

AMANDA: I've had to put up a solitary battle all these years. But you're my right-hand bower! Don't fall down, don't fail!

TOM [gently]: I try, Mother.

AMANDA [with great enthusiasm]: Try and you will SUCCEED! [The notion makes her breathless.] Why, you – you're just *full* of natural endowments! Both of my children – they're *unusual* children! Don't you think I know it? I'm so – *proud!* Happy and – feel I've – so much to be thankful for but – Promise me one thing, Son!

TOM: What, Mother?

AMANDA: Promise, Son, you'll – never be a drunkard!

TOM [turns to her grinning]: I will never be a drunkard, Mother.

AMANDA: That's what frightened me so, that you'd be drinking! Eat a bowl of Purina!

TOM: Just coffee, Mother.

AMANDA: Shredded wheat biscuit?

TOM: No. No, Mother, just coffee.

AMANDA: You can't put in a day's work on an empty stomach. You've got ten minutes – don't gulp! Drinking too-hot liquids makes cancer of the stomach. ... Put cream in.

TOM: No, thank you.

AMANDA: To cool it.

TOM: No! No, thank you, I want it black.

AMANDA: I know, but it's not good for you. We have to do all that we can to build ourselves up. In these trying times we live in, all that we have to cling to is – each other. ... That's why it's so important to – Tom, I – I sent out your sister so I could discuss something with you. If you hadn't spoken I would have spoken to you. [Sits down.]

TOM [gently]: What is it, Mother, that you want to discuss?

AMANDA: *Laura!*

[TOM *puts his cup down slowly.*

LEGEND ON SCREEN: 'LAURA'.
MUSIC: 'THE GLASS MENAGERIE'.]

TOM: – Oh. – Laura . . .

AMANDA [*touching his sleeve*]: You know how Laura is. So quiet but – still water runs deep! She notices things and I think she – broods about them. [TOM *looks up.*] A few days ago I came in and she was crying.

TOM: What about?

AMANDA: You.

TOM: Me?

AMANDA: She has an idea that you're not happy here.

TOM: What gave her that idea?

AMANDA: What gives her any idea? However, you do act strangely. I – I'm not criticizing, understand *that*! I know your ambitions do not lie in the warehouse, that like everybody in the whole wide world – you've had to – make sacrifices, but – Tom – Tom – life's not easy, it calls for – Spartan endurance! There's so many things in my heart that I cannot describe to you! I've never told you but I – *loved* your father. . . .

TOM [*gently*]: I know that, Mother.

AMANDA: And you – when I see you taking after his ways! Staying out late – and – well, you *had* been drinking the night you were in that – terrifying condition! Laura says that you hate the apartment and that you go out nights to get away from it! Is that true, Tom?

TOM: No. You say there's so much in your heart that you can't describe to me. That's true of me, too. There's so much in my heart that I can't describe to *you*! So let's respect each other's –

AMANDA: But, why – *why*, Tom – are you always so *restless*? Where do you *go* to, nights?

TOM: I – go to the movies.

AMANDA: Why do you go to the movies so much, Tom?

TOM: I go to the movies because – I like adventure.

Adventure is something I don't have much of at work, so I go to the movies.

AMANDA: But, Tom, you go to the movies *entirely* too *much*!

TOM: I like a lot of adventure.

[AMANDA *looks baffled, then hurt. As the familiar inquisition resumes he becomes hard and impatient again.* AMANDA *slips back into her querulous attitude towards him.*

   IMAGE ON SCREEN: SAILING VESSEL WITH JOLLY ROGER.]

AMANDA: Most young men find adventure in their careers.

TOM: Then most young men are not employed in a warehouse.

AMANDA: The world is full of young men employed in warehouses and offices and factories.

TOM: Do all of them find adventure in their careers?

AMANDA: They do or they do without it! Not everybody has a craze for adventure.

TOM: Man is by instinct a lover, a hunter, a fighter, and none of those instincts are given much play at the warehouse!

AMANDA: Man is by instinct! Don't quote instinct to me! Instinct is something that people have got away from! It belongs to animals! Christian adults don't want it!

TOM: What do Christian adults want, then, Mother?

AMANDA: Superior things! Things of the mind and the spirit! Only animals have to satisfy instincts! Surely your aims are somewhat higher than theirs! Than monkeys — pigs —

TOM: I reckon they're not.

AMANDA: You're joking. However, that isn't what I wanted to discuss.

TOM [*rising*]: I haven't much time.

AMANDA [*pushing his shoulders*]: Sit down.

TOM: You want me to punch in red at the warehouse, Mother?

AMANDA: You have five minutes. I want to talk about Laura.

[LEGEND: 'PLANS AND PROVISIONS'.]

TOM: All right! What about Laura?

AMANDA: We have to be making some plans and provisions for her. She's older than you, two years, and nothing has happened. She just drifts along doing nothing. It frightens me terribly how she just drifts along.

TOM: I guess she's the type that people call home girls.

AMANDA: There's no such type, and if there is, it's a pity! That is unless the home is hers, with a husband!

TOM: What?

AMANDA: Oh, I can see the handwriting on the wall as plain as I see the nose in front of my face! It's terrifying! More and more you remind me of your father! He was out all hours without explanation! – Then *left*! *Good-bye*! And me with the bag to hold. I saw that letter you got from the Merchant Marine. I know what you're dreaming of. I'm not standing here blindfolded.
Very well, then. Then *do* it!
But not till there's somebody to take your place.

TOM: What do you mean?

AMANDA: I mean that as soon as Laura has got somebody to take care of her, married, a home of her own, independent – why, then you'll be free to go wherever you please, on land, on sea, whichever way the wind blows you!
But until that time you've got to look out for your sister. I don't say me because I'm old and don't matter! I say for your sister because she's young and dependent.
I put her in business college – a dismal failure! Frightened her so it made her sick at the stomach.
I took her over to the Young People's League at the church. Another fiasco. She spoke to nobody, nobody spoke to her. Now all she does is fool with those pieces

of glass and play those worn-out records. What kind of a life is that for a girl to lead?

TOM: What can I do about it?

AMANDA: Overcome selfishness!
Self, self, self is all that you ever think of!

[TOM *springs up and crosses to get his coat. It is ugly and bulky. He pulls on a cap with earmuffs.*]

Where is your muffler? Put your wool muffler on! [*He snatches it angrily from the closet and tosses it around his neck and pulls both ends tight.*] Tom! I haven't said what I had in mind to ask you.

TOM: I'm too late to –

AMANDA [*catching his arm – very importunately. Then shyly*]: Down at the warehouse, aren't there some – nice young men?

TOM: No!

AMANDA: There *must* be – *some* . . .

TOM: Mother –

[*Gesture.*]

AMANDA: Find out one that's clean-living – doesn't drink and – ask him out for sister!

TOM: What?

AMANDA: For *sister*! To *meet*! Get *acquainted*!

TOM [*stamping to door*]: Oh, my *go-osh*!

AMANDA: Will you? [*He opens door. Imploringly.*] Will you? [*He starts down.*] Will you? *Will* you, dear?

TOM [*calling back*]: YES!

[AMANDA *closes the door hesitantly and with a troubled but faintly hopeful expression.*

SCREEN IMAGE: GLAMOUR MAGAZINE COVER.
Spot AMANDA *at phone.*]

AMANDA: Ella Cartwright? This is Amanda Wingfield!
How are you, honey?

How is that kidney condition?

[*Count five.*]

Horrors!

[*Count five.*]

You're a Christian martyr, yes, honey, that's what you are, a Christian martyr!

Well, I just now happened to notice in my little red book that your subscription to the *Companion* has just run out! I knew that you wouldn't want to miss out on the wonderful serial starting in this issue. It's by Bessie Mae Hopper, the first thing she's written since *Honeymoon for Three*.

Wasn't that a strange and interesting story? Well, this one is even lovelier, I believe. It has a sophisticated, society background. It's all about the horsy set on Long Island!

FADE OUT

SCENE FIVE

LEGEND ON SCREEN: 'ANNUNCIATION'. *Fade with music.*
[*It is early dusk on a spring evening. Supper has just been finished in the Wingfield apartment.* AMANDA *and* LAURA *in light-coloured dresses are removing dishes from the table, in the upstage area, which is shadowy, their movements formalized almost as a dance or ritual, their moving forms as pale and silent as moths.*

    TOM, *in white shirt and trousers, rises from the table and crosses toward the fire-escape.*]

AMANDA [*as he passes her*]: Son, will you do me a favour?

TOM: What?

AMANDA: Comb your hair! You look so pretty when your hair is combed! [TOM *slouches on sofa with evening paper. Enormous caption 'Franco Triumphs'.*] There is only one respect in which I would like you to emulate your father.

TOM: What respect is that?

AMANDA: The care he always took of his appearance. He never allowed himself to look untidy. [*He throws down the paper and crosses to fire-escape.*] Where are you going?

TOM: I'm going out to smoke.

AMANDA: You smoke too much. A pack a day at fifteen cents a pack. How much would that amount to in a month? Thirty times fifteen is how much, Tom? Figure it out and you will be astounded at what you could save. Enough to give you a night-school course in accounting at Washington U! Just think what a wonderful thing that would be for you, Son!

    [TOM *is unmoved by the thought.*]

TOM: I'd rather smoke. [*He steps out on the landing, letting the screen door slam.*]

AMANDA [*sharply*]: I know! That's the tragedy of it. ...
[*Alone, she turns to look at her husband's picture.*]

[DANCE MUSIC: 'ALL THE WORLD IS WAITING FOR
THE SUNRISE!']

TOM [*to the audience*]: Across the alley from us was the Paradise Dance Hall. On evenings in spring the windows and
doors were open and the music came outdoors. Sometimes
the lights were turned out except for a large glass sphere
that hung from the ceiling. It would turn slowly about
and filter the dusk with delicate rainbow colours. Then
the orchestra played a waltz or a tango, something that
had a slow and sensuous rhythm. Couples would come
outside, to the relative privacy of the alley. You could see
them kissing behind ash-pits and telegraph poles.
This was the compensation for lives that passed like mine,
without any change or adventure.
Adventure and change were imminent in this year. They
were waiting around the corner for all these kids.
Suspended in the mist over Berchtesgaden, caught in the
folds of Chamberlain's umbrella –
In Spain there was Guernica!
But here there was only hot swing music and liquor,
dance halls, bars, and movies, and sex that hung in the
gloom like a chandelier and flooded the world with brief,
deceptive rainbows. ...
All the world was waiting for bombardments!

[AMANDA *turns from the picture and comes outside.*]

AMANDA [*sighing*]: A fire-escape landing's a poor excuse for
a porch. [*She spreads a newspaper on a step and sits down grace-
fully and demurely as if she were settling into a swing on a
Mississippi veranda.*] What are you looking at?
TOM: The moon.
AMANDA: Is there a moon this evening?
TOM: It's rising over Garfinkel's Delicatessen.

AMANDA: So it is! A little silver slipper of a moon. Have you made a wish on it yet?

TOM: Um-hum.

AMANDA: What did you wish for?

TOM: That's a secret.

AMANDA: A secret, huh? Well, I won't tell mine either. I will be just as mysterious as you.

TOM: I bet I can guess what yours is.

AMANDA: Is my head so transparent?

TOM: You're not a sphinx.

AMANDA: No, I don't have secrets. I'll tell you what I wished for on the moon. Success and happiness for my precious children! I wish for that whenever there's a moon, and when there isn't a moon, I wish for it, too.

TOM: I thought perhaps you wished for a gentleman caller.

AMANDA: Why do you say that?

TOM: Don't you remember asking me to fetch one?

AMANDA: I remember suggesting that it would be nice for your sister if you brought home some nice young man from the warehouse. I think that I've made that suggestion more than once.

TOM: Yes, you have made it repeatedly.

AMANDA: Well?

TOM: We are going to have one.

AMANDA: *What?*

TOM: A gentleman caller!

[THE ANNUNCIATION IS CELEBRATED WITH MUSIC. AMANDA *rises.*

IMAGE ON SCREEN: CALLER WITH BOUQUET.]

AMANDA: You mean you have asked some nice young man to come over?

TOM: Yep. I've asked him to dinner.

AMANDA: You really did?

TOM: I did!

AMANDA: You did, and did he – *accept?*

TOM: He did!

AMANDA: Well, well – well, well! That's – lovely!

TOM: I thought that you would be pleased.

AMANDA: It's definite, then?

TOM: Very definite.

AMANDA: Soon?

TOM: Very soon.

AMANDA: For heaven's sake, stop putting on and tell me some things, will you?

TOM: What things do you want me to tell you?

AMANDA: *Naturally* I would like to know when he's *coming!*

TOM: He's coming tomorrow.

AMANDA: *Tomorrow?*

TOM: Yep. Tomorrow.

AMANDA: But, Tom!

TOM: Yes, Mother?

AMANDA: Tomorrow gives me no time!

TOM: Time for what?

AMANDA: Preparations! Why didn't you phone me at once, as soon as you asked him, the minute that he accepted? Then, don't you see, I could have been getting ready!

TOM: You don't have to make any fuss.

AMANDA: Oh, Tom, Tom, Tom, of course I have to make a fuss! I want things nice, not sloppy! Not thrown together. I'll certainly have to do some fast thinking, won't I?

TOM: I don't see why you have to think at all.

AMANDA: You just don't know. We can't have a gentleman caller in a pigsty! All my wedding silver has to be polished, the monogrammed table linen ought to be laundered! The windows have to be washed and fresh curtains put up. And how about clothes? We have to *wear* something, don't we?

TOM: Mother, this boy is no one to make a fuss over!

AMANDA: Do you realize he's the first young man we've introduced to your sister?

It's terrible, dreadful, disgraceful that poor little sister has never received a single gentleman caller! Tom, come inside! [*She opens the screen door.*]

TOM: What for?

AMANDA: I want to ask you some things.

TOM: If you're going to make such a fuss, I'll call it off, I'll tell him not to come!

AMANDA: You certainly won't do anything of the kind. Nothing offends people worse than broken engagements. It simply means I'll have to work like a Turk! We won't be brilliant, but we will pass inspection. Come on inside. [TOM *follows, groaning.*] Sit down.

TOM: Any particular place you would like me to sit?

AMANDA: Thank heavens I've got that new sofa! I'm also making payments on a floor lamp I'll have sent out! And put the chintz covers on, they'll brighten things up! Of course I'd hoped to have these walls re-papered. ... What is the young man's name?

TOM: His name is O'Connor.

AMANDA: That, of course, means fish – tomorrow is Friday! I'll have that salmon loaf – with Durkee's dressing! What does he do? He works at the warehouse?

TOM: Of course! How else would I –

AMANDA: Tom, he – doesn't drink?

TOM: Why do you ask me that?

AMANDA: Your father *did!*

TOM: Don't get started on that!

AMANDA: He *does* drink, then?

TOM: Not that I know of!

AMANDA: Make sure, be certain! The last thing I want for my daughter's a boy who drinks!

TOM: Aren't you being a little bit premature? Mr O'Connor has not yet appeared on the scene!

AMANDA: But will tomorrow. To meet your sister, and what do I know about his character? Nothing! Old maids are better off than wives of drunkards!

TOM: Oh, my God!

AMANDA: Be still!

TOM [*leaning forward to whisper*]: Lots of fellows meet girls whom they don't marry!

AMANDA: Oh, talk sensibly, Tom – and don't be sarcastic!

[*She has gotten a hairbrush.*]

TOM: What are you doing?

AMANDA: I'm brushing that cow-lick down!

What is this young man's position at the warehouse?

TOM [*submitting grimly to the brush and the interrogation*]: This young man's position is that of a shipping clerk, Mother.

AMANDA: Sounds to me like a fairly responsible job, the sort of a job *you* would be in if you just had more *get-up*.

What is his salary? Have you any idea?

TOM: I would judge it to be approximately eighty-five dollars a month.

AMANDA: Well – not princely, but –

TOM: Twenty more than I make.

AMANDA: Yes, how well I know! But for a family man, eighty-five dollars a month is not much more than you can just get by on. . . .

TOM: Yes, but Mr O'Connor is not a family man.

AMANDA: He might be, mightn't he? Some time in the future?

TOM: I see. Plans and provisions.

AMANDA: You are the only young man that I know of who ignores the fact that the future becomes the present, the present the past, and the past turns into everlasting regret if you don't plan for it!

TOM: I will think that over and see what I can make of it.

AMANDA: Don't be supercilious with your mother! Tell me some more about this – what do you call him?

TOM: James D. O'Connor. The D. is for Delaney.

AMANDA: Irish on *both* sides! *Gracious!* And doesn't drink?

TOM: Shall I call him up and ask him right this minute?

AMANDA: The only way to find out about those things is to make discreet inquiries at the proper moment. When I was a girl in Blue Mountain and it was suspected that a young man drank, the girl whose attentions he had been receiving, if any girl *was*, would sometimes speak to the minister of his church, or rather her father would if her father was living, and sort of feel him out on the young man's character. That is the way such things are discreetly handled to keep a young woman from making a tragic mistake!

TOM: Then how did you happen to make a tragic mistake!

AMANDA: That innocent look of your father's had everyone fooled! He *smiled* – the world was *enchanted*!
No girl can do worse than put herself at the mercy of a handsome appearance!
I hope that Mr O'Connor is not too good-looking.

TOM: No, he's not too good-looking. He's covered with freckles and hasn't too much of a nose.

AMANDA: He's not right-down homely, though?

TOM: Not right-down homely. Just medium homely, I'd say.

AMANDA: Character's what to look for in a man.

TOM: That's what I've always said, Mother.

AMANDA: You've never said anything of the kind and I suspect you would never give it a thought.

TOM: Don't be so suspicious of me.

AMANDA: At least I hope he's the type that's up and coming.

TOM: I think he really goes in for self-improvement.

AMANDA: What reason have you to think so?

TOM: He goes to night school.

AMANDA [*beaming*]: Splendid! What does he do, I mean study?

TOM: Radio engineering and public speaking!

AMANDA: Then he has visions of being advanced in the world! Any young man who studies public speaking is aiming to have an executive job some day!

And radio engineering? A thing for the future! Both of these facts are very illuminating. Those are the sort of things that a mother should know concerning any young man who comes to call on her daughter. Seriously or – not.

TOM: One little warning. He doesn't know about Laura. I didn't let on that we had dark ulterior motives. I just said, why don't you come and have dinner with us? He said okay and that was the whole conversation.

AMANDA: I bet it was! You're eloquent as an oyster. However, he'll know about Laura when he gets here. When he sees how lovely and sweet and pretty she is, he'll thank his lucky stars he was asked to dinner.

TOM: Mother, you mustn't expect too much of Laura.

AMANDA: What do you mean?

TOM: Laura seems all those things to you and me because she's ours and we love her. We don't even notice she's crippled any more.

AMANDA: Don't say crippled! You know that I never allow that word to be used!

TOM: But face facts, Mother. She is and – that's not all –

AMANDA: What do you mean 'not all'?

TOM: Laura is very different from other girls.

AMANDA: I think the difference is all to her advantage.

TOM: Not quite all – in the eyes of others – strangers – she's terribly shy and lives in a world of her own and those things make her seem a little peculiar to people outside the house.

AMANDA: Don't say peculiar.

TOM: Face the facts. She is.

[THE DANCE-HALL MUSIC CHANGES TO A TANGO THAT HAS A MINOR AND SOMEWHAT OMINOUS TONE.]

AMANDA: In what way is she peculiar – may I ask?

TOM [gently]: She lives in a world of her own – a world of –

little glass ornaments, Mother. . . . [*Gets up.* AMANDA *remains holding brush, looking at him, troubled.*] She plays old phonograph records and – that's about all – [*He glances at himself in the mirror and crosses to door.*]

AMANDA [*sharply*]: Where are you going?

TOM: I'm going to the movies. [*Out screen door.*]

AMANDA: Not to the movies, every night to the movies! [*Follows quickly to screen door.*] I don't believe you always go to the movies! [*He is gone.* AMANDA *looks worriedly after him for a moment. Then vitality and optimism return and she turns from the door. Crossing to portières.*] Laura! Laura! [LAURA *answers from kitchenette.*]

LAURA: Yes, Mother.

AMANDA: Let those dishes go and come in front! [LAURA *appears with dish towel. Gaily.*] Laura, come here and make a wish on the moon!

[SCREEN IMAGE: MOON.]

LAURA [*entering*]: Moon – moon?

AMANDA: A little silver slipper of a moon. Look over your left shoulder, Laura, and make a wish!

[LAURA *looks faintly puzzled as if called out of sleep.* AMANDA *seizes her shoulders and turns her at an angle by the door.*]

Now!

Now, darling, *wish*!

LAURA: What shall I wish for, Mother?

AMANDA [*her voice trembling and her eyes suddenly filling with tears*]: Happiness! Good fortune!

[*The violin rises and the stage dims out.*]

CURTAIN

SCENE SIX

[IMAGE: HIGH SCHOOL HERO.]

TOM: And so the following evening I brought Jim home to dinner. I·had known Jim slightly in high school. In high school Jim was a hero. He had tremendous Irish good nature and vitality with the scrubbed and polished look of white chinaware. He seemed to move in a continual spotlight. He was a star in basket-ball, captain of the debating club, president of the senior class and the glee club and he sang the male lead in the annual light operas. He was always running or bounding, never just walking. He seemed always at the point of defeating the law of gravity. He was shooting with such velocity through his adolescence that you would logically expect him to arrive at nothing short of the White House by the time he was thirty. But Jim apparently ran into more interference after his graduation from Soldan. His speed had definitely slowed. Six years after he left high school he was holding a job that wasn't much better than mine.

[IMAGE: CLERK.]

He was the only one at the warehouse with whom I was on friendly terms. I was valuable to him as someone who could remember his former glory, who had seen him win basketball games and the silver cup in debating. He knew of my secret practice of retiring to a cabinet of the washroom to work on poems when business was slack in the warehouse. He called me Shakespeare. And while the other boys in the warehouse regarded me with suspicious hostility, Jim took a humorous attitude toward me. Gradually his attitude affected the others, their hostility wore off and they also began to smile at me as people smile at an oddly fashioned dog who trots across their path at some distance.

I knew that Jim and Laura had known each other at Soldan, and I had heard Laura speak admiringly of his voice. I didn't know if Jim remembered her or not. In high school Laura had been as unobtrusive as Jim had been astonishing. If he did remember Laura, it was not as my sister, for when I asked him to dinner, he grinned and said, 'You know, Shakespeare, I never thought of you as having folks!'

He was about to discover that I did. ....

[LIGHT UPSTAGE.

LEGEND ON SCREEN: 'THE ACCENT OF A COMING FOOT'.

Friday evening. It is about five o'clock of a late spring evening which comes 'scattering poems in the sky'.

A delicate lemony light is in the Wingfield apartment.

AMANDA *has worked like a Turk in preparation for the gentleman caller. The results are astonishing. The new floor lamp with its rose-silk shade is in place, a coloured paper lantern conceals the broken light fixture in the ceiling, new billowing white curtains are at the windows, chintz covers are on chairs and sofa, a pair of new sofa pillows make their initial appearance.*

Open boxes and tissue paper are scattered on the floor.

LAURA *stands in the middle with lifted arms while* AMANDA *crouches before her, adjusting the hem of the new dress, devout and ritualistic. The dress is coloured and designed by memory. The arrangement of* LAURA'S *hair is changed; it is softer and more becoming. A fragile, unearthly prettiness has come out in* LAURA: *she is like a piece of translucent glass touched by light, given a momentary radiance, not actual, not lasting.*]

AMANDA [*impatiently*]: Why are you trembling?

LAURA: Mother, you've made me so nervous!

AMANDA: How have I made you nervous?

LAURA: By all this fuss! You make it seem so important!

AMANDA: I don't understand you, Laura. You couldn't be satisfied with just sitting home, and yet whenever I try to arrange something for you, you seem to resist it. [*She gets up.*]

Now take a look at yourself.

No, wait! Wait just a moment – I have an idea!

LAURA: What is it now?

[AMANDA *produces two powder puffs which she wraps in handkerchiefs and stuffs in* LAURA'*s bosom.*]

LAURA: Mother, what are you doing?

AMANDA: They call them 'Gay Deceivers'!

LAURA: I won't wear them!

AMANDA: You will!

LAURA: Why should I?

AMANDA: Because, to be painfully honest, your chest is flat.

LAURA: You make it seem like we were setting a trap.

AMANDA: All pretty girls are a trap, a pretty trap, and men·expect them to be!

[LEGEND: 'A PRETTY TRAP'.]

Now look at yourself, young lady. This is the prettiest you will ever be!

I've got to fix myself now! You're going to be surprised by your mother's appearance! [*She crosses through portières, humming gaily.*]

[LAURA *moves slowly to the long mirror and stares solemnly at herself. A wind blows the white curtains inward in a slow, graceful motion and with a faint, sorrowful sighing.*]

AMANDA [*off stage*]: It isn't dark enough yet. [LAURA *turns slowly before the mirror with a troubled look.*]

[LEGEND ON SCREEN: 'THIS IS MY SISTER: CELE-
BRATE HER WITH STRINGS!' MUSIC.]

AMANDA [*laughing, off*]: I'm going to show you something.
I'm going to make a spectacular appearance!
LAURA: What is it, Mother?
AMANDA: Possess your soul in patience – you will see!
Something I've resurrected from that old trunk! Styles
haven't changed so terribly much after all. ...

[*She parts the portières.*]

Now just look at your mother!

[*She wears a girlish frock of yellowed voile with a blue silk
sash. She carries a bunch of jonquils – the legend of her youth
is nearly revived.*]

[*Feverishly*]: This is the dress in which I led the cotillion,
won the cakewalk twice at Sunset Hill, wore one spring
to the Governor's ball in Jackson!
See how I sashayed around the ballroom, Laura?

[*She raises her skirt and does a mincing step around the room.*]

I wore it on Sundays for my gentlemen callers! I had it on
the day I met your father –
I had malaria fever all that spring. The change of climate
from East Tennessee to the Delta – weakened resistance –
I had a little temperature all the time – not enough to be
serious – just enough to make me restless and giddy! –
Invitations poured in – parties all over the Delta! – 'Stay
in bed,' said mother, 'you have fever!' – but I just
wouldn't. – I took quinine but kept on going, going! –
Evenings, dances! – Afternoons, long, long rides! Picnics
– lovely! – So lovely, that country in May. – All lacy with
dogwood, literally flooded with jonquils! – That was the
spring I had the craze for jonquils. Jonquils became an
absolute obsession. Mother said, 'Honey, there's no more
room for jonquils.' And still I kept on bringing in more

jonquils. Whenever, wherever I saw them, I'd say, 'Stop! Stop! I see jonquils!' I made the young men help me gather the jonquils! It was a joke, Amanda and her jonquils! Finally there were no more vases to hold them, every available space was filled with jonquils. No vases to hold them? All right, I'll hold them myself! And then I – [*She stops in front of the picture.* MUSIC.] met your father! Malaria fever and jonquils and then – this – boy. . . .

[*She switches on the rose-coloured lamp.*]

I hope they get here before it starts to rain.

[*She crosses upstage and places the jonquils in bowl on table.*]

I gave your brother a little extra change so he and Mr O'Connor could take the service car home.

LAURA [*with altered look*]: What did you say his name was?

AMANDA: O'Connor.

LAURA: What is his first name?

AMANDA: I don't remember. Oh, yes, I do. It was – Jim!

[LAURA *sways slightly and catches hold of a chair.*
   LEGEND ON SCREEN: 'NOT JIM!']

LAURA [*faintly*]: Not – Jim!

AMANDA: Yes, that was it, it was Jim! I've never known a Jim that wasn't nice!

[MUSIC OMINOUS.]

LAURA: Are you sure his name is Jim O'Connor?

AMANDA: Yes. Why?

LAURA: Is he the one that Tom used to know in high school?

AMANDA: He didn't say so. I think he just got to know him at the warehouse.

LAURA: There was a Jim O'Connor we both knew in high school – [*Then, with effort.*] If that is the one that Tom is bringing to dinner – you'll have to excuse me, I won't come to the table.

AMANDA: What sort of nonsense is this?

LAURA: You asked me once if I'd ever liked a boy. Don't you remember I showed you this boy's picture?

AMANDA: You mean the boy you showed me in the year book?

LAURA: Yes, that boy.

AMANDA: Laura, Laura, were you in love with that boy?

LAURA: I don't know, Mother. All I know is I couldn't sit at the table if it was him!

AMANDA: It won't be him! It isn't the least bit likely. But whether it is or not, you will come to the table. You will not be excused.

LAURA: I'll have to be, Mother.

AMANDA: I don't intend to humour your silliness, Laura. I've had too much from you and your brother, both! So just sit down and compose yourself till they come. Tom has forgotten his key so you'll have to let them in, when they arrive.

LAURA [*panicky*]: Oh, Mother – *you* answer the door!

AMANDA [*lightly*]: I'll be in the kitchen – busy!

LAURA: Oh, Mother, please answer the door, don't make me do it!

AMANDA [*crossing into kitchenette*]: I've got to fix the dressing for the salmon. Fuss, fuss – silliness! over a gentleman caller!

[*Door swings shut.* LAURA *is left alone.*

LEGEND: 'TERROR!'

She utters a low moan and turns off the lamp – sits stiffly on the edge of the sofa, knotting her fingers together.

LEGEND ON SCREEN: 'THE OPENING OF A DOOR!'

TOM *and* JIM *appear on the fire-escape steps and climb to landing. Hearing their approach,* LAURA *rises with a panicky gesture. She retreats to the portières.*

The doorbell, LAURA *catches her breath and touches her throat. Low drums.*]

AMANDA [*calling*]: Laura, sweetheart! The door!

[LAURA *stares at it without moving.*]

JIM: I think we just beat the rain.

TOM: Uh-huh. [*He rings again, nervously.* JIM *whistles and fishes for a cigarette.*]

AMANDA [*very, very gaily*]: Laura, that is your brother and Mr O'Connor! Will you let them in, darling?

[LAURA *crosses toward kitchenette door.*]

LAURA [*breathlessly*]: Mother – you go to the door!

[AMANDA *steps out of kitchenette and stares furiously at* LAURA. *She points imperiously at the door.*]

LAURA: Please, please!

AMANDA [*in a fierce whisper*]: What is the matter with you, you silly thing?

LAURA [*desperately*]: Please, you answer it, *please*!

AMANDA: I told you I wasn't going to humour you, Laura. Why have you chosen this moment to lose your mind?

LAURA: Please, please, please, you go!

AMANDA: You'll have to go to the door because I can't!

LAURA [*despairingly*]: I can't either!

AMANDA: *Why?*

LAURA: I'm *sick*!

AMANDA: I'm sick, too – of your nonsense! Why can't you and your brother be normal people? Fantastic whims and behaviour!

[TOM *gives a long ring.*]

Preposterous goings on! Can you give me one reason – [*Calls out lyrically.*] COMING! JUST ONE SECOND! – why you should be afraid to open a door? Now you answer it, Laura!

LAURA: Oh, oh, oh ... [*She returns through the portières. Darts to the victrola and winds it frantically and turns it on.*]

AMANDA: Laura Wingfield, you march right to that door!

LAURA: Yes – yes, Mother!

> [*A faraway, scratchy rendition of 'Dardanella' softens the air and gives her strength to move through it. She slips to the door and draws it cautiously open.*
>
> TOM *enters with the caller,* JIM O'CONNOR.]

TOM: Laura, this is Jim. Jim, this is my sister, Laura.

JIM [*stepping inside*]: I didn't know that Shakespeare had a sister!

LAURA [*retreating stiff and trembling from the door*]: How – how do you do?

JIM [*heartily extending his hand*]: Okay!

> [LAURA *touches it hesitantly with hers.*]

JIM: Your hand's *cold*, Laura!

LAURA: Yes, well – I've been playing the victrola....

JIM: Must have been playing classical music on it! You ought to play a little hot swing music to warm you up!

LAURA: Excuse me – I haven't finished playing the victrola. ... [*She turns awkwardly and hurries into the front room. She pauses a second by the victrola. Then catches her breath and darts through the portières like a frightened deer.*]

JIM [*grinning*]: What was the matter?

TOM: Oh – with Laura? Laura is – terribly shy.

JIM: Shy, huh? It's unusual to meet a shy girl nowadays. I don't believe you ever mentioned you had a sister.

TOM: Well, now you know. I have one. Here is the *Post Dispatch*. You want a piece of it?

JIM: Uh-huh.

TOM: What piece? The comics?

JIM: Sports! [*Glances at it.*] Ole Dizzy Dean is on his bad behaviour.

TOM [*disinterested*]: Yeah? [*Lights cigarette and crosses back to fire-escape door.*]

JIM: Where are *you* going?

TOM: I'm going out on the terrace.

JIM [*goes after him*]: You know, Shakespeare – I'm going to sell you a bill of goods!

TOM: What goods?

JIM: A course I'm taking.

TOM: Huh?

JIM: In public speaking! You and me, we're not the warehouse type.

TOM: Thanks – that's good news.

But what has public speaking got to do with it?

JIM: It fits you for – executive positions!

TOM: Awww.

JIM: I tell you it's done a helluva lot for me.

[IMAGE: EXECUTIVE AT DESK.]

TOM: In what respect?

JIM: In every! Ask yourself what is the difference between you an' me and men in the office down front? Brains? – No! – Ability? – No! Then what? Just one little thing –

TOM: What is that one little thing?

JIM: Primarily it amounts to – social poise! Being able to square up to people and hold your own on any social level!

AMANDA [*off stage*]: Tom?

TOM: Yes, Mother?

AMANDA: Is that you and Mr O'Connor?

TOM: Yes, Mother.

AMANDA: Well, you just make yourselves comfortable in there.

TOM: Yes, Mother.

AMANDA: Ask Mr O'Connor if he would like to wash his hands.

JIM: Aw, no – no – thank you – I took care of that at the warehouse. Tom –

TOM: Yes?

JIM: Mr Mendoza was speaking to me about you.

TOM: Favourably?

JIM: What do you think?

TOM: Well –

JIM: You're going to be out of a job if you don't wake up.

TOM: I am waking up –

JIM: You show no signs.

TOM: The signs are interior.

[IMAGE ON SCREEN: THE SAILING VESSEL WITH JOLLY ROGER AGAIN.]

TOM: I'm planning to change. [*He leans over the rail speaking with quiet exhilaration. The incandescent marquees and signs of the first-run movie houses light his face from across the alley. He looks like a voyager.*] I'm right at the point of committing myself to a future that doesn't include the warehouse and Mr Mendoza or even a night-school course in public speaking.

JIM: What are you gassing about?

TOM: I'm tired of the movies.

JIM: Movies!

TOM: Yes, movies! Look at them – [*A wave toward the marvels of Grand Avenue.*] All of those glamorous people – having adventures – hogging it all, gobbling the whole thing up! You know what happens? People go to the *movies* instead of *moving*! Hollywood characters are supposed to have all the adventures for everybody in America, while everybody in America sits in a dark room and watches them have them! Yes, until there's a war. That's when adventure becomes available to the masses! *Everyone's* dish, not only Gable's! Then the people in the dark room come out of the dark room to have some adventure themselves – Goody, goody! – It's our turn now, to go to the South Sea

Islands – to make a safari – to be exotic, far-off! – But I'm not patient. I don't want to wait till then. I'm tired of the *movies* and I am *about to move*!

JIM [*incredulously*]: Move?

TOM: Yes.

JIM: When?

TOM: Soon!

JIM: Where? Where?

[THEME THREE MUSIC SEEMS TO ANSWER THE QUESTION, WHILE TOM THINKS IT OVER. HE SEARCHES AMONG HIS POCKETS.]

TOM: I'm starting to boil inside. I know I seem dreamy, but inside – well, I'm boiling! – Whenever I pick up a shoe, I shudder a little thinking how short life is and what I am doing! – Whatever that means, I know it doesn't mean shoes – except as something to wear on a traveller's feet! [*Finds paper.*] Look –

JIM: What?

TOM: I'm a member.

JIM [*reading*]: The Union of Merchant Seamen.

TOM: I paid my dues this month, instead of the light bill.

JIM: You will regret it when they turn the lights off.

TOM: I won't be here.

JIM: How about your mother?

TOM: I'm like my father. The bastard son of a bastard! See how he grins? And he's been absent going on sixteen years!

JIM: You're just talking, you drip. How does your mother feel about it?

TOM: Shhh! – Here comes mother! Mother is not acquainted with my plans!

AMANDA [*enters portières*]: Where are you all?

TOM: On the terrace, Mother.

[*They start inside. She advances to them.* TOM *is distinctly shocked at her appearance. Even* JIM *blinks a little. He is making his first contact with girlish Southern vivacity and in spite of the night-school course in public speaking is somewhat thrown off the beam by the unexpected outlay of social charm.*

Certain responses are attempted by JIM *but are swept aside by* AMANDA'S *gay laughter and chatter.* TOM *is embarrassed but after the first shock* JIM *reacts very warmly. Grins and chuckles, is altogether won over.*

[IMAGE: AMANDA AS A GIRL.]

AMANDA [*coyly smiling, shaking her girlish ringlets*]: Well, well, well, so this is Mr O'Connor. Introductions entirely unnecessary. I've heard so much about you from my boy. I finally said to him, Tom – good gracious! – why don't you bring this paragon to supper? I'd like to meet this nice young man at the warehouse! – Instead of just hearing you sing his praises so much!

I don't know why my son is so stand-offish – that's not Southern behaviour!

Let's sit down and – I think we could stand a little more air in here! Tom, leave the door open. I felt a nice fresh breeze a moment ago. Where has it gone to?

Mmm, so warm already! And not quite summer, even. We're going to burn up when summer really gets started. However, we're having – we're having a very light supper. I think light things are better fo' this time of year. The same as light clothes are. Light clothes an' light food are what warm weather calls fo'. You know our blood gets so thick during th' winter – it takes a while fo' us to *adjust* ou'selves! – when the season changes . . .

It's come so quick this year. I wasn't prepared. All of a sudden – heavens! Already summer! – I ran to the trunk an' pulled out this light dress – Terribly old! Historical almost! But feels so good – so good an' co-ol, y' know. . . .

TOM: Mother –

AMANDA: Yes, honey?

TOM: How about – supper?

AMANDA: Honey, you go ask Sister if supper is ready! You know that Sister is in full charge of supper!
Tell her you hungry boys are waiting for it.

[*To* JIM.]

Have you met Laura?

JIM: She –

AMANDA: Let you in? Oh, good, you've met already! It's rare for a girl as sweet an' pretty as Laura to be domestic! But Laura is, thank heavens, not only pretty but also very domestic. I'm not at all. I never was a bit. I never could make a thing but angel-food cake. Well, in the South we had so many servants. Gone, gone, gone. All vestige of gracious living! Gone completely! I wasn't prepared for what the future brought me. All of my gentlemen callers were sons of planters and so of course I assumed that I would be married to one and raise my family on a large piece of land with plenty of servants. But man proposes – and woman accepts the proposal! – To vary that old, old saying a little bit – I married no planter! I married a man who worked for the telephone company! – That gallantly smiling gentleman over there! [*Points to the picture.*] A telephone man who – fell in love with long distance! – Now he travels and I don't even know where! – But what am I going on for about my – tribulations?
Tell me yours – I hope you don't have any!
Tom?

TOM [*returning*]: Yes, Mother?

AMANDA: Is supper nearly ready?

TOM: It looks to me like supper is on the table.

AMANDA: Let me look – [*She rises prettily and looks through portières.*] Oh, lovely! – But where is Sister?

TOM: Laura is not feeling well and she says that she thinks she'd better not come to the table.

AMANDA: What? – Nonsense! – Laura? Oh, Laura!

LAURA [*off stage, faintly*]: Yes, Mother.

AMANDA: You really must come to the table. We won't be seated until you come to the table!

Come in, Mr O'Connor. You sit over there, and I'll – Laura? Laura Wingfield!

You're keeping us waiting, honey! We can't say grace until you come to the table!

[*The back door is pushed weakly open and* LAURA *comes in. She is obviously quite faint, her lips trembling, her eyes wide and staring. She moves unsteadily toward the table.*

LEGEND: 'TERROR!'

Outside a summer storm is coming abruptly. The white curtains billow inward at the windows and there is a sorrowful murmur and deep blue dusk.

LAURA *suddenly stumbles – she catches at a chair with a faint moan.*]

TOM: Laura!

AMANDA: Laura!

[*There is a clap of thunder.*

LEGEND: 'AH!']

[*Despairingly*] Why, Laura, you *are* sick, darling! Tom, help your sister into the living-room, dear!

Sit in the living-room, Laura – rest on the sofa.

Well!

[*To the gentleman caller.*]

Standing over the hot stove made her ill! – I told her that was just too warm this evening, but –

[TOM *comes back in.* LAURA *is on the sofa.*]

Is Laura all right now?

TOM: Yes.

AMANDA: What *is* that? Rain? A nice cool rain has come up!

[*She gives the gentleman caller a frightened look.*]

I think we may – have grace – now ...

[TOM *looks at her steadily.*]

Tom, honey – you say grace!

TOM: Oh ...
'For these and all thy mercies –'

[*They bow their heads,* AMANDA *stealing a nervous glance at* JIM. *In the living-room* LAURA, *stretched on the sofa, clenches her hand to her lips, to hold back a shuddering sob.*]

God's Holy Name be praised –

THE SCENE DIMS OUT

SCENE SEVEN

A SOUVENIR

Half an hour later. Dinner is just being finished in the upstage area which is concealed by the drawn portières.

[*As the curtain rises* LAURA *is still huddled upon the sofa, her feet drawn under her, her head resting on a pale blue pillow, her eyes wide and mysteriously watchful. The new floor lamp with its shade of rose-coloured silk gives a soft, becoming light to her face, bringing out the fragile, unearthly prettiness which usually escapes attention. There is a steady murmur of rain, but it is slackening and stops soon after the scene begins; the air outside becomes pale and luminous as the moon breaks out. A moment after the curtain rises, the lights in both rooms flicker and go out.*]

JIM: Hey, there, Mr Light Bulb!

[AMANDA *laughs nervously.*

LEGEND: 'SUSPENSION OF A PUBLIC SERVICE'.]

AMANDA: Where was Moses when the lights went out? Ha-ha. Do you know the answer to that one, Mr O'Connor?

JIM: No, Ma'am, what's the answer?

AMANDA: In the dark!

[JIM *laughs appreciatively.*]

Everybody sit still. I'll light the candles. Isn't it lucky we have them on the table? Where's a match? Which of you gentlemen can provide a match?

JIM: Here.

AMANDA: Thank you, sir.

JIM: Not at all, Ma'am!

AMANDA: I guess the fuse has burnt out. Mr O'Connor,

can you tell a burnt-out fuse? I know I can't and Tom is a total loss when it comes to mechanics.

[SOUND: GETTING UP: VOICES RECEDE A LITTLE TO KITCHENETTE.]

Oh, be careful you don't bump into something. We don't want our gentleman caller to break his neck. Now wouldn't that be a fine howdy-do?

JIM: Ha-ha!

Where is the fuse-box?

AMANDA: Right here next to the stove. Can you see anything?

JIM: Just a minute.

AMANDA: Isn't electricity a mysterious thing?
Wasn't it Benjamin Franklin who tied a key to a kite?
We live in such a mysterious universe, don't we? Some people say that science clears up all the mysteries for us. In my opinion it only creates more!
Have you found it yet?

JIM: No, Ma'am. All these fuses look okay to me.

AMANDA: Tom!

TOM: Yes, Mother?

AMANDA: That light bill I gave you several days ago. The one I told you we got the notices about?

[LEGEND: 'HA!']

TOM: Oh. – Yeah.

AMANDA: You didn't neglect to pay it by any chance?

TOM: Why, I –

AMANDA: Didn't! I might have known it!

JIM: Shakespeare probably wrote a poem on that light bill, Mrs Wingfield.

AMANDA: I might have known better than to trust him with it! There's such a high price for negligence in this world!

JIM: Maybe the poem will win a ten-dollar prize.

AMANDA: We'll just have to spend the remainder of the evening in the nineteenth century, before Mr Edison made the Mazda lamp!

JIM: Candlelight is my favourite kind of light.

AMANDA: That shows you're romantic! But that's no excuse for Tom.

Well, we got through dinner. Very considerate of them to let us get through dinner before they plunged us into ever-lasting darkness, wasn't it, Mr O'Connor?

JIM: Ha-ha!

AMANDA: Tom, as a penalty for your carelessness you can help me with the dishes.

JIM: Let me give you a hand.

AMANDA: Indeed you will not!

JIM: I ought to be good for something.

AMANDA: Good for something? [*Her tone is rhapsodic.*] *You?* Why, Mr O'Connor, nobody, *nobody*'s given me this much entertainment in years – as you have!

JIM: Aw, now, Mrs Wingfield!

AMANDA: I'm not exaggerating, not one bit! But Sister is all by her lonesome. You go keep her company in the parlour! I'll give you this lovely old candelabrum that used to be on the altar at the church of the Heavenly Rest. It was melted a little out of shape when the church burnt down. Lightning struck it one spring.

Gypsy Jones was holding a revival at the time and he intimated that the church was destroyed because the Episcopalians gave card parties.

JIM: Ha-ha.

AMANDA: And how about you coaxing Sister to drink a little wine? I think it would be good for her! Can you carry both at once?

JIM: Sure. I'm Superman!

AMANDA: Now, Thomas, get into this apron!

[*The door of kitchenette swings closed on* AMANDA'S *gay*

laughter; the flickering light approaches the portières.

LAURA *sits up nervously as he enters. Her speech at first is low and breathless from the almost intolerable strain of being alone with a stranger.*

THE LEGEND: 'I DON'T SUPPOSE YOU REMEMBER ME AT ALL!'

In her first speeches in this scene, before JIM'S *warmth overcomes her paralysing shyness,* LAURA'S *voice is thin and breathless as though she has just run up a steep flight of stairs.*

JIM'S *attitude is gently humorous. In playing this scene it should be stressed that while the incident is apparently unimportant, it is to* LAURA *the climax of her secret life.*]

JIM: Hello, there, Laura.
LAURA [*faintly*]: Hello. [*She clears her throat.*]
JIM: How are you feeling now? Better?
LAURA: Yes. Yes, thank you.
JIM: This is for you. A little dandelion wine. [*He extends it toward her with extravagant gallantry.*]
LAURA: Thank you.
JIM: Drink it – but don't get drunk!

[*He laughs heartily.* LAURA *takes the glass uncertainly; laughs shyly.*]

Where shall I set the candles?
LAURA: Oh – oh, anywhere. . . .
JIM: How about here on the floor? Any objections?
LAURA: No.
JIM: I'll spread a newspaper under to catch the drippings. I like to sit on the floor. Mind if I do?
LAURA: Oh, no.
JIM: Give me a pillow?
LAURA: What?
JIM: A pillow!
LAURA: Oh . . . [*Hands him one quickly.*]
JIM: How about you? Don't you like to sit on the floor?

LAURA: Oh – yes.

JIM: Why don't you, then?

LAURA: I – will.

JIM: Take a pillow! [LAURA *does. Sits on the other side of the candelabrum.* JIM *crosses his legs and smiles engagingly at her.*] I can't hardly see you sitting way over there.

LAURA: I can – see you.

JIM: I know, but that's not fair, I'm in the limelight. [LAURA *moves her pillow closer.*] Good! Now I can see you! Comfortable?

LAURA: Yes.

JIM: So am I. Comfortable as a cow! Will you have some gum?

LAURA: No, thank you.

JIM: I think that I will indulge, with your permission. [*Musingly unwraps it and holds it up.*] Think of the fortune made by the guy that invented the first piece of chewing gum. Amazing, huh? The Wrigley Building is one of the sights of Chicago. – I saw it summer before last when I went up to the Century of Progress. Did you take in the Century of Progress?

LAURA: No, I didn't.

JIM: Well, it was quite a wonderful exposition. What impressed me most was the Hall of Science. Gives you an idea of what the future will be in America, even more wonderful than the present time is! [*Pause. Smiling at her.*] Your brother tells me you're shy. Is that right, Laura?

LAURA: I – don't know.

JIM: I judge you to be an old-fashioned type of girl. Well, I think that's a pretty good type to be. Hope you don't think I'm being too personal – do you?

LAURA [*hastily, out of embarrassment*]: I believe I will take a piece of gum, if you – don't mind. [*Clearing her throat.*] Mr O'Connor, have you – kept up with your singing?

JIM: Singing? Me?

LAURA: Yes. I remember what a beautiful voice you had.

JIM: When did you hear me sing?

[VOICE OFF STAGE IN THE PAUSE]

VOICE [*off stage*]:

> O blow, ye winds, heigh-ho,
> A-roving I will go!
>> I'm off to my love
>> With a boxing glove –
> Ten thousand miles away!

JIM: You say you've heard me sing?

LAURA: Oh, yes! Yes, very often . . . I don't suppose – you remember me – at all?

JIM [*smiling doubtfully*]: You know I have an idea I've seen you before. I had that idea soon as you opened the door. It seemed almost like I was about to remember your name. But the name that I started to call you – wasn't a name! And so I stopped myself before I said it.

LAURA: Wasn't it – Blue Roses?

JIM [*springs up. Grinning*]: Blue Roses! – My gosh, yes – Blue Roses! That's what I had on my tongue when you opened the door!
Isn't it funny what tricks your memory plays? I didn't connect you with high school somehow or other.
But that's where it was; it was high school. I didn't even know you were Shakespeare's sister!
Gosh, I'm sorry.

LAURA: I didn't expect you to. You – barely knew me!

JIM: But we did have a speaking acquaintance, huh?

LAURA: Yes, we – spoke to each other.

JIM: When did you recognize me?

LAURA: Oh, right away!

JIM: Soon as I came in the door?

LAURA: When I heard your name I thought it was probably you. I knew that Tom used to know you a little in high school. So when you came in the door –
Well, then I was – sure.

JIM: Why didn't you *say* something, then?

LAURA [*breathlessly*]: I didn't know what to say, I was – too surprised!

JIM: For goodness' sakes! You know, this sure is funny!

LAURA: Yes! Yes, isn't it, though ...

JIM: Didn't we have a class in something together?

LAURA: Yes, we did.

JIM: What class was that?

LAURA: It was – singing – Chorus!

JIM: Aw!

LAURA: I sat across the aisle from you in the Aud.

JIM: Aw.

LAURA: Mondays, Wednesday, and Fridays.

JIM: Now I remember – you always came in late.

LAURA: Yes, it was so hard for me, getting upstairs. I had that brace on my leg – it clumped so loud!

JIM: I never heard any clumping.

LAURA [*wincing at the recollection*]: To me it sounded like – thunder!

JIM: Well, well, well, I never even noticed.

LAURA: And everybody was seated before I came in. I had to walk in front of all those people. My seat was in the back row. I had to go clumping all the way up the aisle with everyone watching!

JIM: You shouldn't have been self-conscious.

LAURA: I know, but I was. It was always such a relief when the singing started.

JIM: Aw, yes, I've placed you now! I used to call you Blue Roses. How was it that I got started calling you that?

LAURA: I was out of school a little while with pleurosis. When I came back you asked me what was the matter. I said I had pleurosis – you thought I said Blue Roses. That's what you always called me after that!

JIM: I hope you didn't mind.

LAURA: Oh, no – I liked it. You see, I wasn't acquainted with many – people. ...

JIM: As I remember you sort of stuck by yourself.

LAURA: I – I – never have had much luck at – making friends.

JIM: I don't see why you wouldn't.

LAURA: Well, I – started out badly.

JIM: You mean being –

LAURA: Yes, it sort of – stood between me –

JIM: You shouldn't have let it!

LAURA: I know, but it did, and –

JIM: You were shy with people!

LAURA: I tried not to be but never could –

JIM: Overcome it?

LAURA: No, I – I never could!

JIM: I guess being shy is something you have to work out of kind of gradually.

LAURA [*sorrowfully*]: Yes – I guess it –

JIM: Takes time!

LAURA: Yes –

JIM: People are not so dreadful when you know them. That's what you have to remember! And everybody has problems, not just you, but practically everybody has got some problems.

You think of yourself as having the only problems, as being the only one who is disappointed. But just look around you and you will see lots of people as disappointed as you are. For instance, I hoped when I was going to high school that I would be further along at this time, six years later, than I am now – You remember that wonderful write-up I had in *The Torch*?

LAURA: Yes! [*She rises and crosses to table.*]

JIM: It said I was bound to succeed in anything I went into! [LAURA *returns with the annual.*] Holy Jeez! *The Torch!* [*He accepts it reverently. They smile across it with mutual wonder.* LAURA *crouches beside him and they begin to turn through it.* LAURA's *shyness is dissolving in his warmth.*]

LAURA: Here you are in *The Pirates of Penzance!*

JIM: [*wistfully*]: I sang the baritone lead in that operetta.

LAURA [*raptly*]: So – beautifully!

JIM [*protesting*]: Aw –

LAURA: Yes, yes – beautifully – beautifully!

JIM: You heard me?

LAURA: All three times!

JIM: No!

LAURA: Yes!

JIM: All three performances?

LAURA [*looking down*]: Yes.

JIM: Why?

LAURA: I – wanted to ask you to – autograph my programme.

JIM: Why didn't you ask me to?

LAURA: You were always surrounded by your own friends so much that I never had a chance to.

JIM: You should have just –

LAURA: Well, I – thought you might think I was –

JIM: Thought I might think you was – what?

LAURA: Oh –

JIM [*with reflective relish*]: I was beleaguered by females in those days.

LAURA: You were terribly popular!

JIM: Yeah –

LAURA: You had such a – friendly way –

JIM: I was spoiled in high school.

LAURA: Everybody – liked you!

JIM: Including you?

LAURA: I – yes, I – I did, too – [*She gently closes the book in her lap.*]

JIM: Well, well, well! – Give me that programme, Laura. [*She hands it to him. He signs it with a flourish.*] There you are – better late than never!

LAURA: Oh, I – what a – surprise!

JIM: My signature isn't worth very much right now. But some day – maybe – it will increase in value!

Being disappointed is one thing and being discouraged is something else. I am disappointed but I am not discouraged. I'm twenty-three years old.

How old are you?

LAURA: I'll be twenty-four in June.

JIM: That's not old age!

LAURA: No, but –

JIM: You finished high school?

LAURA [*with difficulty*]: I didn't go back.

JIM: You mean you dropped out?

LAURA: I made bad grades in my final examinations. [*She rises and replaces the book and the programme. Her voice strained.*] How is – Emily Meisenbach getting along?

JIM: Oh, that kraut-head!

LAURA: Why do you call her that?

JIM: That's what she was.

LAURA: You're not still – going with her?

JIM: I never see her.

LAURA: It said in the Personal Section that you were – engaged!

JIM: I know, but I wasn't impressed by that – propaganda!

LAURA: It wasn't – the truth?

JIM: Only in Emily's optimistic opinion!

LAURA: Oh –

[LEGEND: 'WHAT HAVE YOU DONE SINCE HIGH SCHOOL?'

JIM *lights a cigarette and leans indolently back on his elbows smiling at* LAURA *with a warmth and charm which lights her inwardly with altar candles. She remains by the table and turns in her hands a piece of glass to cover her tumult.*]

JIM [*after several reflective puffs on a cigarette*]: What have you done since high school? [*She seems not to hear him.*] Huh? [LAURA *looks up.*] I said what have you done since high school, Laura?

LAURA: Nothing much.

JIM: You must have been doing something these six long years.

LAURA: Yes.

JIM: Well, then, such as what?

LAURA: I took a business course at business college –

JIM: How did that work out?

LAURA: Well, not very – well – I had to drop out, it gave me – indigestion –

[JIM *laughs gently.*]

JIM: What are you doing now?

LAURA: I don't do anything – much. Oh, please don't think I sit around doing nothing! My glass collection takes up a good deal of time. Glass is something you have to take good care of.

JIM: What did you say – about glass?

LAURA: Collection I said – I have one – [*She clears her throat and turns away, acutely shy.*]

JIM [*abruptly*]: You know what I judge to be the trouble with you?

Inferiority complex! Know what that is? That's what they call it when someone low-rates himself!

I understand it because I had it, too. Although my case was not so aggravated as yours seems to be. I had it until I took up public speaking, developed my voice, and learned that I had an aptitude for science. Before that time I never thought of myself as being outstanding in any way whatsoever!

Now I've never made a regular study of it, but I have a friend who says I can analyse people better than doctors that make a profession of it. I don't claim that to be necessarily true, but I can sure guess a person's psychology, Laura! [*Takes out his gum.*] Excuse me, Laura. I always take it out when the flavour is gone. I'll use this scrap of paper to wrap it in. I know how it is to get it stuck on a shoe.

Yep – that's what I judge to be your principal trouble. A lack of amount of faith in yourself as a person. You don't have the proper amount of faith in yourself. I'm basing that fact on a number of your remarks and also on certain observations I've made. For instance that clumping you thought was so awful in high school. You say that you even dreaded to walk into class. You see what you did? You dropped out of school, you gave up an education because of a clump, which as far as I know was practically non-existent! A little physical defect is what you have. Hardly noticeable even! Magnified thousands of times by imagination!

You know what my strong advice to you is? Think of yourself as *superior* in some way!

LAURA: In what way would I think?

JIM: Why, man alive, Laura! Just look about you a little. What do you see? A world full of common people! All of 'em born and all of 'em going to die!

Which of them has one-tenth of your good points! Or mine! Or anyone else's, as far as that goes – Gosh! Everybody excels in some one thing. Some in many!

[*Unconsciously glances at himself in the mirror.*]

All you've got to do is discover in *what!*
Take me, for instance.

[*He adjusts his tie at the mirror.*]

My interest happens to lie in electro-dynamics. I'm taking a course in radio engineering at night school, Laura, on top of a fairly responsible job at the warehouse. I'm taking that course and studying public speaking.

LAURA: Ohhhh.

JIM: Because I believe in the future of television!

[*Turning back to her.*]

I wish to be ready to go up right along with it. Therefore

I'm planning to get in on the ground floor. In fact I've already made the right connexions and all that remains is for the industry itself to get under way! Full steam –

[*His eyes are starry.*]

Knowledge – Zzzzzp! *Money* – Zzzzzzp! – *Power!*
That's the cycle democracy is built on!

[*His attitude is convincingly dynamic.* LAURA *stares at him, even her shyness eclipsed in her absolute wonder. He suddenly grins.*]

I guess you think I think a lot of myself!

LAURA: No – o-o-o, I –

JIM: Now how about you? Isn't there something you take more interest in than anything else?

LAURA: Well, I do – as I said – have my – glass collection –

[*A peal of girlish laughter from the kitchen.*]

JIM: I'm not right sure I know what you're talking about. What kind of glass is it?

LAURA: Little articles of it, they're ornaments mostly! Most of them are little animals made out of glass, the tiniest little animals in the world. Mother calls them a glass menagerie!
Here's an example of one, if you'd like to see it!
This one is one of the oldest. It's nearly thirteen.

[MUSIC: 'THE GLASS MENAGERIE'.
He stretches out his hand.]

Oh, be careful – if you breathe, it breaks!

JIM: I'd better not take it. I'm pretty clumsy with things.

LAURA: Go on, I trust you with him!

[*Places it in his palm.*]

There now – you're holding him gently!

Hold him over the light, he loves the light! You see how the light shines through him?

JIM: It sure does shine!

LAURA: I shouldn't be partial, but he is my favourite one.

JIM: What kind of a thing is this one supposed to be?

LAURA: Haven't you noticed the single horn on his forehead?

JIM: A unicorn, huh?

LAURA: Mmmm-hmmm!

JIM: Unicorns, aren't they extinct in the modern world?

LAURA: I know!

JIM: Poor little fellow, he must feel sort of lonesome.

LAURA [*smiling*]: Well, if he does he doesn't complain about it. He stays on a shelf with some horses that don't have horns and all of them seem to get along nicely together.

JIM: How do you know?

LAURA [*lightly*]· I haven't heard any arguments among them!

JIM [*grinning*]: No arguments, huh? Well, that's a pretty good sign! Where shall I set him?

LAURA: Put him on the table. They all like a change of scenery once in a while!

JIM [*stretching*]: Well, well, well, well –
Look how big my shadow is when I stretch!

LAURA: Oh, oh, yes – it stretches across the ceiling!

JIM [*crossing to door*]: I think it's stopped raining. [*Opens fire-escape door.*] Where does the music come from?

LAURA: From the Paradise Dance Hall across the alley.

JIM: How about cutting the rug a little, Miss Wingfield?

LAURA: Oh –

JIM: Or is your programme filled up? Let me have a look at it. [*Grasps imaginary card.*] Why, every dance is taken! I'll just have to scratch some out. [WALTZ MUSIC: 'LA GOLONDRINA'.] Ahhh, a waltz! [*He executes some sweeping turns by himself then holds his arms toward* LAURA.]

LAURA [*breathlessly*]: I – can't dance!

JIM: There you go, that inferiority stuff!
  Come on, try!

LAURA: Oh, but I'd step on you!

JIM: I'm not made out of glass.

LAURA: How – how – how do we start?

JIM: Just leave it to me. You hold your arms out a little.

LAURA: Like this?

JIM: A little bit higher. Right. Now don't tighten up, that's
  the main thing about it – relax.

LAURA [*laughing breathlessly*]: It's hard not to.
  I'm afraid you can't budge me.

JIM: What do you bet I can't? [*He swings her into motion.*]

LAURA: Goodness, yes, you can!

JIM: Let yourself go, now, Laura, just let yourself go.

LAURA: I'm –

JIM: Come on!

LAURA: Trying!

JIM: Not so stiff – Easy does it!

LAURA: I know but I'm –

JIM: Loosen th' backbone! There now, that's a lot better.

LAURA: Am I?

JIM: Lots, lots better! [*He moves her about the room in a clumsy
  waltz.*]

LAURA: Oh, my!

JIM: Ha-ha!

LAURA: Oh, my goodness!

JIM: Ha-ha-ha! [*They suddenly bump into the table. JIM stops.*]
  What did we hit on?

LAURA: Table.

JIM: Did something fall off it? I think –

LAURA: Yes.

JIM: I hope that it wasn't the little glass horse with the horn!

LAURA: Yes.

JIM: Aw, aw, aw. Is it broken?

LAURA: Now it is just like all the other horses.

JIM: It's lost its –

LAURA: Horn!

It doesn't matter. Maybe it's a blessing in disguise.

JIM: You'll never forgive me. I bet that that was your favourite piece of glass.

LAURA: I don't have favourites much. It's no tragedy, Freckles. Glass breaks so easily. No matter how careful you are. The traffic jars the shelves and things fall off them.

JIM: Still I'm awfully sorry that I was the cause.

LAURA [*smiling*]: I'll just imagine he had an operation. The horn was removed to make him feel less – freakish!

[*They both laugh.*]

Now he will feel more at home with the other horses, the ones that don't have horns. . . .

JIM: Ha-ha, that's very funny!

[*Suddenly serious.*]

I'm glad to see that you have a sense of humour. You know – you're – well – very different! Surprisingly different from anyone else I know!

[*His voice becomes soft and hesitant with a genuine feeling.*]

Do you mind me telling you that?

[LAURA *is abashed beyond speech.*]

I mean it in a nice way . . .

[LAURA *nods shyly, looking away.*]

You make me feel sort of – I don't know how to put it! I'm usually pretty good at expressing things, but – This is something that I don't know how to say!

[LAURA *touches her throat and clears it – turns the broken unicorn in her hands.*
Even softer.]

Has anyone ever told you that you were pretty?

[PAUSE: MUSIC.
LAURA *looks up slowly, with wonder, and shakes her head.*]

Well, you are! In a very different way from anyone else. And all the nicer because of the difference, too.

[*His voice becomes low and husky.* LAURA *turns away, nearly faint with the novelty of her emotions.*]

I wish that you were my sister. I'd teach you to have some confidence in yourself. The different people are not like other people, but being different is nothing to be ashamed of. Because other people are not such wonderful people. They're one hundred times one thousand. You're one times one! They walk all over the earth. You just stay here. They're common as – weeds, but – you – well, you're – *Blue Roses!*

[IMAGE ON SCREEN: BLUE ROSES.
MUSIC CHANGES.]

LAURA: But blue is wrong for – roses ...
JIM: It's right for you! – You're – pretty!
LAURA: In what respect am I pretty?
JIM: In all respects – believe me! Your eyes – your hair – are pretty! Your hands are pretty!

[*He catches hold of her hand.*]

You think I'm making this up because I'm invited to dinner and have to be nice. Oh, I could do that! I could put on an act for you, Laura, and say lots of things without being very sincere. But this time I am. I'm talking to you sincerely. I happened to notice you had this inferiority complex that keeps you from feeling comfortable with people. Somebody needs to build your confidence up and make you proud instead of shy and turning away and – blushing – Somebody – ought to –

Ought to – *kiss* you, Laura !

[*His hand slips slowly up her arm to her shoulder.*
MUSIC SWELLS TUMULTUOUSLY.
He suddenly turns her about and kisses her on the lips.
When he releases her, LAURA *sinks on the sofa with a bright, dazed look.*
JIM *backs away and fishes in his pocket for a cigarette.*
LEGEND ON SCREEN: 'SOUVENIR'.]

Stumble-john !

[*He lights the cigarette, avoiding her look.*
There is a peal of girlish laughter from AMANDA *in the kitchen.*
LAURA *slowly raises and opens her hand. It still contains the little broken glass animal. She looks at it with a tender, bewildered expression.*]

Stumble-john !
I shouldn't have done that – That was way off the beam.
You don't smoke, do you ?

[*She looks up, smiling, not hearing the question.*
He sits beside her a little gingerly. She looks at him speechlessly – waiting.
He coughs decorously and moves a little farther aside as he considers the situation and senses her feelings, dimly, with perturbation.
Gently.]

Would you – care for a – mint ?

[*She doesn't seem to hear him but her look grows brighter even.*]
Peppermint – Life-Saver ?
My pocket's a regular drug store – wherever I go ...

[*He pops a mint in his mouth. Then gulps and decides to make a clean breast of it. He speaks slowly and gingerly.*]

Laura, you know, if I had a sister like you, I'd do the
same thing as Tom. I'd bring out fellows and – introduce
her to them. The right type of boys of a type to – appreciate her.

Only – well – he made a mistake about me.

Maybe I've got no call to be saying this. That may not
have been the idea in having me over. But what if it was?
There's nothing wrong about that. The only trouble is
that in my case – I'm not in a situation to – do the right
thing.

I can't take down your number and say I'll phone.

I can't call up next week and – ask for a date.

I thought I had better explain the situation in case you –
misunderstand it and – hurt your feelings. . . .

> [*Pause.*
>   *Slowly, very slowly,* LAURA'S *look changes, her eyes re-*
> *turning slowly from his to the ornament in her palm.*
>   AMANDA *utters another gay laugh in the kitchen.*]

LAURA [*faintly*]: You – won't – call again?

JIM: No, Laura, I can't.

> [*He rises from the sofa.*]

As I was just explaining, I've – got strings on me.

Laura, I've – been going steady!

I go out all of the time with a girl named Betty. She's a
home-girl like you, and Catholic, and Irish, and in a great
many ways we – get along fine.

I met her last summer on a moonlight boat trip up the
river to Alton, on the *Majestic*.

Well – right away from the start it was – love!

> [LEGEND: 'LOVE!'
>   LAURA *sways slightly forward and grips the arm of the*
> *sofa. He fails to notice, now enrapt in his own comfortable*
> *being.*]

Being in love has made a new man of me!

[*Leaning stiffly forward, clutching the arm of the sofa,* LAURA *struggles visibly with her storm. But* JIM *is oblivious, she is a long way off.*]

The power of love is really pretty tremendous!
Love is something that – changes the whole world, Laura!

[*The storm abates a little and* LAURA *leans back. He notices her again.*]

It happened that Betty's aunt took sick, she got a wire and had to go to Centralia. So Tom – when he asked me to dinner – I naturally just accepted the invitation, not knowing that you – that he – that I –

[*He stops awkwardly.*]

Huh – I'm a stumble-john!

[*He flops back on the sofa.*
   The holy candles in the altar of LAURA'S *face have been snuffed out.*
   There is a look of almost infinite desolation.
   JIM *glances at her uneasily.*]
I wish that you would – say something. [*She bites her lip which was trembling and then bravely smiles. She opens her hand again on the broken glass ornament. Then she gently takes his hand and raises it level with her own. She carefully places the unicorn in the palm of his hand, then pushes his fingers closed upon it.*] What are you – doing that for? You want me to have him? Laura? [*She nods.*] What for?
LAURA: A – souvenir . . .

[*She rises unsteadily and crouches beside the victrola to wind it up.*

   LEGEND ON SCREEN: 'THINGS HAVE A WAY OF TURNING OUT SO BADLY!'

OR IMAGE: GENTLEMAN CALLER WAVING
GOOD-BYE! - GAILY.

[*At this moment* AMANDA *rushes brightly back in the
front room. She bears a pitcher of fruit punch in an old-
fashioned cut-glass pitcher and a plate of macaroons. The
plate has a gold border and poppies painted on it.*]

AMANDA: Well, well, well! Isn't the air delightful after
the shower? I've made you children a little liquid refresh-
ment.

[*Turns gaily to the gentleman caller.*]

Jim, do you know that song about lemonade?
              'Lemonade, lemonade
                   Made in the shade and stirred with a spade -
                   Good enough for any old maid!'

JIM [*uneasily*]: Ha-ha! No - I never heard it.

AMANDA: Why, Laura! You look so serious!

JIM: We were having a serious conversation.

AMANDA: Good! Now you're better acquainted!

JIM [*uncertainly*]: Ha-ha! Yes.

AMANDA: You modern young people are much more
serious-minded than my generation. I was so gay as a
girl!

JIM: You haven't changed, Mrs Wingfield.

AMANDA: Tonight I'm rejuvenated! The gaiety of the
occasion, Mr O'Connor!

[*She tosses her head with a peal of laughter. Spills lemonade.*]

Oooo! I'm baptizing myself!

JIM: Here - let me -

AMANDA [*setting the pitcher down*]: There now. I discovered
we had some maraschino cherries. I dumped them in,
juice and all!

JIM: You shouldn't have gone to that trouble, Mrs Wingfield.

AMANDA: Trouble, trouble? Why, it was loads of fun! Didn't you hear me cutting up in the kitchen? I bet your ears were burning! I told Tom how outdone with him I was for keeping you to himself so long a time! He should have brought you over much, much sooner! Well, now that you've found your way, I want you to be a very frequent caller! Not just occasional but all the time. Oh, we're going to have a lot of gay times together! I see them coming!

Mmm, just breathe that air! So fresh, and the moon's so pretty!

I'll skip back out – I know where my place is when young folks are having a – serious conversation!

JIM: Oh, don't go out, Mrs Wingfield. The fact of the matter is I've got to be going.

AMANDA: Going, now? You're joking! Why, it's only the shank of the evening, Mr O'Connor!

JIM: Well, you know how it is.

AMANDA: You mean you're a young working man and have to keep working men's hours. We'll let you off early tonight.

But only on the condition that next time you stay later. What's the best night for you? Isn't Saturday night the best night for you working men?

JIM: I have a couple of time-clocks to punch, Mrs Wingfield. One at morning, another one at night!

AMANDA: My, but you *are* ambitious! You work at night, too?

JIM: No, Ma'am, not work but – Betty! [*He crosses deliberately to pick up his hat. The band at the Paradise Dance Hall goes into a tender waltz.*]

AMANDA: Betty? Betty? Who's – Betty!

[*There is an ominous cracking sound in the sky.*]

JIM: Oh, just a girl. The girl I go steady with! [*He smiles charmingly. The sky falls.*]

[LEGEND: 'THE SKY FALLS'.]

AMANDA [a long-drawn exhalation]: Ohhhh. ... Is it a serious romance, Mr O'Connor?

JIM: We're going to be married the second Sunday in June.

AMANDA: Ohhhh – how nice!

Tom didn't mention that you were engaged to be married.

JIM: The cat's not out of the bag at the warehouse yet.
You know how they are. They call you Romeo and stuff like that.

[He stops at the oval mirror to put on his hat. He carefully shapes the brim and the crown to give a discreetly dashing effect.]

It's been a wonderful evening, Mrs Wingfield. I guess this is what they mean by Southern hospitality.

AMANDA: It really wasn't anything at all.

JIM: I hope it don't seem like I'm rushing off. But I promised Betty I'd pick her up at the Wabash depot, an' by the time I get my jalopy down there her train'll be in. Some women are pretty upset if you keep 'em waiting.

AMANDA: Yes, I know – The tyranny of women!

[Extends her hand.]

Good-bye, Mr O'Connor.
I wish you luck – and happiness – and success! All three of them, and so does Laura! – Don't you, Laura?

LAURA: Yes!

JIM [taking her hand]: Good-bye, Laura. I'm certainly going to treasure that souvenir. And don't you forget the good advice I gave you.

[Raises his voice to a cheery shout.]

So long, Shakespeare!
Thanks again, ladies – Good night!

[*He grins and ducks jauntily out.*]

    Still bravely grimacing, AMANDA *closes the door on the gentleman caller. Then she turns back to the room with a puzzled expression. She and* LAURA *don't dare face each other.* LAURA *crouches beside the victrola to wind it.*]

AMANDA [*faintly*]: Things have a way of turning out so badly.

I don't believe that I would play the victrola.

Well, well – well –

Our gentleman caller was engaged to be married!

Tom!

TOM [*from back*]: Yes, Mother?

AMANDA: Come in here a minute. I want to tell you something awfully funny.

TOM [*enters with macaroon and a glass of lemonade*]: Has the gentleman caller gotten away already?

AMANDA: The gentleman caller has made an early departure. What a wonderful joke you played on us!

TOM: How do you mean?

AMANDA: You didn't mention that he was engaged to be married.

TOM: Jim? Engaged?

AMANDA: That's what he just informed us.

TOM: I'll be jiggered! I didn't know about that.

AMANDA: That seems very peculiar.

TOM: What's peculiar about it?

AMANDA: Didn't you call him your best friend down at the warehouse?

TOM: He is, but how did I know?

AMANDA: It seems extremely peculiar that you wouldn't know your best friend was going to be married!

TOM: The warehouse is where I work, not where I know things about people!

AMANDA: You don't know things anywhere! You live in a dream; you manufacture illusions!

[*He crosses to door.*]

Where are you going?

TOM: I'm going to the movies.

AMANDA: That's right, now that you've had us make such fools of ourselves. The effort, the preparations, all the expense! The new floor lamp, the rug, the clothes for Laura! All for what? To entertain some other girl's fiancé! Go to the movies, go! Don't think about us, a mother deserted, an unmarried sister who's crippled and has no job! Don't let anything interfere with your selfish pleasure! Just go, go, go – to the movies!

TOM: All right, I will! The more you shout about my selfishness to me the quicker I'll go, and I won't go to the movies!

AMANDA: Go, then! Then go to the moon – you selfish dreamer!

[TOM *smashes his glass on the floor. He plunges out on the fire-escape, slamming the door.* LAURA *screams – cut by door.*

Dance-hall music up. TOM *goes to the rail and grips it desperately, lifting his face in the chill white moonlight penetrating the narrow abyss of the alley.*

LEGEND ON SCREEN: 'AND SO GOOD-BYE ...'

TOM'S *closing speech is timed with the interior pantomime. The interior scene is played as though viewed through soundproof glass.* AMANDA *appears to be making a comforting speech to* LAURA *who is huddled upon the sofa. Now that we cannot hear the mother's speech, her silliness is gone and she has dignity and tragic beauty.* LAURA'S *dark hair hides her face until at the end of the speech she lifts it to smile at her mother.* AMANDA'S *gestures are slow and graceful, almost dancelike, as she comforts the daughter. At the end of her speech she glances a moment at the father's picture – then withdraws through the portières. At the close of* TOM'S *speech,* LAURA *blows out the candles, ending the play.*]

TOM: I didn't go to the moon, I went much further — for time is the longest distance between two places —

Not long after that I was fired for writing a poem on the lid of a shoebox.

I left Saint Louis. I descended the steps of this fire-escape for a last time and followed, from then on, in my father's footsteps, attempting to find in motion what was lost in space — I travelled around a great deal. The cities swept about me like dead leaves, leaves that were brightly coloured but torn away from the branches.

I would have stopped, but I was pursued by something.

It always came upon me unawares, taking me altogether by surprise. Perhaps it was a familiar bit of music. Perhaps it was only a piece of transparent glass —

Perhaps I am walking along a street at night, in some strange city, before I have found companions. I pass the lighted window of a shop where perfume is sold. The window is filled with pieces of coloured glass, tiny transparent bottles in delicate colours, like bits of a shattered rainbow.

Then all at once my sister touches my shoulder. I turn around and look into her eyes . . .

Oh, Laura, Laura, I tried to leave you behind me, but I am more faithful than I intended to be!

I reach for a cigarette, I cross the street, I run into the movies or a bar, I buy a drink, I speak to the nearest stranger — anything that can blow your candles out!

[LAURA *bends over the candles.*]

— for nowadays the world is lit by lightning! Blow out your candles, Laura — and so good-bye. . . .

[*She blows the candles out.*]

THE SCENE DISSOLVES

READ MORE IN PENGUIN

In every corner of the world, on every subject under the sun, Penguin represents quality and variety – the very best in publishing today.

For complete information about books available from Penguin – including Puffins, Penguin Classics and Arkana – and how to order them, write to us at the appropriate address below. Please note that for copyright reasons the selection of books varies from country to country.

In the United Kingdom: Please write to *Dept. EP, Penguin Books Ltd, Bath Road, Harmondsworth, West Drayton, Middlesex UB7 ODA*

In the United States: Please write to *Consumer Sales, Penguin Putnam Inc., P.O. Box 999, Dept. 17109, Bergenfield, New Jersey 07621-0120*. VISA and MasterCard holders call 1-800-253-6476 to order Penguin titles

In Canada: Please write to *Penguin Books Canada Ltd, 10 Alcorn Avenue, Suite 300, Toronto, Ontario M4V 3B2*

In Australia: Please write to *Penguin Books Australia Ltd, P.O. Box 257, Ringwood, Victoria 3134*

In New Zealand: Please write to *Penguin Books (NZ) Ltd, Private Bag 102902, North Shore Mail Centre, Auckland 10*

In India: Please write to *Penguin Books India Pvt Ltd, 210 Chiranjiv Tower, 43 Nehru Place, New Delhi 110 019*

In the Netherlands: Please write to *Penguin Books Netherlands bv, Postbus 3507, NL-1001 AH Amsterdam*

In Germany: Please write to *Penguin Books Deutschland GmbH, Metzlerstrasse 26, 60594 Frankfurt am Main*

In Spain: Please write to *Penguin Books S. A., Bravo Murillo 19, 1° B, 28015 Madrid*

In Italy: Please write to *Penguin Italia s.r.l., Via Benedetto Croce 2, 20094 Corsico, Milano*

In France: Please write to *Penguin France, Le Carré Wilson, 62 rue Benjamin Baillaud, 31500 Toulouse*

In Japan: Please write to *Penguin Books Japan Ltd, Kaneko Building, 2-3-25 Koraku, Bunkyo-Ku, Tokyo 112*

In South Africa: Please write to *Penguin Books South Africa (Pty) Ltd, Private Bag X14, Parkview, 2122 Johannesburg*

READ MORE IN PENGUIN

Penguin Twentieth-Century Classics offer a selection of the finest works of literature published this century. Spanning the globe from Argentina to America, from France to India, the masters of prose and poetry are represented in by the Penguin.

If you would like a catalogue of the Twentieth-Century Classics library, please write to:

Penguin Marketing, 27 Wrights Lane, London W8 5TZ

(Available while stocks last)

READ MORE IN PENGUIN

A SELECTION OF PLAYS

Edward Albee	**Who's Afraid of Virginia Woolf?**
	Three Tall Women
Alan Ayckbourn	**Joking Apart and Other Plays**
James Baldwin	**The Amen Corner**
Dermot Bolger	**A Dublin Quartet**
Bertolt Brecht	**Parables for the Theatre**
Albert Camus	**Caligula and Other Plays**
Anton Chekhov	**Plays (The Cherry Orchard/Three Sisters/ Ivanov/The Seagull/Uncle Vanya)**
Brian Friel	**Molly Sweeney**
Henrik Ibsen	**A Doll's House/League of Youth/Lady from the Sea**
Eugène Ionesco	**Rhinoceros/The Chairs/The Lesson**
Ben Jonson	**Three Comedies (Volpone/The Alchemist/ Bartholomew Fair)**
D. H. Lawrence	**Three Plays (The Collier's Friday Night/ The Daughter-in-Law/The Widowing of Mrs Holroyd)**
Mike Leigh	**Abigail's Party/Goose-Pimples**
Arthur Miller	**Death of a Salesman**
Peter Shaffer	**The Royal Hunt of the Sun**
	Equus
Bernard Shaw	**Plays Pleasant**
	Pygmalion
	John Bull's Other Island
Sophocles	**Three Theban Plays (Oedipus the King/ Antigone/Oedipus at Colonus)**
Keith Waterhouse	**Jeffrey Bernard is Unwell and Other Plays**
Arnold Wesker	**Plays, Volumes 1-7**
Oscar Wilde	**The Importance of Being Earnest and Other Plays**
Thornton Wilder	**Our Town/The Skin of Our Teeth/The Matchmaker**
Tennessee Williams	**Cat on a Hot Tin Roof/The Milk Train Doesn't Stop Here Anymore/The Night of the Iguana**

BY THE SAME AUTHOR

The Rose Tattoo and Other Plays

The Rose Tattoo · Camino Real · Orpheus Descending

The Rose Tattoo, set in a Sicilian peasant community opens with news of a violent death. 'In the blind and frenzied efforts of the widow, Serafina, to comprehend the mysteries of her dead husband,' Tennessee Williams wrote, 'we sense and learn more about him than would have been possible through direct observation of the living man, the Dionysian himself.'

The New York Times described *Camino Real* as 'a symbolic portrait of the American poet ... of genius lavishly misspent, a defiant play about defeat ... a lovely play, a play of genuinely poetic vision ... oddly prophetic about its author'.

In the corrupt hell of a Southern township, the backcloth for *Orpheus Descending*, a wandering guitar-player meets his Eurydice.

Baby Doll and Other Plays

Baby Doll · Something Unspoken · Suddenly Last Summer

'A work of art – an absorbing study of frustration, poverty and racial intolerance' – *Daily Telegraph*

Tennessee Williams's famous Hollywood screenplay *Baby Doll* opens with Archie Lee's wife driving him to distraction, as she has refused to consummate the marriage until the day of her twentieth birthday. Enter Silva Vacarro, Archie's rival both in business and for the fluffy affections of Baby Doll, and the tension rapidly reaches breaking-point.

This volume also contains *Something Unspoken*, a brilliantly comic study of female tyranny, and *Suddenly Last Summer*, which tells the story of a man's escape from his possessive mother and the revenge she plans for the girl who liberated him.

BY THE SAME AUTHOR

'Williams has a long reach and a genuinely dramatic imagination . . . He is constantly pressing his own limits. He creates shows, as all of us must, but he possesses the restless inconsolability with his solutions which is inevitable in a genuine writer' – Arthur Miller

Cat on a Hot Tin Roof and Other Plays

Cat on a Hot Tin Roof, one of his masterpieces, conveys his vision of the dark, primitive elements that lurk beneath the superficial civilization of the American South. One hot summer night in the house of the Mississippi Delta's richest cotton-planter, a family imprisoned by the past is torn apart by the revelations of feelings of lust, greed and envy.

In *The Milk Train Doesn't Stop Here Anymore* Mrs Goforth, an ageing American actress, dictates her memoires in a luxurious Mediterranean retreat, aware that she is running out of time.

The Night of the Iguana is set in an isolated Mexican hotel in 1940. A group of very different people are brought together by chance. They include a tough hotel proprietor, a defrocked clergyman, a middle-aged spinster who is weary of travelling the world with her poet grandfather, and a family of jubilant Nazis.

Period of Adjustment and Other Plays

Period of Adjustment first hit Broadway in 1960 and remains a brilliantly sardonic and entertaining comedy. Opening one Christmas Eve in Memphis, Tennessee, it portrays two couples, one just married, caught in a sudden crisis of loneliness and sexual and emotional inhibition.

This volume also contains *Summer and Smoke*, a love story set in Mississippi in 1916; and *Small Craft Warnings*, commonly agreed to be the best of Tennessee Williams' later plays. With its action concentrated into a single evening in a bar on the Californian coast, it is a drama of survival executed with characteristic passion and power to move.

'An insistent and even a heroic presence, a troubled spirit who never stopped trying to move us with the amplified music of our own hearts' – *Newsweek*